New Technology @ Work

New computer and communications technologies have acted as the catalyst for a revolution in the way goods are produced and services delivered, leading to profound changes in the way work is organized and the way jobs are designed. This important new book examines the nature, setting and impact of new technologies on work, organization and management.

Conventional debates about new technology often invoke optimistic visions of enhanced democracy, rising skills and economic abundance; others predict darker scenarios such as the destruction of jobs through labour-eliminating devices. This book proposes an alternative perspective, arguing that technology can be powerful, but in and of itself has no independent causal powers. It considers the impact of new technologies on manufacturing, clerical, administrative and call centre employment, in both managerial and professional arenas, and introduces the growing phenomena of telework. The book also assesses the important political and economic forces that restrict or facilitate the flow of new technologies on national and global levels.

New Technology @ Work is an illuminating and thought-provoking text that will prove invaluable to all serious students of business, management and technology.

Paul Boreham is Professor of Political Science and Director of the University of Queensland Social Research Centre. His research interests include employment and organization studies, comparative political economy and social inequality and he has published ten books and numerous articles and chapters on these topics.

Rachel Parker is Professor of Management in the Faculty of Business at Queensland University of Technology. Her research interests include innovation, technology transfer and entrepreneurship.

Paul Thompson is Professor of Organisational Analysis and Head of Department of Human Resource Management in the Business School at the University of Strathclyde. His research interests focus on skill and work organization, control and resistance, organizational restructuring and changing economies.

Richard Hall is Associate Professor of Work and Organisational Studies at the University of Sydney and is a Co-Director of the International Centre for Research in Organizational Discourse, Strategy and Change. His research interests concern work, employment, new technology and organizational change.

New Technology @ Work

Paul Boreham
Rachel Parker
Paul Thompson
and Richard Hall

Routledge
Taylor & Francis Group

LONDON AND NEW YORK

First published 2008
by Routledge
2 Park Square, Milton Park, Abingdon, Oxon OX14 4RN

Simultaneously published in the USA and Canada
by Routledge
270 Madison Ave, New York, NY 10016

Routledge is an imprint of the Taylor & Francis Group, an informa business

© 2008 Paul Boreham, Rachel Parker, Paul Thompson and Richard Hall

Typeset in Times New Roman by
Book Now Ltd, London
Printed and bound in Great Britain by
MPG Books Ltd, Bodmin

British Library Cataloguing in Publication Data
A catalogue record for this book is available from the British Library

Library of Congress Cataloging in Publication Data
New technology [at] work/Paul Boreham ... [et al.].
        p. cm.
On t.p. "[at]" appears as "at" sign.
Includes bibliographical references.
1. Technological innovations. 2. Organizational change. I. Boreham, Paul.
HD45.N45 2007
338′.064–dc22   2007027004

ISBN10: 0–415–26896–6 (hbk)
ISBN10: 0–415–26897–4 (pbk)
ISBN10: 0–203–64700–9 (ebk)

ISBN13: 978–0–415–26896–7 (hbk)
ISBN13: 978–0–415–26897–4 (pbk)
ISBN13: 978–0–203–64700–4 (ebk)

Contents

Figures

Tables

Preface

This book is about the ways in which new information and communication technologies have enabled changes in the way work is organized in contemporary society. The book takes up two major themes about new technologies that may be briefly summarized as follows: a critical response to those accounts that accord to technology an independent role in determining workplace change; an emphasis on the social processes that influence the way that technology is utilized in the workplace; and a focus on the manner in which technological developments have been applied in quite different ways to different segments of the employed population.

Between them, the authors bring a great deal of experience and research into work organization and management, employment and the labour process, and sociology and political economy. This interdisciplinary perspective led each of us individually to question the hyperbole that characterizes a great deal of the academic and popular accounts of new technology, and the narrowness of many of the claims based on the perspective of single disciplines. Our collaboration on this project has extended over several years, and has led to both a refinement of our analysis and confirmation of the need to extend the study of new technologies beyond that of the popular business writers and futurists who currently populate the field.

The book draws on knowledge we have all accumulated over many years of research and writing about work and its organization. This has not been a development that has proceeded in a vacuum: we all owe a debt of gratitude to those with whom we have collaborated, and others too numerous to single out with whom we have had discussions and debates in a wide variety of locales around the world.

Finally, we would like to thank those who have made a material contribution to the preparation of the book. In particular, we would like to recognize Rebecca Coates, who worked patiently to help to improve the form and content of the manuscript, and our editors at Routledge, who have been tolerant of the necessarily complicated gestation process of a book whose authors have struggled to co-ordinate a complex activity across time and place despite the exaggerated benefits of information and communication technologies.

Acronyms

ACD	Automated Call Distributor
AMH	Automated Material Handling
AMHs	Automated Material Handling system
AMTs	Advanced Manufacturing Technologies
ANT	Actor Network Theory
APEC	Asia Pacific Economic Co-operation forum
ARS	Automated Retrieval System
ASS	Automated Storage System
ATM	Automated Teller Machine
CAD	Computer Aided Design
CAI	Computer Aided Inspection
CAM	Computer Aided Manufacturing
CAP	Computer Aided Planning
CCM	Call Centre Manager
CEF	Capital Extensive Firm
CEO	Chief Executive Officer
CM	Cellular Manufacturing
CNC	Computer Numerical Control
CQI	Continuous Quality Improvement
CRM	Customer Relationship Management
CSR	Customer Service Representative
ECaTT	European Electronic Commerce and Telework Trends
EDP	Electronic Design Process/Electronic Data Processing
EPOS	Electronic Point of Sales
ERPs	Enterprise Resource Planning system
EU	European Union
FDI	Foreign Direct Investment
FMCs	Flexible Manufacturing Cells
FMS	Flexible Manufacturing System
GATT	General Agreement on Tariffs and Trade
GBL	Global Body Line
GCSR	Globalizing Competition State Regime
GDP	Gross Domestic Expenditure

GERD	Gross Domestic Expenditure on Research and Development
GT	Group Technology
HPWO	High Performance Work Organization
HR	Human Resource
HRIS	Human Resource Information System
HRM	Human Resource Management
ICT	Information and Communication Technology
ILO	International Labour Organization
IMD	International Institutions of Management Development
IMF	International Monetary Fund
IS	Information System
IT	Information Technology
ITAC	International Telework Association and Council
IVF	The Swedish Institute of Production Engineering Research
JIT	Just in Time
KM	Knowledge Management
LPT	Labour Process Theorists/Theory
MNC	Multinational Corporation
MIS	Management Information System
MOT	Management of Technology
NAFTA	North American Free Trade Agreement
NC	Numerically Controlled
NIDL	New International Divisions of Labour
NPM	New Public Management
NSI	National Systems of Innovation
OECD	Organization for Economic Co-operation and Development
PC	Personal Computer
PDA	Personal Digital Assistant
R&D	Research and Development
SCM	Supply Chain Management
SCOT	Social Construction of Technology
SIBIS	Statistical Indicators Benchmarking the Information Society
SPC	Statistics Process Control
SSK	Sociology of Scientific Knowledge
TQM	Total Quality Management
TS	Technological Systems
UK	United Kingdom
UNECE	United Nations Economic Commission for Europe
US	United States
USA	United States of America
WTO	World Trade Organization

1 Introduction:
New Technology @ Work

We are constantly told that we are living through a period of unprecedented technological change, with new products and systems such as the Internet transforming the way in which we communicate, work, do business, even make friends and meet partners. Many of these changes, including iconic products such as the iPod, are experienced mainly in the sphere of consumption. This is a book about new technology at work, yet the gap is not as large as it might seem. After all, iPods have to be made in factories and sold by service workers in shops. More broadly, many contemporary information and communication technologies (ICTs) straddle workplace, home and civil society, even if their uses differ across the specific locations.

Most of the chapters in this book seek to examine the nature, settings and impacts of new technologies on work, organization and management. What we want to do in the first part of this opening chapter is to discuss and understand more broadly the nature and limits to the power of technology. Whilst Chapter 2 examines in greater depth the various theories of technology and society, here we take a preliminary look at some of the themes of such theorizing and how they are represented in popular contemporary discourses such as those in business literatures. Such discourses tend to invest huge significance in the powers of technology. This includes driving and triggering change (the power *of*) and shaping the character of the change (the power *to*). Sometimes these views are called *technological determinism* – the idea that technology determines the pace and content of social change. Within such frameworks some commentators invoke optimistic visions of enhanced democracy, rising skills and economic abundance; others prefer darker scenarios of the destruction of jobs through labour-eliminating devices and the decline of privacy through total surveillance. As will become obvious in subsequent chapters, most social scientists do not endorse the more apocalyptic visions and are more sceptical about the impacts of technology. But the idea of all-powerful technologies is deeply rooted in popular discourses and, as we shall see below, has had some support within different branches of social science.

The legacy of technological determinism

In the 1950s and 1960s technology did not have the prominence it does today and was not associated with the kind of controversies and contending visions that can

be found in contemporary debates. Technology was seen as a neutral force uncon-
nected to social designs and relations – its evolution inevitable and its effects
benign. One of the most widespread theories of the 1950s was the 'logic of industrialism'. All societies that follow the industrialization path are shaped by universal technological and economic imperatives that result in common characteristics
such as hierarchical large scale organizations, urbanization, and the increasing
role of government in society. Managers, civil servants and other experts were
seen as part of a technocratic elite that would run the private and public sector in
the wider interest of all. Whilst such notions have more to do with the machinery
of governance than machines at work, these images of technocratic expertise reinforced the idea of a neutral, benign technological development. As the first stirrings
of a post-industrial future became apparent with the rise of scientific-technical
industries and labour, the labels for the society changed, but the technocratic
images persisted.

At a more micro workplace level, the influence of technological determinism
was more apparent. Most research focussed on the plant and how the technical and
social or human organization fitted together, as this was the best basis for efficiency and work satisfaction. Within such plant sociology, the emphasis was
increasingly put on the power of technology in general, and the currently dominant
form of mass production in particular. One of the best known studies, Walker and
Guest's *Man on the Assembly Line* (1952), referred to mass production as 'a code
of law governing ... behaviour and way of life in the factory' (1952: 2). Workers
had to adjust to the 'commanding machinery' of mass production.

The assembly line and mass production also played a prominent role in the
influential studies of Blauner (1964), but as part of a quartet that included craft,
machine-tending and continuous process. He saw the work process and work satisfaction as determined mainly by structural differentiation related to changing
technologies. The distinctive feature of his argument is that technologies were
developing in an inverted U curve that began with craft relations, hit a low point
for work satisfaction with mass production, but would return to relations of
greater autonomy and skill as technologies such as continuous process in chemicals and brewing began to be automated. This optimism about the trajectory of
technology and automation was common to a lot of (post-) industrial sociology
and social theory in this period (Kumar 1978).

Technological determinism could also be seen in the allied discipline of organization theory. Woodward's (1958) survey-based studies of firms found that
styles of management and formal work organization were determined primarily
by technology. For example, the span of control lengthened as technological
complexity increased. As with industrial sociology, a space was still seen for
varying managerial practice within technological constraints, but the technology
itself was left unexamined and unproblematic.

Such arguments had begun to diminish as social change and new theories
changed the way we looked at technology. Braverman (1974) and what became
known as labour process theory (Thompson 1989) were particularly influential in
this. His argument was that Taylorist methods – measuring, fragmenting and

standardizing work – had remained at the core of managerial practice in the twentieth century. These methods gave capital powerful tools to deskill expensive craft labour and control new work processes. But it was when Taylorism was combined with scientific technical advances such as mechanization that such changes were most far reaching. New forms of machinery offer capital the opportunity to extend by mechanical means what had previously been attempted primarily by means of organization and discipline.

From this viewpoint, science and technology are not neutral productive forces, but are imprinted with social relations of ownership and control in the capitalist labour process. To return to our previous idea of technology embodying two types of power, Braverman brings together the idea that technology has the power to trigger change, but that change is conditioned by the power of capital to fashion the work process to its own ends. It is not technological determinism because different conceptions of machinery embody alternative designs and uses reflected in particular forms of management and organization.

This perspective allowed Braverman and his followers to critique the dominant view of automation as qualitatively different from mechanization. There is a continuum between the two, precisely because technological developments are incorporated into the same underlying Taylorist methods of organizing the labour process. When Braverman was writing *Labor and Monopoly Capital* the first wave of what became known as new technology based on the microprocessor was just beginning. The design capacities of the microchip were seen as an ideal vehicle for managerial shaping of work arrangements, whether further removing skills or increasing electronic surveillance. In the 1970s, the microchip was extending the technological reach of management into office and white-collar sectors that had been previously less touched by deskilling and direct controls. Illustrations were given through the examination of the impact of computer aided design on the work of draughtsmen and of word processing on secretaries. Even computer programming could be industrialized and sub-divided through standardized programs and packages (Kraft 1979). We will look at this in detail in Chapters 4 and 5.

We are not concerned here with the precise or detailed effects examined in later chapters, nor with the qualifications, constraints and variations to such trends made clear by Braverman and labour process theorists. What is important is the conceptual point – the perspective broke with determinism by uncovering the link between managerial motives and technological change. The microchip showed that systems could be designed for different purposes – the technology contains possibilities for different types of skill and work organization.

Such emphases were somewhat lost in wider popular discourses on new technology and the microchip. Picking up on a mixture of the real (e.g. ATM machines replacing bank tellers) and the imaginary (the automated factory) this 'third industrial revolution', as it was often referred to, was projected by many commentators as likely to lead to the collapse or end of work (Jenkins and Sherman 1979; Rifkin 1995). The World Centre for Computer Sciences and Human Resources predicted that, by the end of the 1980s, 50 million people would be without work because of ICTs (Braham 1985). Clearly the doom-laden scenarios didn't come to pass. Whilst one could rehearse the predictable economic and political factors that intervened, the important point for our purposes is that what some saw as a technological imperative, with a clear set of consequences and effects, had been allowed to set much of the terms of debate. At the beginning of such a cycle, hype and over-sold predictions associated with a techno-economic paradigm are characteristic features. That was to be reproduced with a vengeance as we moved to a new paradigm.

ICTs, the Internet and the 'new economy'

The idea of an information age had been around for a considerable time in post-industrial discourses and in the minds of popular business writers and 'futurists' such as Toffler (1970), who conceived of it as a revolution equivalent to its agri-cultural and industrial forerunners. Such arguments were given much greater force by the emergence of a new generation of ICT, notably the Internet. Suddenly we were all heading rapidly down the information superhighway to a new economy and new society where, as Webster observes, it is believed that 'Work will be transformed, education upturned, corporate structures revitalized, democracy itself re-assessed – all because of the "information revolution"' (2002: 4).

For our purposes, the most interesting projections were those that envisaged new employment systems and business models. Much of this focussed on elec-tronic networks, where ICT would facilitate flexibility and communication processes that would replace hierarchies, command and control, by flatter organ-izations, collaboration and collegiality. Another popular commentator, Rifkin (2000) sees an age of access displacing market capitalism, where a hyper-speed network economy renders the ownership of physical capital redundant and intel-lectual capital the primary resource. Liberated from real world borders and their geographic anchor in material production, informational products and services can thus float free of physical space and the traditional business cycle of boom and bust. The rapid expansion and success of dotcom and other 'new economy' firms in the late 1990s merely served to confirm this set of beliefs.

Such arguments are not confined to the populist end of the spectrum. The most influential and detailed contemporary account of technology-influenced social change is provided by Castells (1996, 2001). Summarizing his view of the gen-eral trends, he refers to 'The new economy, spearheaded by e-business, is not an on-line economy, but an economy powered by information technology, depend-ent on self-programmable labor, and organized around computer networks' (2001: 99). Castells is not a simple technological determinist. Aside from clearly stating that technological systems are social products, he distinguishes between an informational *mode of development* (based on ICT innovations) and the capi-talist *mode of production*. Under the combination of the two – informational cap-italism – whilst the market economy still exists, ICT has profoundly altered its operation, and information has become 'the fundamental source of productivity and power' (1996: 21). In turn this has enabled markets to make a great leap for-ward. As Jessop observes, 'Castells argues that capitalism has finally become pervasive because the new infrastructure provided by ICTs has enabled the capitalist mode of production to overcome the limits of time and space and become truly global' (2003: 5). The Internet embodies the capacity of an electronically networked society to allow companies and individuals alike to coordinate complex and decentralized activities across time and space.

Castells also outlines a changed conception of trends in work and employment. An increasing number of jobs will be based on informational occupations such as those in software engineering, biotechnology and advertising. Highly educated and qualified, such labour is also self-programmable – capable, not only of exercising intellective skills in the jobs, but of retraining and renewing their knowledge in portfolio careers. Self-programmable labour can only flourish in the new flat, networked organizations, leaving behind the old rigid hierarchies. He does acknowledge that there is a significant residue of 'generic' labour – people who lack the access to the kind of skills and knowledge to secure a place in informational capitalism. Able only to execute orders, their marginality makes them vulnerable to replacement by machines or cheaper routine employees in developing countries.

Rather than simply being a new technology 'booster', Castells, in common with most social scientists, is thus able to present a more complex picture that sees unevenness, gainers and losers across individuals, groups and nations. The theme of divergent realities is reflected in other literatures that focus on the impact of ICT on the workplace. Amongst the most influential has been Zuboff's (1988) conception of informated labour that draws on her detailed case studies in manufacturing and service settings. She lays out two alternative futures for work and power within a common trend towards the age of the smart machine. Information technology contains a duality that allows companies to automate or informate. While the former will reproduce or deepen the old hierarchical relations and Tayloristic work design, the latter will allow employees to understand and manipulate information, imbuing work with more comprehensive meaning. The informated workplace holds up a mirror to the worker so that his or her actions are rendered visible and precise. But whilst that provides an opportunity for surveillance, management recognized the greater need for 'intellective skills' and critical judgement, and therefore for positive motivation and enhanced cognitive abilities that will flow from less control and more mutual learning and collegial relationships.

Whilst the literature on technological transformations at work throws up more nightmarish scenarios of electronic surveillance (Sewell 1998), if we examine the writings of popular business writers, social scientists such as Castells and those in between like Zuboff, we find that though the labels sometimes change – information age, digital economy, knowledge economy – the power of new ICTs is the persistent feature. This is expressed through three projected kinds of change:

- society-wide notions of a new economy or new business models based on e-commerce;
- new networked, dispersed and decentralized organizational forms;
- new forms of work and employment relations, from autonomous labour to a growing army of freelancers and e-lancers.

An evaluation of many of these claims forms the basis of later chapters. For example Chapters 2, 3 and 4 examine some of the arguments about autonomy and control at work, Chapter 5 looks at corporate structures and organizational forms and Chapter 6 examines the extent and character of employment relations involving teleworkers. Leaving that level of detail until later chapters, we want to make some comments on the more general themes of technology and social transformation.

ICTs undeniably make a difference, and sometimes a decisive one. Massively enhanced capacity for storage and circulation has increased the information-intensive character of many goods and services. Castells is right to note that real-time feedback between companies and customers can enable more efficient and differentiated supply of services. Most importantly, they allow companies to manage more complex product and supply chains. One of the consequences is that large transnationals can disaggregate the work process and re-assemble it in dispersed locations across the globe (Huws 2003). Offshoring of call centres to India provides a good example.

However, whether the emergence of powerful new ICTs justifies the re-definition of a whole economy and society is another matter. Castell's notion of informational capitalism tries to create a workable conceptual hybrid, but the separation of mode of production and informational mode of development allows capitalism to slip into the background whilst the technological revolution becomes the motor of change (Webster 2002: 120). For all his qualifications to technological determinism, Castells continues with the optimism and belief in largely benign outcomes characteristic of post-industrial and post-Fordist pundits. Whilst he acknowledges that the 'new economy' is volatile, he is impatient with critics who argue that it has been over-valued and over-hyped. Indeed, he blames sceptical academic economists for diminishing expectations of innovation and growth (2001: 108).

Webster is one of a variety of writers who emphasize the considerable continuity in economy and work systems, and the power of markets to harness the potential of ICTs in search of ways to commodify new areas of social life. Industries at the heart of the 'new economy' bear out such judgements. Whilst the early stages of the creation of new products and markets appear to be based on very different and more open forms of competition and organization, a process of consolidation and concentration of capital invariably follows. As Schiller, shows in *Digital Capitalism* with respect to the Internet:

> Smaller companies that specialised in what were initially niche markets at the frontier of the liberalisation process worked the new territory. When they succeeded, major traditional suppliers either snapped them up or rushed to develop similar applications of their own.
>
> (Schiller 1999: 28)

As in other sectors, mergers and acquisitions have been the primary engine of concentration. A particular objective has been to facilitate vertical integration that can link up control of content with channels of distribution; an objective aided by the increased convergence of telecommunications, broadcasting and computing technologies. As such concentration increases, the enthusiasm for free, unpatented open-source software comes up against the reality of a corporate grab for control over form and content. The only remarkable thing about these trends is just how quickly the Internet has moved from its military and public sector origins, through the period of pluralism, to corporate domination. For all the access potential available for the information-hungry and resourceful, 'The days when the Net appeared to exist outside the laws of capitalism are just about over' (HotWired, quoted in Golding 1996: 70).

The emergence of peer-to-peer file-sharing and self-production and distribution through websites such as myspace.com has led many commentators to herald the demise of the traditional music industry business model. The new wave of artists can by-pass the corporate world and write, record and distribute music without the traditional record deal. Again, this is a somewhat romantic and short-term view. As a recent study puts it:

> ... as the response to the initial wave of file-sharing demonstrates, the resilience, power and capacity for adaptation of the record companies should not be under-estimated. Within a few years, these companies have largely recovered the ground lost and, through huge investment in legal downloading services, have re-located the existing business model (with its attendant exclusive ownership of intellectual property rights) seamlessly, if not entirely painlessly, to the web.
>
> (Thompson, Jones and Warhurst 2007: 636)

Whilst new technologies diversify and sometimes accelerate the points of entry into the music business, the record companies are still signing up any promising acts and buying up the blogs, websites and other cyberspace outlets that showcase talent. Rupert Murdoch's media empire has already bought up myspace.com, the main web forum to listen to and discuss new bands. These and other examples demonstrate that the big challenge for corporate capital is to locate, enclose and exploit new forms of intellectual property. ICTs open up greater possibilities within this search, but do not prescribe the form or content. Ownership and control of productive assets is still the central question, no matter what the array of new economy theorists say.

It is not only with respect to business models that we can observe a process of continuity. As Webster (2002: 115) notes, for all the claims of novelty surrounding the work of Castells and other writers about the character and effects of new technologies, they are strikingly similar to previous waves of post-industrial discourse. Not only are they technocratic, there is the same aura of optimism. The idea, for example, that as information and knowledge diffuse throughout the world, 'the entire labour force could and should become self-programmable' (2002: 95) seems extraordinarily naïve. Generic labour is neither residue nor uniformed choice by employers, but a specific outcome of contemporary work design whereby more and more jobs are programmed through expert systems or scripted service interactions. Employees have to execute orders, not because they lack the skills, but because they are not given the opportunity to do otherwise.

In this opening chapter, we have tried to set out and examine some of the popular conceptions of new technology at work and in society. Such writings have manifested a strong streak of technological determinism – a linear logic in which technology powers change and has a set of identifiable and largely positive effects. Our perspective in this book is different. We are not trying to stand such claims on their head by saying that technology has no influence or that it can be completely malleable. Technology can be powerful, but, in and of itself, it has no independent causal powers. It makes a difference to our working or other lives when it is invested with specific purposes by human agents (managers, policy makers, etc.) and is embedded in particular social relations (e.g. ownership and control of resources, national institutions).

This has been an extremely brief exposition. In the following chapter we return to the variety of contending perspectives on technology and society, before applying the insights to particular territories and issues in the chapters that follow. In the remainder of this chapter, we provide a more detailed overview of the way in which our argument unfolds in the chapters that follow.

New technology at work: a reassessment

Particular theoretical perspectives that characterize the literature about new technologies make different claims about the role and character of technologies and the nature of the relationship between technology and its social and organizational context. The following chapter critically reviews some of the most significant contributions to the social study of technology to provide a background to our subsequent substantive chapters. Our objective is to build a more nuanced analytical approach characterized by a synthesis of existing political-materialist perspectives that highlight the ways in which new technology can be used to facilitate managerial control over work and work organization, and social constructivist approaches that emphasize the way in which social processes play a critical role in shaping, creating and constituting the nature and impact of technology. The central argument of Chapter 2 is that, despite the weight of research undertaken on new technology at work from a social constructivist perspective, the case for a political materialist account remains compelling. In particular, contemporary research questions demand a theoretical approach which recognizes that the processes of selecting, implementing and deploying technology are *political* processes and that the impact of technology on work is critically mediated by managerial, organizational, politico-economic and institutional factors. Our approach, which is sensitive to both the material characteristics and outcomes of new technology and the social shaping of both technologies and their implementation, can be applied to the study of new technology at organizational, sectoral and national levels, and it is to these issues that we turn in the following chapters.

Manufacturing organizations were among the first to take up integrated computer technologies and communications systems that utilized data to design and control the manufacturing process. In Chapter 3 we focus on the view that the widespread adoption of new technologies and management practices will result in the convergence of manufacturing production and related management systems across nations. What becomes clear from our analysis of the impact of cross-national differences in the application of technologies for management and the organization of work is that there are many other forces involved that filter the take-up of new technologies. Both the application of new technologies and the adoption of management techniques and work practices are intimately associated with the institutional characteristics and policy frameworks of nations and the dominant strategic orientations of business organizations in different national contexts. Any notion of a universal convergence of manufacturing management and the organization of work is quite strongly refuted by these findings.

In contrast with manufacturing, clerical work has been characterized by a much slower pace of technological innovation. For most of the twentieth century, mechanization and technological change had little impact on the way office work was undertaken. In the 1980s and 1990s computers and information and communications technologies enabled a significant rationalization of activity in the 'electronic office', and the way this rationalization has evolved is the topic of Chapter 4. The progressive development of technological change in the office has been uneven, at least in the view of many commentators. There is a positive assessment that information or electronic offices have enabled an enhancement of skills and autonomy for many categories of office employees. However, the arrival of the call centre with their regimented and controlled work practices has thrown some of these assessments into disarray. In our assessment, the social process of organizational change has facilitated a division within the office between routinized, technologically intensive operations and smaller scale operations that use technology in a creative and innovative manner. In other words, new technology in the office allows a versatile and adaptable approach to organizational change. Such change has generally been subordinate to the market and work organization goals of corporate executives and systems designers.

While the strategic objectives of corporate managers influence the framework within which organizational change takes place, they may find themselves both the masters of and subject to new technologies. In Chapter 5 we turn to the role played by new technologies in reshaping how organizations are coordinated and how managers and experts are themselves managed. The first issue is that new technologies are said to pose a challenge to the working arrangements of managers in terms of increased flexibility of time and place, promoting project-focussed collaborative networks characterized by loose amalgamations of autonomous individuals, capital and technology. However, many recent changes in managerial roles are just as likely to be the outcome of downsizing and the expansion of responsibilities across the remaining layers. Our view is that ICT facilitates such diversity and experimentation. However, we should be cautious about attributing changes in organization structure to ICTs and not exaggerate their role as drivers of change. As environments and organizational structures become more complex, so has there been a tendency for diversification of types of control and co-ordination. Hierarchies continue to co-exist with markets and more horizontal forms of coordination.

The second issue discussed in Chapter 5 concerns the view that the knowledge of managers and professional workers is increasingly subject to codification and rationalization through the use of technological systems integrated with organizational practices. Certainly the evidence from recent UK surveys suggests that the sharpest fall in task discretion has been among technical and professional employees. Contemporary performance management systems are grounded in highly computerized metrics and measurement, and supply performance indicators that can be assessed by corporate executives. However, much of the evidence we consider suggests that there are also inherent limits to technological mechanisms and expertise. Given its tacit character and the high level of expert knowledge involved, knowledge work cannot be easily routinized and managed. The process appears to be much more about managing the tension between creativity and control and the boundaries between tacit and explicit knowledge.

One of the most prominent examples of the application of new information and computer technologies on the contemporary work of managers and professionals is the rise of the virtual organization. Chapter 6 reviews the contradictory implications for organizational design and governance of computer mediated communication and distributed work settings. Until recently, the framework of modern work organization has been developed and maintained within the physical boundaries of the workplace enabling trust and control to be embedded in organizational structure. The production of goods and services, controls over productivity and the rate of output are formally and informally determined by organizational systems such as hierarchical structures and the co-ordination of discrete tasks. However, there is now a rapidly increasing category of (tele)workers and others with distributed work arrangements who generally work outside and across organizational boundaries in an emerging pattern of employment that is potentially independent of time and place and the physical networks of communication available within conventional workplaces.

Virtual organization almost always involves cooperative work across distributed work settings where communication and information sharing is provided by advanced technological systems. Many of the workers in these organizations have potentially greater autonomy in time management and are removed from the pace and rhythms of the workplace. This has sparked a recurring theme in a great deal of the popular management literature on these new organizational forms which has emphasized their democratic potential. However, while new information and communication technologies have the potential to facilitate democratic or participatory employment practices, those who assume that these arrangements are a necessary component of the virtual workplace underestimate the social and political issues involved in establishing a corporate environment based on trust between employees and managers that would be necessary for high levels of decision-making autonomy. On the contrary, the studies that we review indicate that managers and system developers tend to implement information technology that embodies existing institutionalized practices, forms of control and authority relationships. Trust and the decision-making autonomy that goes with it are elements which are always likely to be in tension with managerial regulation of the work process. There is simply no reason to believe that management principles are likely to be determined by technological imperatives detached from the political, social and economic context that mediates the impact of new technology on the contemporary workplace.

The importance of social and political forces at the national level is also highlighted in Chapter 7 which explores the interplay between technological change and globalization and examines debates concerning the implications of these trends for work and employment. New patterns of interaction in the international economy in the areas of international finance, trade, the activities of multinational corporations and the development and diffusion of technology are discussed, and the implications for what some have described as the globalized knowledge economy are examined. Our argument suggests that it is both advances in information, communications and media technologies as well as economic policies that remove restrictions on international market transactions that lie behind the globalization of economic activity.

Taken together, these developments have led to a growing division between a segment of the workforce that has experienced real benefits from technological developments and globalization in terms of high growth in real wages and the benefits of high quality, high-skilled employment, and a low-skilled segment in increasingly insecure employment that lacks the capacity to re-skill for new industries. In many national contexts this latter group is relatively unprotected because of the declining influence of trade unions and pressure to deregulate labour markets where trade unions and labour market regulation have traditionally protected the wages and conditions of low skilled employees. The chapter argues that national institutions and the policies of national governments remain important in mediating the effect of globalization and technological transformation on work and employment.

Chapter 8 focusses more directly on the role of the nation state – its policy settings and institutional framework. The chapter is principally concerned with innovation, which includes the development and uptake of technology, the introduction of new products or processes, the introduction of different forms of work organization or management structures and approaches to new market opportunities. Our analysis highlights the continuing differences in advanced economies in key national institutions such as the state, the industrial relations system, the system of education and training, the structure of business organizations and the role of intermediary organizations such as the finance sector and industry associations. This national institutional framework has been shown to be important in terms of the way in which it affects innovation and ultimately influences the uptake of particular kinds of knowledge-intensive activities.

The aim of the chapter is to draw a conceptual distinction between competitive and coordinated market economies. The former have an emphasis on market relations and autonomous business units. In the latter, relations within corporations (between management and employees) and with external organizations and institutions (including other firms, suppliers, customers, research institutions and educational institutions) are more developed and regulated. These settings are not always consistent and some countries depart from the general pattern. However, it seems that alongside success in medium-high and high technology production, coordinated economies have achieved success in knowledge industries that is more broadly transmitted throughout society through a high level of income equality and social cohesion.

The final chapter aims to draw together the key themes developed in the previous chapters concerning the use of new technology in the workplace, the implications for the organization of contemporary work and the impact of new technologies on levels of employment in the various industry sectors. There are two important questions that arise out of the previous discussion. The first concerns the impact of new technology on structural change and the *quantity* of jobs that are destroyed or generated in the process. The second question focuses on the *quality* of jobs and levels of skill and participation in workplace decision-making that have developed out of technological changes. The main focus is on the way in which both the quantity and the quality of jobs have changed as a result of the manner in which new technologies have been introduced into the workplace and utilized to manage production. Our argument is that these are political questions about which social groups have differential power resources to influence decisions to develop and implement new technologies. Political power as it pertains to the organization of work will, in turn, be influenced by: levels of unionization; the strength of institutions that represent employer or employee interests in industrial relations or broader policy arenas; dominant policy agendas; and the ideological predispositions of political parties in power.

The general theme that shapes our argument throughout the book may be summarized as follows. Technology itself has no independent causal powers but it can make a significant difference to our working and other lives when it is invested with specific purposes by human agents (managers, policy makers) and is embedded in particular social relationships and institutions. An important consideration that underlies the debate about new technology at work is that decisions that influence the implementation of new technology in various national settings are part of an ongoing process of change which will be very likely to constrain future choices and to set a trajectory for the workplace of the future.

2   Organizational change

Theories of technological change at work

Technology has long been seen as central to organizational, social and economic change. Beyond some of the more simplistic accounts that see technology as directly and unconditionally determining the nature of change at work and in society, there persists a rich tradition of the social study of technology at work. This tradition has attempted to interpret the complex relations between technology, social processes and work organization as a means of understanding a range of phenomena: the impact of technology on work, the impact of social processes and social agency on technology and, most recently, the nature of organizational change as *sociotechnical* change (Badham 2005). In the course of this work, virtually all the dimensions of technological change have been questioned: the ontological status of technology itself (material or constructed), the possibility that technologies actually have 'effects', the relationship between technology and work, the capacity of managers, workers, users, consumers and other actors (human and non-human!) to shape, construct and enact technology, and the very experience of technological change itself.

A review of the social study of technology undertaken over the past 30-odd years suggests the existence of four principal approaches: technologically determinist, managerialist, political materialist and social constructivist. While there are (sometimes fundamental) disagreements between the elements of each of these four perspectives on technology at work, the critical review which informs our study seeks to derive its theoretical and research propositions from all of these approaches and the debates they have inspired. In other words we ask: what can we learn from almost four decades of the social study of technology at work? What do the theoretical debates, empirical investigations and the weight of evidence suggest about the claims of these different approaches?

Attempts to categorize the main theoretical approaches to technology at work have typically distinguished between those approaches that focus on the features of the technology and its impact, and those that emphasize the role of the social context and the role of social actors in the construction or shaping of the technology in the organization. Traditional studies tended to do the former, while more recent approaches have tended to do the latter. In more recent times there have been a number of attempts to reconcile both approaches (Orlikowski 1992; McLoughlin 1999; Badham 2005).

Liker, Haddad and Karlin (1999) utilize a simple two-dimensional matrix ('technology focus' versus 'contextual focus' and 'static' versus 'dynamic' approaches) to generate four general approaches to the analysis of technology impacts: 'Technological Determinism' (static technology focus), 'Management of Technology' (dynamic technology focus), 'Political Interests' (static contextual focus) and 'Interpretivist' (dynamic contextual focus) approaches. Liker *et al.*'s static–dynamic dimension appears to be based on the predictability (static) or unpredictability (dynamic) of the impact of technology (1999: 580). This implies that 'static' is virtually coterminous with 'determinist'.

McLoughlin (1999: 8–10) bases his classification on the different metaphors for technology that tend to be employed by different theoretical traditions. 'Technologically determinist' approaches tend to represent technology as 'machine', 'organism', 'information system' or as evolutionary process. In opposition to technological determinism, McLoughlin notes the emergence of more critical approaches that have highlighted the adverse consequences of technology, including its role in enhancing management surveillance and control and its consequences for worker skills and power. These approaches are linked to 'strategic choice/organizational politics' perspectives which argue that the use and deployment of a given technology is the result of the complex interaction between organizational power struggles and the purposive intent of managers and key stakeholders. This category thus resembles the 'Political Interests' perspective identified by Liker *et al.* 'Social constructivist' approaches rely on metaphors of 'actor-networks', 'ensembles' and 'texts' depending on the specific variant. And finally McLoughlin distinguishes 'Social Shaping' perspectives that see technology as the 'embodiment' or 'crystallization' of social processes and histories.

Informed by both these attempts at classification, we propose a slightly more elaborated schema as shown in Figure 2.1.

This schema attempts to locate some of the most prominent approaches to the study of technology at work in terms of whether their prime explanatory focus is technological, political or social and whether their accounts of technology at work tend to be relatively 'simple' – identifying one or a small number of variables as causal – or 'complex' – identifying multiple variables as causal. Figure 2.1 accommodates most of the specific theoretical approaches reviewed in this chapter, although it does not do justice to the subtlety and complexity of many of these approaches; nor does it convey the inter-relationships between some of them. From the perspective of schools of thought or analytical traditions there are, as suggested above, arguably four clusters:

1   Technological determinism, which tends to focus on the characteristics of the technology, and which also includes Management of Technology (MOT) approaches to technology selection.
2   MOT approaches, which are primarily concerned with processes of implementation, and afford a very significant role to management agency in the implementation process. These approaches share much with early strategic choice approaches, although these latter perspectives are discussed in the

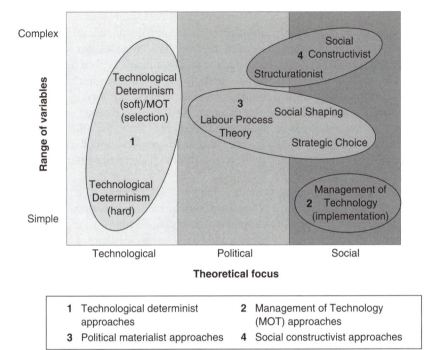

Figure 2.1 Approaches to the social study of technology.

context of the Political Materialist tradition because this is the direction in which subsequent strategic choice work tended to move.

3 Political materialist approaches which take a political focus and include Labour Process Theory (LPT) approaches and many of the social shaping approaches along with the later strategic choice perspectives.

4 Social constructivist approaches which take a strongly social focus and countenance a high degree of complexity in their accounts of technology at work, and include the Social Construction of Technology (SCOT) school, Actor Network Theory approaches and, most recently, a range of perspectives informed by theories of structuration.

Technological determinism and management of technology approaches

As discussed in the previous chapter, technological determinism – the idea that technological artefacts have certain identifiable, objective and deterministic qualities that affect or even determine individual, group, organizational and societal behaviour and dynamics – continues to occupy an important if contested place in the field. On one hand, technologically determinist perspectives have been thoroughly and repeatedly discredited as naïve, simplistic, myopic, reductionist and functionalist. Indeed, it is virtually *de rigueur* for contemporary researchers on technology to disavow any hint of technological determinism as a precursor to their subsequent analysis (irrespective of their subsequent reliance on technologically determinist assumptions). On the other hand, the idea that technologies *do* have discernable effects on individuals, organizations and even societies continues to be alluring, and the central question addressed by technological determinism – what are the organizational, workplace or societal effects of a particular technology? – continues to attract interest. As some have noted (e.g. Winner 1977), if technologies did not have any discernable effects then there would be little point in studying them. While we have some sympathy with the pragmatism of that position, as will be seen in the course of this chapter, the matter is not quite so straightforward.

Technological determinism comes in hard and soft variants. The hard version asserts that technologies have predictable consequences and that outcomes (such as organizational change, for example) can be explained wholly or predominately in terms of the technology, its design and characteristics. As noted in the previous chapter there are optimistic and pessimistic variations on these themes. Hard technological determinism is unsustainable – the empirical record offers little support for the claim that technological change is predictable or that it can be fully explained by the characteristics of the technology itself.

A softer version of technological determinism that asserts that the characteristics of the technology, along with other variables, are likely to have an impact on organizational change in instances of new technology at work, is more compelling. Soft technological determinism might simply direct our analytical attention to the characteristics of the technological artefact in question. We also accept the more controversial claim that technological artefacts have a material reality: qualities and characteristics that, while not determinist, can still limit, influence or shape outcomes at the workplace, organizational or even societal level. Therefore we accept that technological artefacts can have material characteristics that might help explain organizational change, but insist that the impact of these characteristics will inevitably be mediated by a range of political, institutional and social factors and processes.

Management of Technology approaches tend to focus on the processes of technology selection and implementation (Liker *et al.* 1999: 582). Technology selection is guided by organizational strategy, but once organizational strategy has been settled, selection is primarily a matter of identifying the technological artefact that will deliver the desired results. In this sense, then, selection is determined by the characteristics of the technology; hence the classification of MOT (selection) approaches as technologically determinist. From an MOT perspective, however, implementation is a highly social process, although one that can be seen to be relatively 'straightforward' in the sense that it is a predictable process of management completing specific implementation steps according to a planned sequence. MOT suggests that, armed with an appropriate implementation methodology, managers can ensure implementation outcomes that are optimal for the organization (Huber 1990; Bloomfield and Coombs 1992; Preece 1995). Provided management follows the appropriate steps, technology implementations can be managed so as to ensure optimal outcomes for organizations.

We see MOT approaches as politically and analytically deficient. MOT approaches address a distinctively managerialist problematic, and pay little attention to the interests or perspectives of workers whose interests might not correspond with those of managerial efficiency, disclosing a distinctively 'unitarist' assumption regarding organizational interests. MOT approaches also have difficulty in accounting for diverse outcomes (which often results from the same technology), failed or suboptimal implementations, and the unintended consequences which often seem to flow from technology implementations. MOT can only explain these in terms of managerial failure to adhere to the specified implementation steps and tend to ignore the possibility of the role of other contextual variables in accounting for technology and organizational change.

Political materialist perspectives

The idea that technologies have an independent material 'reality' and form, and that their implementation or introduction in an organization or social context will have consequences and impacts that affect the objective conditions under which people work, interact and organize (what we conceive of as 'materialism'), is of course entirely consistent with technological determinism and what were described earlier as MOT approaches. However, the political materialist perspectives discussed here diverge from both technological determinism and MOT at fundamental points. Political materialist perspectives tend to share with both a concern to take the technology and its objective and apparent characteristics 'seriously' (Orlikowski and Iacono 2001). However, whereas technological determinism claims that the material characteristics of the technology will have a more or less determinate impact on organization and people, largely independent of the organizational context (Woodward 1958, 1965), political materialist perspectives see the organizational impact and effect of any technology as decisively shaped by struggles between a range of social and political actors and forces – capital, labour, the state, consumers, producers, etc. – at (potentially) societal, organizational and workplace levels. On the other hand, political materialist approaches differ from MOT approaches by problematizing the process of 'managing' the technology. Political materialist approaches reject the unitarist view of the organization implicit in the MOT formulation – rather than the possibility of achieving an outcome that is unambiguously optimal for the organization, its managers and workers, these approaches assert that there are different sets of interests that can be ascribed to different groups of workers, managers and other actors that are variously met, or not met, by various implementations of different technologies.

A central theme of political materialist approaches is therefore that technologies and their implementation are socially shaped by political processes and struggles that are infused by the interests of different actors. Labour Process Theory (LPT), inspired by Braverman's (1974) famous reconsideration of Marx's theory of the labour process in capitalism, was one of the first to develop a critical analysis of new technology at work informed by these ideas. A strategic choice approach associated with the work of Child (1973), which initially emphasized the role of managers and organizations in making deliberate choices about technologies and their implementation, converged with aspects of the evolving LPT approach in the sense that Child's (1984, 1985) later analysis afforded a greater role for structural interests in shaping choice. Social shaping approaches, which came to see social shaping as economic shaping (MacKenzie and Wajcman 1999: 13), can also be considered to be political materialist in character.

Braverman and labour process theory

The central claim of Braverman's (1974) famous and influential thesis concerning the capitalist labour process was that in contemporary capitalism, capitalists ensured effective control over the labour process by using the techniques and strategies of scientific management (or 'Taylorism') to separate the role of conception (planning and designing work processes, methods and tasks) from the role of execution (undertaking the tasks). Taylorism had critical implications for the work of workers and managers alike: the fragmentation of jobs into a series of discrete work tasks that in themselves required relatively little skill, training or understanding of the broader work process and production system led to a deskilling of work that had traditionally been undertaken by relatively skilled craft workers. The more intellectual, conceptual and strategic parts of jobs (determining how and in what order various work tasks should be undertaken) were concentrated in the hands of managers. The key problem for management under Taylorism, according to Braverman, was not the design of the most efficient and profitable work methods, but rather ensuring that workers undertaking deskilled and degraded work worked assiduously and efficiently, and according to what would now be known as standard operating procedures. Originally this required extensive direct surveillance and oversight by supervisors (so called 'direct control'). The critical role for technology in the capitalist labour process was, however, its capacity to automate aspects of work and thereby reduce the direct control burden shouldered by supervisors, leading hands and middle managers of various kinds. Thus, for example, workers on a manufacturing assembly line were effectively controlled by the machinery itself: the pace of work, the order in which tasks were executed and the specific actions and methods for completing a work task were determined in significant part by the operation of the technology as implemented. As such, technology was seen by Braverman to enhance control and deskill non-managerial work.

Commentators (e.g. Liker *et al.* 1999) often overlook the fact that deskilling was not seen by Braverman to be the *inevitable* result of technological change at work. Tendencies to deskilling were not inherent in the technology itself, according to Braverman, but were characteristic of technological change *in the capitalist labour process* because technology could and would be used by capitalists to increase or maintain control over the labour process – the 'central problem of management in capitalism' (McLoughlin and Clark 1994: 44–5). In any event, the key conclusion to be drawn from Braverman's analysis of technology at work is that technology in the capitalist labour process will be used to deskill work as a means of increasing capitalist control over the labour process.

Criticisms of the deskilling thesis and implications for the labour process theory of technology

Criticisms of Braverman's deskilling thesis have been described and debated in detail elsewhere (Wood 1982; Thompson 1989; McLoughlin and Clark 1994). While there is little point in reviewing them comprehensively here, they have provided direction to subsequent work on technology at work that has been undertaken in the labour process tradition. Four main avenues of critique of the deskilling thesis can be readily identified.

First, it was apparent to critics of Braverman that deskilling and automation of work tasks is not the only, nor the most rational control strategy available to capital. Particularly in the case of more complex work, where it is rational for capital to encourage workers to exercise discretion and judgement in the execution of their tasks, capitalists will control work through strategies of 'responsible autonomy' (Friedman 1977) under which a degree of autonomy is afforded workers in exchange for their commitment to achieving the goals sought by management. Setting aside questions of the accuracy or prevalence of responsible autonomy, it is apparent that many contemporary control strategies rely on much more than simply deskilling and automation. The key implication for the study of technology in organizations is not that technology is inevitably used for deskilling, but rather that technology can be used to enhance managerial control. It follows that we need to be alert to the potential role of technology in the mix of control strategies used in contemporary work organizations.

Second, it was widely noted that Braverman's analysis suggested that 'management' tended to operate as a monolithic, unified group in seeking to control the labour process of all 'workers'. This, it was claimed, ignored the fact that there is typically great diversity within 'management' – supervisors, middle managers, line managers, operational managers, senior managers are all likely to have different interests and concerns and different orientations towards a whole range of strategies including labour use and work organization strategies. To ascribe a simple uniformity of purpose and intent amongst all managers in an organization (let alone across an entire sector or economy) was portrayed as naïve. Certainly subsequent empirical analysis has pointed to the divisions and differences between different kinds of managers even within the same organization, and the relatively small number of studies (e.g. Harley, Wright, Hall and Dery 2006) which have looked at management attitudes to technology implementations have confirmed this picture of complexity. This does not mean that there might not be a general tendency for management driving technology implementations to be concerned to enhance their control of the labour process of operational workers, but it does mean that technology implementation decisions and processes are likely to be more complicated than a simple 'control-through-deskilling' logic might suggest. We need to recognize that technology will not simply be used or interpreted uniformly by all managers – managers and workers will have diverse interests at the workplace level, and specific technologies and technology implementations will have complex and variable implications for different organizational members.

Third, Braverman's thesis was also widely discredited on the grounds that it tended to under-emphasize the reality of (worker) resistance in the face of deskilling. It is clear that management does not, and cannot, act unilaterally in deskilling, automating, dividing, reconfiguring and reorganizing work through the use of technology (or indeed by other means). Workers will often resist, subvert or refashion the implementation or introduction of new technologies, just as much as they might resist any attempts at change – a simple fact long recognized in even the clearly non-critical organizational change literatures. Evidently, then, the realities of worker resistance, as well as the ever-present possibilities of worker consent (Burawoy 1979), further complicate any simple control-through-deskilling-and-automation account of technology implementation and change. In addition, then, to recognizing that managers' responses to technological change will be diverse, we must recognize diversity in worker reactions to technological change: consent, compliance, accommodation, as well as various forms of passive and active resistance are all possible. Nevertheless, perhaps the more important point is that managerial attempts to secure complete control (through technological or other means) will never be perfect, owing in part to the 'persistence of resistance' (Thompson and Harley 2007).

Fourth, and possibly most decisively, Braverman's thesis has been challenged by the weight of empirical studies of technology and deskilling/upskilling, and the apparent trends in work organization and restructuring since the time of his writing over 30 years ago. There are a number of lines of argument and research that have sought to demonstrate the falsity or limitations of the deskilling thesis in empirical terms: some of these promoted the ideas of post-Fordism (Piore and Sabel 1984) and then more recently the information society/knowledge economy (Castells 2001); another stream of research much more sympathetic to Labour Process Theory concluded, on the basis of detailed empirical studies of the effects of technologies on skills at work, that both upskilling and deskilling outcomes are always possible in practice (Wilkinson 1983; Boddy and Buchanan 1986; McLoughlin 1989, 1999); other more openly critical of LPT have proposed a generalized if not universal upskilling associated with the proliferation of ICTs (Adler 1992); yet another stream of research focussed on the potential of new technology to achieve heightened control through the enhanced surveillance of work (Zuboff 1988; Sewell and Wilkinson 1992).

While empirical studies rendered any strong version of the deskilling thesis untenable, alternative generalizing paradigms have proven to be no more persuasive. The post-Fordist future of empowered, functionally flexible workers has failed to materialize as a general trend. In Chapter 1 it was suggested that the ideas of the post-industrial, information society/information economy are similarly naïve and over-stated. Yet with LPT approaches somewhat discredited by the failure of the deskilling thesis to stand up to empirical scrutiny, the time was ripe for alternative accounts. In the early 1990s Adler (1992) heralded a new consensus which accepted that, in general terms, new technology was in fact leading to aggregate levels of upskilling. His collection of studies included an examination of the effects of new technology on workers and managers at Digital Equipment Corporation (Hirschhorn and Mokray 1992), a revised analysis of aggregate skill levels across US occupations (Attewell 1992), as well as Kern and Schumann's (1992) revision of their earlier research (which had supported the deskilling thesis). The conclusion drawn from these studies, by Adler, was that contemporary competitive pressures were driving forms of automation and technological transformation that demanded 'both new upgraded skills and new broadened roles' (1992: 10). While Adler clearly concluded that the dominant trend, on the basis of these kinds of empirical studies, was in the direction of upskilling, he conceded that 'upgrading tendencies will typically manifest themselves in a somewhat chaotic manner, often leaving pockets of de-skilling and layoffs' (1992: 8). Despite Adler's apparent enthusiasm to write the obituary for the deskilling thesis, some of the studies in his collection suggest that deskilling was more widespread than he suggested. For example, Senker's (1992) contribution argued that while an upskilling of work was *needed* in contemporary UK manufacturing, the reality was that management in the sector typically remained opposed to upskilling, thus compromising the benefits that might otherwise have accrued to British manufacturing organizations undertaking technological change. Rather than a generalized trend for deskilling or upskilling, Senker's study reaffirms contingency and the role of management as well as a range of workplace, organizational, institutional and economy-wide variables in explaining the effects of new technology – themes that were becoming more relevant in second-wave LPT studies of new technology.

Although discredited, LPT approaches to technology did not wither and die in the wake of the deskilling debate. In a series of studies conducted in the 1980s, researchers broadly sympathetic to LPT, and cognizant of the critiques of the deskilling thesis, examined the introduction of a variety of new technologies in diverse work settings, explicitly considering the impact of those technologies on worker's skills and experience of work. These studies (e.g. Buchanan and Boddy 1983; Clark, McLoughlin, Rose and King 1988; Baldry and Connelly 1986; McLoughlin 1989, 1990) suggest that, while deskilling is certainly not inevitable in the case of new technology, it is a common tendency. But the most significant insight of these studies was the recognition that the effect of new technology (on skills, control, power and the experience of work) depended on the contingent interaction of managerial choice and power, worker power, resistance and creativity, and the organization of work (the division of labour, the organization of the labour process, forms of control), as much as it depended on the nature of the technology itself. Studies in this tradition are considered in more detail in Chapter 3 where we discuss the implications of the combination of technologies (including AMTs) with managerial strategies such as JIT and TQM in manufacturing. These studies confirm that the impact of new technology is contingent on the way that technology is configured and implemented. This was a theme that had been earlier emphasized by strategic choice perspectives (considered below). However, for the LPT researchers, those decisions were not seen to result from any unfettered managerial choice, but were, rather, decisively shaped by the organization of work, the political-economic environment of the organization and the struggles between labour and capital.

Power, political interests and strategic choice

The idea that technologies as implemented were best understood as the result of the strategic choice of powerful organizational decision-makers was promoted by Child in the early 1970s. McLoughlin (1999) argues that what is most significant about Child's approach was that it highlighted the role of power, and conceived the process of technological selection and implementation as a political process. Wilkinson (1983) highlighted the organization and its technology as the product of struggle between key actors at the workplace level: management, unions and workers. Wilkinson's study further echoes second-wave LPT in concluding that the outcome of these struggles is contingent on the way in which conflicts, negotiations and compromises are played out at the organizational level. The nature of political struggles over technology at the organizational level was further elaborated by those such as Clark *et al.* (1988) identifying 'critical junctures' at which key decisions about the design, configuration, operation and evaluation of a given technology were determined.

While there is much to commend the emphasis on politics in the strategic choice/organizational politics approach, it does suffer from a number of weaknesses. First, to the extent that these approaches focus on political power-plays at the organizational level, environmental factors and broader structural realities (that are fundamentally political) might be downplayed. Thus for example, a technological outcome might be explained by the relative power resources available to various coalitions within an organization and their capacity to mobilize those resources at specific 'critical junctures'. However, the broader political economy of the organization and the technology implementation might be decisive and might help explain why, for example, managerial preference trumps union opposition to a particular implementation. Second, while these approaches are political, they are not necessarily strongly materialist. These approaches can descend into a kind of political determinism where the material characteristics of the technology are prone to be under-emphasized and the account of the material implications of the technology as implemented might be underdeveloped.

More compelling and persuasive accounts of technological change that adopt a genuinely political materialist perspective have sought to combine a sensitivity to the micro-dynamics of workplace politics with a recognition of the political-economic and institutional environment in which organizations operate. Noble's (1979) study of automatically controlled machine tools remains perhaps *the* classic example of this approach. Noble asked why the technology of automatically controlled machine tools took the form that it did – a form that was feasible for some firms and not others, and a form that facilitated enhanced, but far from perfect, managerial control over the labour process of machinists. Two candidates for the automation of machine tools emerged in post-war manufacturing: the 'record–playback' method which recorded the physical manipulations of a machinist on magnetic tape for later automatic replay; and the 'numerical control' (NC) method which converted the technical specifications of a finished part into a numerical code which was then stored on an NC tape. The former technology retained the skill of the machinist in the labour process; the latter largely eliminated the need for that skill. In time NC prevailed over record–playback. Yet the ascendancy of NC could not be explained simply by any clear technical superiority of NC, nor simply by the power dynamics at the workplace level; rather Noble's detailed account reveals the importance of the 'social context' in which NC was developed. Noble identifies the 'horizontal relations of production' – the relations between manufacturing firms and the leading role of the US Air Force – and the 'vertical relations of production' – the relations between management and labour – as critical to the story. He explains that NC technology was made possible only by the intervention of the Air Force which effectively created a market for NC. Firms were forced to follow, lured by lucrative Air Force contracts. As a result, record–playback, despite its lower cost and greater feasibility for smaller firms, was abandoned as a technology. But Noble notes that the ascendancy of the more expensive and complex NC technology was also consistent with the vertical relations of production: NC allowed employers to reduce their dependence on the skills of machinists. In Noble's analysis of NC technology therefore we can see the convergence of the political economy of machining, dominated by an Air Force keen to control a smaller number of large contractors utilizing a sophisticated, consistent and ultimately flexible technology, with the workplace politics of management in large firms seeking to enhance its control over a labour process traditionally controlled by skilled machinists.

In line with the tradition of LPT, however, it was noted by Noble that management's attempt to control the labour process of machinists was far from completely successful. Problems with the technology, worker resistance and shopfloor mobilization combined to ensure that machinists continued to exercise significant control over the labour process. Subsequent work on the impact of computer numerical control (CNC) systems confirmed the importance of processes of workplace negotiation, accommodation and compromise. CNC systems, it was observed, could, therefore, be implemented in different ways, affording more or less control and discretion to workers on the shopfloor. Different configurations of CNC were seen to be influenced by the relative power of labour and management at workplace, sectoral and national levels (Anderson 1988; Hampson 1999).

Since the work of Noble (1979), Wilkinson (1983), Buchanan and Boddy (1983) and McLoughlin and his colleagues in the 1980s, distinctively LPT approaches to technology at work have been more difficult to identify. There are a number of reasons for this. First, LPT was discredited by the failure of the deskilling thesis. Amongst other things, this probably dampened the enthusiasm of LPT researchers for grand generalizations and theory building, in the name of LPT at least. Second, theoretical claims of the kind that might come from a political materialist position were also exposed to the increasingly intense critique of post-structuralist approaches that came to dominate the social study of technology in the 1990s. Third, the rise and rise of information and communication technologies (ICTs) as the key technological form and (arguably) prime impetus for technological change in recent times has presented significant challenges to social researchers and theorists of all inclinations. As a result, not only has LPT lost its exclusive claim to the franchise on critical studies of work and organization, it is also struggling to sustain a political materialist approach to technology at work.

Since the early 1990s, most studies of technology that have been informed by LPT and might still be classified as political materialist in orientation have gone in one of two directions. On the one hand, several studies have focussed on the impact of new technologies in specific sectors and particular kinds of workplaces. For example, categories of analysis common in LPT, such as power, control, resistance, discretion, autonomy, work intensification and skill have been pressed into service in the analysis of new technologies and call centre work (Bain and Taylor 2000; Callaghan and Thompson 2001), banking (Regini, Kitay and Baethge 1999; Autor, Levy and Murnane 2002), the software labour process (Kraft 1977; Friedman and Cornford 1989; Beirne, Ramsay and Panteli 1998; Barrett 2005), grocery warehousing and distribution (Wright and Lund 1997; Lund and Wright 2003) and various kinds of customer service work (e.g. Sturdy 2001). While these studies are rich and informative they have not typically advanced a political materialist *theory* of new technology at work; generalizations are difficult where case studies in specific industries are undertaken and where explanations are developed in terms of the contingencies of specific workplaces and industries; a kind of 'plant particularism' has been the result.

On the other hand, the general conclusion that might be derived from many of these studies, and the earlier studies reviewed above – that there are multiple social forces that explain the form and impact of new technologies at work – has led to work that corresponds to the social shaping approach associated with the work of MacKenzie and Wajcman (1985, 1999).

Social shaping approaches

Social shaping approaches tend to identify the social, institutional, economic and cultural factors and forces that shape the direction and rate of technological innovation, the form of technology and the outcomes or impacts of technology (Williams and Edge 1996: 868). These approaches can be considered to be political materialist in tenor because they accept that technological artefacts have material characteristics and implications that are significant, and they can accommodate an analysis of political struggle as part of the central casual dynamic of social shaping. Social shaping differs from LPT approaches, however, in the sense that these approaches accept a very broad range of factors as shaping technology and its effects, and fail to privilege particular social forces such as political economy and labour–capital struggles as decisive. The main factors that social shaping sees as relevant are the technology itself, economics, social factors and the state.

Social shaping approaches highlight the role that technological factors play in technology design. What social shapers mean by this is that prior technological developments, artefacts and experiences are critical to future technological developments. New technologies do not suddenly emerge from the 'flash of inspiration' of a genius inventor (MacKenzie and Wajcman 1999: 7–8). Rather, new technologies build on previous technologies and, rather than revolutionary or radical new inventions, technological innovation is normally characterized by a process of steady and incremental development.

Economic considerations and influences are seen as critical. New technologies are not simply the result of technical improvements but are also the result of cost calculations. Hughes's (1979) study of Edison's 'invention' of the light bulb is invoked as the classic example to demonstrate that technical reasoning is often bound up with economic reasoning. In brief, the reason why Edison's light bulb triumphed over alternatives, was not its technological superiority, but its economic feasibility – Edison understood that to be cost-effective, light bulb filaments needed to use a relatively tiny amount of (expensive) copper. But as MacKenzie and Wajcman assert (1999: 13), economic considerations and calculations are themselves shaped by social factors: what counts as costs and benefits and how the future potential costs and benefits of any technology are evaluated will be shaped by the social context. Here, MacKenzie and Wajcman's conception of 'social context' approximates our understanding of political economy – economic calculations are shaped by social factors such as incentives for new technologies and production methods, the cost of labour and capital, the nature and maturity of the market for various products and services, and so forth.

Social shaping also admits into its analysis the role of the state as a variable shaping technology and its effects. However, it might be argued that the social shapers' notion of the state is relatively narrow. When invoking the state as part of their accounts, social shapers often point to the very prominent role played by military interests in shaping the trajectory of technological innovation (MacKenzie and Wajcman 1999: 16). As Noble's analysis of NC technologies and the cases of jet engines, nuclear energy, electronics and computers readily attest, the military industrial complex has been a critical influence on the path of technological development. However, we contend that this does not give due attention to the role of the state in shaping the prevailing political economy and thus its role in affecting the context for the economic and market calculations discussed above.

It is also notable that for all its capacity to accommodate a broad range of factors into the explanation of the forms taken by technology, social shaping approaches do not focus attention on the impact of technology *at work*. This is hardly surprising, given that social shaping approaches do not have, and do not purport to have, a developed theory of work, industrial relations, political economy or the capitalist labour process. Nevertheless, we see this as a weakness when it comes to analysing technology at work.

In one sense, social shaping approaches straddle both the political materialist tradition and the social constructivist tradition discussed in the next section. As noted above, these approaches are clearly materialist in their conception of technology and its implications. However, they share with social constructivist perspectives a distaste for social structures or 'wider social relations such as those of class, gender and ethnicity' because 'often what is more immediately relevant are "local" considerations …' (MacKenzie and Wajcman 1999: 18–19). As will become clear in our review of social constructivist approaches, we see this rejection of the role of social structures as a critical weakness for theoretical approaches to understanding technology at work.

Contemporary labour process theory and technology at work reconsidered

As noted earlier, LPT's potential contribution to understanding technology at work was discredited, to some degree, by its failure to confirm the original deskilling thesis and by the potency of subsequent post-structuralist attacks on its materialism and structuralism. We contend, however, that a politically materialist approach remains the most promising lens through which to analyse new technology at work and that LPT has much more to contribute. Rather than simply criticizing LPT for becoming mired in the deskilling debate of the 1970s and 1980s, for becoming distracted by debates with the post-structuralists over the 'missing subject' in the 1980s and 1990s, and for restricting itself to detailed case studies of technology implementations in particular workplaces and sectors ever since, we believe LPT has much to offer to an enhanced appreciation of the role of technology in facilitating control and mediating skill change. One of the most significant and enduring contributions of LPT has been the analysis of the control-resistance dynamic. The most significant contribution of a revitalized Labour Process Theory of technology at work may well be the analysis of the role of contemporary technologies in facilitating new regimes of control at work.

The 'plant particularism' of recent LPT research on technology at work may have militated against our ability to derive new theories. However, it is possible to see in this work, and related politically materialist research discussed further in Chapters 4 and 5, the emergence of a new account of the role of technology, and in particular information and communications technology (ICT), in instituting and facilitating new forms of control at work. The theoretical account sketched here is based on the capacity of ICT to facilitate enhanced managerial control through standardization, automation, direct technological control and work intensification.

New ICT is being used to establish and implement *standardized work procedures and processes*. This standardization tendency comes in many forms and variants, some of which echo classical examples of deskilling. For example, innovations in computer programming have facilitated the commoditization of elements of the software labour process (Beirne *et al.* 1998; Greenbaum 1998). Thus, structured programming directs programmers through specific steps and stages, drawing on previously programmed and tested lines of code that can be re-used and be re-assembled into a complete program. Again, while this might not be a straightforward case of deskilling, commoditization has removed some of the creativity and innovation from programming work, compelling programmers to follow pre-determined pathways to the final software product, and promoting a more 'industrial' model of software programming into the bargain.

Another example from the finance industry also demonstrates the way that new technologies can promote and enforce business process standardization, with important implications for skills, discretion, autonomy and control. In one finance company studied by one of the authors (see Buchanan and Hall 2003), management had introduced an automated program for quickly assessing the credit-worthiness of applicants for motor vehicle finance. Operators, with no financial assessment experience or expertise, would simply enter basic information concerning the financial and personal details of applicants acquired over the phone, and the program would reject or accept the application. While exceptional cases still had to be referred to credit assessment officers, the number of these officers had been significantly reduced, and the capacity of credit assessors to intervene and exercise their professional judgement in assessing applications had been severely attenuated. The important point for management, however, was that the processing time for credit applications had been massively reduced. These kinds of programs are now widely used in all high-volume credit application processing settings (Meder 2004).

Using technology to enforce standardized work processes has been especially prominent in customer service and call centre work in particular – areas where extensive LPT-inspired work has been undertaken over the past fifteen years (see Chapter 4 for a review of this research). The combination of online scripts, ACD systems and active computer-based monitoring of call centre operators' task performance, ensures standardized service encounters designed to maximize efficiency, and severely limits the discretion and autonomy of call centre operators in undertaking basic work tasks (Bain and Taylor 2000; van den Broek 2004).

New ICTs have also facilitated easier and faster *information transfer and data processing*. The solution of the so-called hardware and software problems in IT development in the 1970s and 1980s meant that computer systems then had the capacity to centrally gather, store, process and disseminate vast volumes of data relatively quickly and cheaply. This data processing revolution has had profound consequences for the organization of work in many areas including banking and finance. In the case of banking, centralized data processing centres restructured the work performed in bank branches (by relocating much data processing work to remote, centralized locations) and demanded the collection and communication of data in standardized form. Amongst other things, this transformed the work of branch managers by removing their traditional power to make many lending decisions (Kitay 1999). The introduction of key banking technologies such as automatic teller machines, phone banking and internet banking further transformed banking work, leading to the elimination of many bank teller jobs, the fragmentation of banking careers and the creation of new kinds of relatively low-skilled banking jobs with truncated or non-existent career paths (e.g. data processors, call centre operators and customer service officers). The case of the impact of data processing and other ICTs in banking reiterates a consistent theme in political materialist approaches to technology and work – it is not the technology itself that determines work organizational outcomes, but the interaction between the technology's capacity (to centrally process mass data, for example) and the decisions taken by organizations (to establish centralized data processing centres, for example); decisions which are themselves shaped by organizational and sectoral struggles between labour and capital, the nature of the product, service and labour markets, and the prevailing division of labour in the organization and sector.

Recent LPT studies have continued to demonstrate the ways in which technologies are used to *directly and indirectly control the pace of work*. LPT has highlighted forms of technologically-driven control that have emerged beyond the machine-pacing of work (demonstrated by examples such as Wilkinson's (1983) plating factory, and conceptualized as 'technical control' by Edwards (1979)). Some of the clearest examples are again to be found in the call centre industry. Here, automated call processing ensures that incoming calls are streamed to operators, with minimum downtime between calls resulting in an 'assembly line in the head' (Taylor and Bain 1999). The technological control of this work is further supported by the widespread use of large electronic display boards publicly showing real-time performance data of operators, teams and entire centres. But using technology to regulate the pace of work can take even more subtle and indirect forms, especially in the case of more complex and highly skilled work. Consider, for example, the use of online reporting and billing templates for lawyers designed to compel the time-charging of a set number of designated time units (Woolley 2005) (six minute blocks in the case of most large UK and Australian law firms, for example) to clients. The tyranny of 'billable hours' as the key performance measure for practising lawyers in large law firms provides a stark example of the use of technology to indirectly control the pace of professional work. It also provides an example of how technology can be used by capital to increase the control of worker productivity without resort to deskilling.

As many of the above examples also demonstrate, the use of new ICT is often associated with *work intensification*. Evidently, using technology to increase the pace of work either directly or indirectly as described above, will often lead to increasing the intensity of work. However work intensification can also be associated with increasing the range and scope of tasks and responsibilities that are classified as part of the job without a corresponding increase in resources or compensation. The widespread provision by companies of laptop computers, email, hand-held personal digital assistants (PDAs) and blackberries provides a case in point. For all the convenience and accessibility afforded by these devices, it is commonplace for workers to report that they now find it difficult to 'get away from their work', as the existence of these technologies leads to expectations that many professional workers in particular will 'always be on call' (Mazmanian, Yates and Orlikowski 2006).

Another example is provided by the proliferation of integrated IT systems such as Enterprise Resource Planning systems (ERPs) such as SAP and PeopleSoft. One of the commonly reported effects of ERPs is that they often replace periodic (e.g. monthly) reporting cycles with the requirement to report operational data in real time. For example, in a manufacturing setting, process workers might be required to enter data relating to the consumption of various raw materials as those materials are consumed, thus triggering automated requests for stock replenishment. The pattern observed in a number of case studies of ERP implementations (Hall 2002, 2005) has been that organizations have been able to eliminate some of the clerical workers previously responsible for collating and entering this data, while simply adding the reporting responsibilities to the work tasks of process workers. While workers and their supervisors in these cases sometimes welcome the upskilling of their jobs (which now include data entry and basic computer use) they typically lament the work intensification that results.

Some of the most prominent new examples of ICT which have caught the research attention of LPT researchers in recent years thus demonstrate that, while new technologies might not necessarily be being used by managers to simply deskill workers, they *are* being used in increasingly diverse and subtle ways to enhance managerial control over work and the labour process. However, while this is a marked tendency in contemporary organizations, there is nothing inevitable about the use of these ICTs to enhance managerial control – technology might facilitate increased control, but it is not a driver of control.

On the key question of technology and control, Child's (1984) distinction between 'decentralization' and 'delegation' remains instructive. In response to those who saw in new ICTs the prospect of significant decentralization of decision-making and the concession of managerial power and authority to workers and work groups, Child noted that management was more likely to delegate certain decisions-making powers while retaining centralized control over key strategic decisions. Indeed this has been the key trend most consistently promoted by most large-scale IT system implementations undertaken by large organizations since the early 1990s: delegating responsibilities down organizational hierarchies while maintaining and intensifying centralized control. Enterprise systems such as ERPs purport to provide organizations with a single platform and a series of integrated sub-systems (or 'modules') for entire areas of operation – financials, logistics, Human Resources (HR), etc. (Davenport 2000; Monk and Wagner 2006). Once configured, these systems require users to enter data according to predefined protocols in standardized form, and demand that users and groups adhere to predefined business processes or steps in order to complete tasks. These systems are designed to ensure consistency in data and information across the organization (because of standardized formats), to eliminate duplication of data entry (because data need only be entered once in the system), and to ensure that data is 'real-time' (because data is designed to be entered or is automatically entered at the time a business process is undertaken). This technology provides management with access to more accurate and more up-to-date information on operational performance, including the performance of individual workers, teams, and departments. ERP technologies also offer a means for organizations to drive business process change by effectively compelling users to follow specific methods and procedures – typically, 'best practice' operating procedures embedded in the routines dictated by the ERP (Davenport 2000: Chapter 5). In this way, ERPs can be used by managers to enhance their control over both process and performance.

ERPs can have diverse and complex implications for organizations and workers. Again, to underline the critique of technological determinism, ERPs do not have clearly deterministic consequences. Amongst other things, much depends on how the systems are 'configured' and the extent to which the systems are 'customized'. To underline the more general point of political materialist approaches to technology, implementation (and the business process design decisions, configuration decisions and customization decisions that are integral to that implementation process) is a political process with material outcomes.

ERPs can result in workers who report being empowered, to some extent, through the technology. For example, at one Australian bank implementing an ERP, at least some branch managers reported that the data and analytical reports provided by the ERP allowed them to develop a more strategic approach to the financial management and performance evaluation of their branches (Dery, Hall and Wailes 2006). More commonly, however, ERPs appear to result in workers being subjected to more disciplined business process regimes which serve to restrict autonomy and discretion. For example, at one fast-moving consumer goods manufacturer in Australia, workers in a regional depot reported that, whereas they previously had discretion to pick and choose local suppliers, the ERP procurement module meant that they were now compelled to use only certified suppliers that were designated as pre-entered options in the system (Hall 2005).

ERPs can also expose individual and group work performance to more detailed management scrutiny. At one Australian university implementing an ERP, departmental finance managers reported that their and their department's compliance with new accrual accounting procedures could now be more easily monitored by central management as a result of the ERP (Hall 2005). Finally, as noted earlier, ERPs also often intensify work. This was also demonstrated by the 'OzUni' case – departmental managers confirmed that the new reporting requirements introduced as a result of the ERP had significantly added to their workload (Hall 2005).

ERPs are, of course, only one kind of new technology at work. Nevertheless, they are a particularly common and substantial form of technology investment for contemporary organizations – the vast majority of large organizations in advanced industrial economies have implemented enterprise systems since the 1990s, and the costs of implementations range from half a million dollars to hundreds of millions of dollars (Monk and Wagner 2006: 32). They are also the prime contemporary example of an integrated, configurable IT system (Fleck 1994). Moreover, while ERPs are unique in terms of their scale and scope, in terms of their contribution to management control they exemplify trends seen with other organization-wide IT systems such as Management Information Systems (MIS), Human Resource Information Systems (HRIS) and Knowledge Management

(KM) systems. For this reason, the kinds of trends apparent with ERPs are likely to be characteristic of large, organization-wide IT systems more generally.

As the examples noted in this section have attempted to demonstrate, the forms of control afforded by new ICTs go beyond 'technical control' (or a more contemporary variant such as 'technological control'). The forms of control facilitated by enterprise-wide, integrated and configurable IT systems are not typically as direct as technical control, where technology directly and immediately controls, for example, the pace of work, the order of work tasks, and even, potentially, the way in which work tasks are undertaken. Here, by contrast, we see a complex interaction between the material capacities of the technology, the specificities of the system as implemented, the decisions of management (at various levels), the input, lobbying and resistant actions of workers and unions, the influence of system vendors and IT consultants, and the operation of other systems, management techniques, forms of work organization and standard operating procedures. We see the emergence of a kind of 'systemic control' facilitated by enterprise-wide IT systems which we regard as emblematic of contemporary regimes of technology-facilitated control at work.

Political–materialist approaches such as those inspired by LPT have traditionally been strong on identifying the material consequences of technological change, the material qualities of the technologies and how they are linked to labour process and work organizational change, and the macro political structures which underscore the workplace and organizational struggles over technology. On the other hand, these approaches have not been as strong in describing and analysing the social processes through which technologies are designed, operationalized, implemented and experienced. The role of 'the social' in understanding technology at work has however received extensive attention from social constructivist perspectives – the focus of the next part of this chapter.

Social constructivist perspectives

A wealth of research and theory development about new technology at work has been undertaken over the past 20 years from a social constructivist perspective. As noted in the introduction, political materialist and social constructivist perspectives started from very different origins. Whereas LPT (and, to some extent, other political materialist approaches) drew heavily from structuralist traditions such as Marx's political economy and theory of the labour process, social constructivism draws on more recent post-structuralist traditions which have questioned the links between social structures (e.g. class, ethnicity and status) and social action central to structuralist thinking in the social sciences.

Some commentators (e.g. McLaughlin, Rosen, Skinner and Webster 1999) classify these approaches under the category of 'SST' – the 'social study of technology'– while others prefer the term 'interpretivist' (e.g. Liker *et al.* 1999). Regardless of the terminology used, the central claim that unites these approaches is again based on a rejection of technological determinism – the idea that technological change is the result of the inherent qualities and characteristics of a given technology. On the contrary, according to social constructivists, technological change is the result of the various ways in which individuals and groups comprehend, understand, interpret, act upon and use the technology (what might be termed 'processes of social construction'). In other words, a strong version of social constructivism implies that simply knowing the technical characteristics of any new technology at work will not tell us anything about the ultimate ways in which that technology will be used, or the organizational consequences or developments that might follow. Thus, what is critical for social constructivists is not the technical capacities or technical origins of a technology or a technological artefact, but the ways in which different groups and individuals at work conceive of and enact that technology (Grint and Woolgar 1997: 10).

Strong social constructivist approaches claim that technology is necessarily a social construction. This does not mean that a technological artefact is simply a figment of one's imagination (cf. MacKenzie and Wajcman 1999: 18), but it does imply that it is impossible to analyse technology other than by recognizing the way that people interpret its design, understand its function, comprehend its usefulness, and actually use it. Amongst other things, this means that it is impossible to distinguish between 'the technical' and 'the social'; rather, as will be seen in this section, social constructivists tend to talk about 'the social' and 'the technical' constituting a 'seamless web' that can be thought of as a 'socio–technical ensemble' (Bijker 1993). The implications, problems and potential value of this approach are discussed later in this chapter. First, the key lines of social constructivist theories of technology are outlined.

The social construction of technology (SCOT)

Orthodox understandings of scientific knowledge have typically assumed that scientific knowledge is the result of rational and linear processes of scientific deduction and reasoning. In the 1970s the 'sociology of scientific knowledge' (SSK) movement began questioning this assumption by pointing to the way in which decisive and unpredictable turns at key points, apparently shaped by social questions and considerations as much as scientific or technical ones, influenced the path of scientific knowledge development.

From the early 1980s a group of theorists inspired by SSK began studying the historical emergence of various technologies, asking the general question: why does a particular technology take the form that it does? The suggestion of these SCOT theorists was that the form of a given technology cannot be explained by an objective, linear and rational process of technological enhancement and improvement, but rather by processes in which the social claims of different groups influenced (or failed to influence) the process of development. The classic study was Pinch and Bijker's (1984) study of the emergence of the modern safety bicycle. Their detailed study demonstrated that the shift from the high-wheeled models of the 1870s to the smaller-wheeled 'safety bicycles' of the early twentieth century was not the result of any clear technological superiority, but the result of the influential role of key constituents – young men who wanted to travel fast and women and older men who wanted a relatively safe form of transport – and the capacity of designers to meet these twin objectives. In this sense, the safety bicycle was socially constructed rather than determined by any predictable technological trajectory.

The first key concept in SCOT is the idea of *interpretive flexibility* – the meaning of any particular technological artefact (such as a bicycle or a desktop computer) is open to a variety of interpretations. To take a simple example, a desktop computer in a family home is interpreted differently by different users: for one member of a family it might be thought of as a word processing device on which to complete university assignments; for another, a communication device for sending and receiving emails; for yet another, a virtual shop in which to view, evaluate and purchase commodities. The second key idea is that of *closure*. SCOT theorists claim that, at some point, the prevailing meaning of a particular artefact becomes settled, 'closed' or 'stabilized', such that controversies over the best use for a particular artefact begin to fade and a generally accepted meaning of what, for example, a bicycle is and what it is used for becomes widely accepted. For SCOT theorists, competing social claims as to the meaning of an artefact are promoted by *relevant social groups*. These groups will often be designers, consumers and users and other 'stakeholders'. Relevant social groups share various assumptions and understandings, values and capacities for action – what SCOT refers to as their *technological frame*.

Despite its weaknesses and problems (discussed below), SCOT has drawn attention to two key points: first, the meaning, use, ultimate form and (hence potentially) the implications of a given technology are socially constructed by people and groups; second, technologies emerge and become stabilized in form, not because they technically 'work better' than previous technologies, but because they (more or less) meet the demands of relevant social groups.

SCOT has important implications for our understanding of new technology at work. For example, SCOT highlights the indeterminacy of any new technology, and suggests that that indeterminacy is two-fold: the meaning of a technology may be open to dispute and controversy for a period of time, even after it is designed and implemented; and to the extent that artefacts remain interpretively flexible, their meaning may well differ for different groups of workers, managers and other organizational members. At the least, this implies that implementers of new technologies at work concerned with questions of uptake and efficiency might need to consider how different user groups socially construct those technologies, rather than assuming that those technologies have a self-evident purpose or attractiveness.

Despite its influence, SCOT has attracted extensive criticism. While these criticisms are discussed more fully below, one weakness of the approach has been its limited capacity to explain exactly how relevant social groups work to establish or secure closure, and why a stabilized meaning of a particular artefact eventually emerges. A second strand of social constructivist approaches to technology known as 'actor network theory' (ANT) is often seen to offer greater insights into the role of social groups in these processes of closure and stabilization (Bruun and Hukkinen 2003).

Actor network theory (ANT)

ANT's approach to technology (Callon 1986; Law and Callon 1992; Latour 1996) is similar to SCOT's in the sense that both see technology as the result of processes of social construction and both reject any possibility of drawing a distinction between the social and the technological. However ANT's analytical emphasis is more clearly focussed on the processes of actor-network building, disassembly and reconstruction which it sees as the heart of the processes of social construction. Actor-networks are arrangements of relations between human and non-human 'actants' and might include individual people, groups, organizations as well as technical, material and natural entities that are regarded as agents (Callon 1986). Treating both human and non-human actants as capable of action is evidently counter-intuitive and one of the most controversial aspects of ANT. In any event, ANT sees the process of actor-networks as constituting technology, and technological change as one involving a number of steps (see McLoughlin 1999: 94–7; Grint and Woolgar 1997: 28–31):

- *Translation* – The process of enrolment through which the interests of various actors are brought into line with those of certain key actors who are seeking to establish an actor-network.
- *Problematization* – The process by which key actors depict scenarios and define certain key problems for different actors to which enrolment in their actor-network constitutes a solution.
- *Displacements* – The mobilization of various entities which ensures that the actor-network becomes and maintains stabilization.

ANT theorists therefore see the social construction process as one of key actors persuading others, through various rhetorical strategies, to see the emergent technology in their way. Successful and powerful actor-networks can assume a position of dominance or authority, such that Latour (1987 quoted in McLoughlin 1999: 94), for example, speaks of the way in which anyone engaging with a technology is virtually compelled to 'pass through' the meanings and assumptions promoted by the key actors. McLoughlin (1999) notes that Bill Gates' Microsoft technological regime can be seen in this way: as effectively consisting of a dominant actor-network that has successfully enrolled a wide range of people (users), organizations (clients, software and hardware producers, manufacturers of peripherals, retailers), technological artefacts (compatible programs, printers, local area networks) and even practices (using Internet Explorer to surf the Internet, for example). In this way, successful actor-networks establish certain constructions of technology as 'indispensable'; and, as any computer user knows, Microsoft's products, services and ways of doing things are hard to avoid. Amongst other technological phenomena, ANT theorists have applied the framework to the analysis of the emergence, contestation and stabilization of technologies at work such as telework (Jackson and van der Wielen 1998b) and email (Brigham and Corbett 1997).

Criticisms of SCOT, ANT and social constructivism

One line of criticism directed at SCOT, ANT and related approaches comes from commentators who are sympathetic to the constructivist assumptions that are its foundation. This criticism concerns the question of closure or stabilization. Some (Orlikowski 2000; Grint and Woolgar 1997) have questioned whether complete closure or total stabilization of any technology can ever be possible. It was noted above that SCOT accounts appear to be weak in explaining why a particular form of closure ultimately occurs. However, despite its greater detailed attention to the processes and interactions of social construction, ANT still claims that stabilization occurs at some point. If we accept that technology is inevitably a social construction, then on what grounds can we say that at a certain point the meaning of the technology becomes settled, and thus attains a degree of certainty or fixity that makes it immune from (or less amenable to) processes of social construction? In response, Grint and Woolgar (1997) propose a more thoroughgoing social constructivism which refutes the suggestion that a technology (or any phenomenon for that matter) can ever become fully fixed, stabilized or in any sense objective – technology, even when prevailing views about its meaning and potential becomes relatively widespread, is always a social construction and different social constructions of a particular technology can always exist. In this way, Grint and Woolgar adopt an anti-essentialist position and see this as the defining quality of a genuinely social constructivist approach. While this might satisfy Grint and Woolgar's aspirations to achieve constructivist purity, we contend that it only exacerbates other problems.

From our perspective, one of the critical weaknesses with SCOT, ANT and social constructivist approaches more generally is their tendency to relativism. SCOT and ANT approaches are committed to the principle of 'general symmetry' – the idea that all social constructions should be treated equivalently. This means that there is no a priori valid reason for concluding that one social construction of an artefact is any better than any other social construction. This commits social constructivists to an agnostic, relativist stance when it then comes to questions of evaluation, leaving them unable and unprepared to assess whether one particular construction is any more compelling than any other (Winner 1993). In fairness to social constructivists, their point is not to answer the question: what is a particular technology and what is it really used for? Rather, the question they ask is: how is it that a particular form of technology or a particular social construction of a technology comes to prevail? However, this seems to displace the problem rather than resolve it: how can social constructivists confidently identify one social construction as prevailing or dominant, and another one marginal or subordinate?

The relativism implicit in social constructivism becomes a more significant problem when we return again to accounts of closure or stabilization. On the one hand, SCOT approaches tend to suggest that a stabilized meaning emerges consensually, as over time controversy fades and a consensus emerges. On the contrary, we would contend that processes of dispute and debate over the meaning and import of any given technology is a more political and conflictual process than suggested by this account. Drawing from the lessons of political materialist accounts, technology (especially technology at work) is something that different groups contest, struggle over and make competing claims about. And we agree with the likes of Langdon Winner (1980) that technologies have politics and that technology implementations at workplaces can lead to 'winners' and 'losers'. While any one of the examples discussed in the course of analysing political materialist approaches above would suffice, recall the examples relating to the implementation of ERP systems in the Australian university. In that case the ERP and the procedures and requirements associated with its implementation rendered the financial affairs of departments more transparent to central management monitoring and surveillance. This restricted the freedom of these departmental managers and administrative staff, gave them less scope for autonomous decision-making and decreased their power to use resources independently of central management control and scrutiny. More generally, in those cases where technologies lead to deskilling or job loss, it seems disingenuous and naïve to see the affected workers as anything other than 'losers' in the technology implementation process. These are the material consequences that political materialist approaches seek to identify; yet social constructivism forecloses such a project.

Social constructivist approaches emphasize the social process inherent in technological development, but in doing so they tend to deflect attention from the *outcomes* or *implications* of technological development. This downplaying of the consequences of technological change is a consequence of the constructivist approach – neither technology nor the social can be regarded as determinant, it is impossible to identify or assess the extent to which any outcome might be associated with any specific cause, and outcomes cannot be confidently comprehended objectively anyway, because they, like other social phenomena, are social constructions. A further analytical problem emerges – social constructivist accounts are often very descriptive and particularistic. Because any particular empirical instance of technological change or implementation is the result of potentially unique social constructions, generalizations are difficult to draw. To the extent that particular outcomes at particular workplaces might be explained by social constructivists, they can only ever be explained in terms unique to the circumstances and historical and cultural specificities of that case. As a result, it is difficult, if not impossible, to draw any generalizable conclusions from social constructivist accounts.

A further consequence of this attention to process is a relative neglect of context (organizational, political, economic and social). Latour (2004) has declared that context is the enemy of ANT because ANT is committed to understanding technology implementations in the terms of the actors themselves, their social constructions and their immediate actions. (Actors' social constructions will, of course, potentially include perceptions of the context, but constructivists have little faith in identifying any contextual elements that might exist independently of the social constructions of actors.) This echoes constructivism's disavowal of anything which is structural – that is something which exists independently of the actors' social constructions but which shapes actors' actions and behaviour.

Again, we see this as naïve and as resigning social constructivist accounts to political impotency. We would argue that understanding context and social and political structures is critical to a compelling account of any new technology.

Recalling political materialist approaches, we argue that, in addition to questions such as why and how has the technology taken the form it has, it is important to ask what are the consequences of any particular technology and any particular social construction of that technology for workers, managers and others (McLoughlin 1999: 117). In order to even hypothesize that any particular technology configuration is likely to be adverse or beneficial for a particular group of workers, it is necessary to have reference to social structures (class, occupation, status, organizational membership) that decisively shape and condition, if not determine, their interests.

The final problem we identify in social constructivist accounts concerns the question of the limits to interpretive flexibility. This problem is most relevant for those such as Grint and Woolgar (1997) who call for a thoroughgoing social constructivism which is genuinely anti-essentialist. As noted above, this implies that technological artefacts, for example, be recognized as necessarily social constructions whose meaning and import is dependent on their social construction. Artefacts do not exist independently of social construction and they therefore cannot have any *essential* or objective character. Again this seems counterintuitive, even absurd if taken to its logical conclusion. It is one thing to accept that the meaning and import of technological artefacts might be disputed and subjected to processes of social construction in which different constructions compete for (conditional and contingent) acceptance in a workplace, organization or society. It is, however, surely another to accept that technologies can be anything, i.e. that there are *no* limits to interpretive flexibility. A computer might be a games console or a communication device depending on how it is constructed by users, but it seems farcical to say it is 'a cup of coffee' (Tsoukas 1993).

Grint and Woolgar (1997) make perhaps the most sustained attempt to maintain this anti-essentialist position. To be fair to them, neither they nor other social constructivists are trying to make absurd claims. Thus they concede that 'of course, not any construction is possible; the construction of technological capacity is not itself unconstrained' (1997: 10). However, Grint and Woolgar studiously avoid making any claims as to how these constructions are constrained. One obvious constraint would seem to be associated with the material qualities of the technology itself – the range of potential constructions is surely constrained by some limits set by the material characteristics of the technology which must exist independently of the process of social construction. However, social constructivism, as we have seen, denies the possibility that there is some material set of characteristics inherent to the technology that can be separated from social construction. It is unclear therefore where constraints might come from.

Grint and Woolgar (1997: 10) go on to state that 'some constructions turn out to be more resilient and robust than others' and that the business of social constructivism is to account for why some are more 'resilient and robust than others'.

We heartily commend this enterprise. But again, it is not clear how those such as Grint and Woolgar can escape their own logic, because any empirical evaluation of which of two competing constructions is in fact more resilient and robust must also be subject to the charge that it is also a social construction.

In addition to supporting the social constructivists' quest of explaining why it is that some constructions prevail over others, we also believe that it important to ask, as political materialists do, what are the effects of these constructions on actors (workers, managers, etc.)? While it might be expected that social constructivists would eschew such questions, Grint and Woolgar do concede that 'the social constructivist argument does not deny that material artefacts have constraining influences upon actors. But it does hold a question mark over what those constraints are' (1997: 23). In opposition to Grint and Woolgar, we argue that it is a more fruitful social scientific endeavour to attempt to answer that question, however conditionally. Doing so, as we have suggested above, requires some acceptance of the materiality of artefacts and some acceptance that technologies are prone to have material consequences for actors, and that those consequences can be both evaluated and, to some extent, attributed to a variety of factors. The range of factors that have been highlighted by political materialist approaches include the interests, choices, strategies and power resources of management, workers, and unions, the material characteristics and capacities of the technological artefact, the operation of organizational systems, policies and practices, and the broader political economy of the organization, the sector and the economy. The factors that have been highlighted by the social constructivist approaches surveyed so far are limited to the social constructions and associated discourses of various actors and groups. One of the critical weaknesses of social constructivism's account of technology is its inability to explain the reasons why different and specific social constructions emerge (and why others do not). The main reasons for this is constructivism's anti-structuralism: the denial that social structures influence or even contextualize any process of social construction, or indeed any social behaviour.

Structurationist approaches

Some more recent technology research, sympathetic to social constructivism, has attempted to overcome some of these problems and weaknesses by recovering a role for structures in the explanation of technology at work. Some commentators (e.g. Klein and Kleinman 2002) have called for SCOT to be complemented by a theory of social structure that would better enable social constructivists to account for the prevalence of some constructions of technology over others. 'To understand the capacity of groups to shape a technology, we need to know where the groups are situated within some structural matrix' (Klein and Kleinman 2002: 40). The authors argue that the reasons why some actors' constructions of technology are more influential than others has to do with their access to resources, and that that access is related to social structures. Klein and Kleinman identify economic resources, political resources, cultural resources and 'technological legacies' as relevant.

While Klein and Kleinman's structuralist approach is welcomed, their primary concern is still with explaining how the meaning of a particular technological arte-fact becomes stabilized. As argued earlier, another weakness of the social constructivist perspective is its lack of attention to the material effects of technologies on workers and work organization. There is no apparent reason why social constructivism's sensitivity to the range of potential constructions of technology cannot be applied to the process of technology construction understood as an ongoing and conflictual (rather than ultimately consensual) process, where there is no moment of complete and final 'closure' of the technology, and where different constructions have different material impacts and implications for organizational members and organizational change. In recent work, Wanda Orlikowski comes closest to realizing this project in her application of structuration theory and adoption of a 'practice lens' for studying technology in organizations.

Structurationist perspectives have, for some time, been seen to offer a promising way forward in explaining the social causes and consequences of new technology, especially ICTs (Weick 1990; DeSanctis and Poole 1994; Roberts and Grabowski 1995; Jones 1999; Jones, Orlikowski and Munir 2004). 'Structures' are not seen to be social structures standing outside or behind social action, but are understood as embedded or inscribed in technologies. Orlikowski, in referring to the SCOT tradition, argues that structuration is the process through which 'dominant interests are reflected in the form and functioning of the technology' (2000: 405). Orlikowski first highlights, but then departs from, this interpretation of the role of structuration in two ways: first, she rejects the social constructivist idea that technologies can ever reach final stabilization or closure; second, invoking Giddens' (1984, 1998) original account of structuration, she rejects the idea that structures can be 'embodied' in technolgies because (according to Giddens) structures cannot have a material reality independent of the actions of actors. The implication of these revisions is that technologies are being constantly constructed and reconstructed by actors and groups, and that it is only in the process of engaging with technologies that structures can be enacted by users and thus understood as influencing (or 'structuring') action.

Orlikowski's (2000) 'practice lens' approach involves studying the ways in which different actors and groups enact structures of technology use (which she calls 'technologies-in-practice') through their use and engagement with those technologies. Her study of the use of Lotus Notes software technology in a number of different organizations reveals very different patterns of usage which she understands in terms of distinct 'technologies-in-practice' that structure subsequent use of those technologies in those organizational settings: her study revealed technologies-in-use variously described as 'collaborative', 'collective problem-solving', 'individual productivity', 'limited use' and so forth.

Orlikowski's approach brings, in our view, some much needed structure to social constructivist accounts of the processes of social construction. However, her explicit commitment to seeing structures as the result of actors' enactment, rather than as having some material existence independent of those actions, cannot be fully sustained. Her own models of each of the technologies-in-practice she identifies in her case studies of Notes usage reveal the existence and importance of 'other social structures along with the technology-in-practice' (2000: 411). For example, these structures include a 'cooperative culture' and 'individual and collective incentive structures' in one organization ('Alpha') and a 'learning orientation', a 'cooperative culture' and a 'team incentive structure' in another ('Zeta'). As is turns out, these 'other social structures' (i.e. structures beyond those implicit in the use of the technology) are relevant to her explanation of how and why the particular technolgies-in-use emerged in each of the case study organizations. At least one subsequent study that has attempted to apply her technologies-in-practice approach (Dery *et al.* 2006) also found that various other organizational structures were key to the explanation of how different technology practices had emerged.

The key point for present purposes is that, while social constructivist accounts of technology at work can be improved through the notion of structuration, there still appears to be a need to refer to organizational and social structures if we are to convincingly explain the diversity of technological applications and impacts that can be seen in contemporary organizations.

Conclusions: advancing a political materialist theory of new technology at work

Our critical review of political materialist and social constructivist approaches to technology at work has suggested that there is much to be gained from a reinvigorated politically materialist account that also recognizes the importance of processes of social construction that shape the impact and experience of technology at the organizational level. Political materialist perspectives need to recognize that struggles and conflicts over technology at work are not 'once and for all' matters, where a final and definitive version of the technology emerges and then affects work organization and behaviour in any predictable, deterministic fashion. Despite its weaknesses and problems, the wealth of social constructivist work has demonstrated that 'the social' and 'the technological' are bound up with each other – they are mutually constitutive, rather than separate. We contend, however, that it is still analytically valid to retain a notion of the technological artefact as a material phenomenon existing independently of social action; however we concede that technology only makes sense if it is analysed in its social context. Putting the well-rehearsed and ultimately unsatisfying epistemological and ontological debates to one side, we see this cognizance of social context as a pragmatic point of convergence between political materialist and social constructivist approaches.

If we accept the need for an approach which retains the core political materialist convictions – that technologies have material characteristics and material consequences, and that politics at several levels shapes the implementation and consequences of technologies – but which also accepts the key role of social context, one key question is: what is the nature of the social context in which we need to study new technology at work? As noted in this chapter, the form and effects of technology at work will be shaped by a number of forces and factors including:

- the material characteristics of the technological artefact;
- the decisions and choices of management;
- the struggles between management, workers, unions and others over the form and implementation of the technology;
- organizational structures, practices, traditions and policies, including the way in which work is organized;
- the way in which technologies are interpreted, articulated, promoted, engaged with and used by different workers, managers and organizational groups, as well as by other actors including technology vendors and consultants;
- the political economy of the organization, its industry sector and the institutional structure of competition, supply chains and markets in which the organization is embedded; and,
- the state and its institutions and policies.

Most of the theories of technology at work canvassed in this chapter focus, understandably, on dynamics and relations at the workplace or organizational level. However, as the social shaping approach suggests, technological change and development will also be influenced by state policies, practices and agencies. As we argue in Chapters 7, 8 and 9, these policies, practices and institutions tend to follow distinct cross-national patterns of variation. Our approach seeks to locate technological change and the labour process in the context of institutional ensembles that operate at sectoral, national, international and global levels. Thus the analysis in this book seeks to accommodate developments and dynamics at these levels as well as at the level of the workplace and organization. The theoretical approach we take in this regard is decisively influenced by National Technological Systems theory.

Beyond the organization: the role of national technological systems and systems of innovation

The ways in which technologies are developed, implemented and deployed in organizations are influenced not just by processes and relations at the organization level; they are also affected by sectoral level, national level and supra national level dynamics. While a number of theoretical frameworks exist for the analysis of these dynamics, we contend that the approach which is most consistent with our commitment to a politically materialist interpretation of technology at work is that represented by the technological systems (TS) and national systems of innovation (NSI) literatures (Lundvall 1992; Edquist 1997). These approaches share with political materialism a recognition that 'the technological' – in this case, the technological system – has material consequences for the nature of social, economic and organizational change, and that the system itself is the result of historical and contemporary political struggles and compromises.

The TS and NSI approaches, which are more fully developed and applied in Chapters 7 and 8, also share with comparative political economy approaches a strong emphasis on the role played by state and sectoral level institutional arrangements in shaping technological innovation, diffusion and implementation. State institutions are, for example, most obviously relevant in their capacity to generate innovation policies (such as support for, and provision of R&D) and infrastructure expenditure (such as support for, and provision of, high speed internet infrastructure). However, TS and NSI approaches recognize the effect of a broad range of institutions, policies and practices in shaping technological innovation and change, and understand these institutions, policies and practices as constituting a system. The institutions highlighted by this approach typically include state agencies and departments, educational institutions, the industrial relations system including employer associations, unions and labour regulatory institutions, skill formation and training institutions, financial sector institutions, and industry representative and advocacy institutions. Together, this ensemble of institutions is seen to constitute a national technological and innovation system that is characterized by certain ways of innovating and implementing and deploying technologies (Kristensen 1996).

Consistent with political materialism, we use the NSI approach as a means of identifying and analysing national systems as political systems, in that institutional configurations are forged through historical and political processes, and they result in distinctive outcomes in terms of innovation and technological use and deployment. National systems of innovation can be interpreted as 'coordinated' or 'competitive' and, while the picture is complex, it is apparent that different political forms of these national systems tend to be associated with different modes of technology investment, deployment and innovation, resulting in different outcomes for organizations and workers.

Conclusion

Technology, then, does not develop, operate or have implications or impacts that are independent or autonomous at any level: organizational, national or global. Rather, technology and its effects are shaped by a wide range of social and political factors and dynamics. However, we reject the conclusion that analysing the effects of technology on work therefore becomes wholly a matter of contingency, social agency and circumstantial specificity. Unlike some social constructivists, we reject the notion that generalizations cannot be drawn or that evaluations cannot be made. On the contrary, we seek to highlight that the selection, implementation, shaping and implications of technology at work are phenomena that are intensely political and socially significant.

We have argued that an adequate theory of new technology at work must accommodate both the materiality of technology and its effects, and the political character of its social context. This latter point compels us to critically consider the ways in which managerial agency, worker resistance and action, management techniques, prevailing forms of work organization, organizational structures and practices, and the complex of political and economic institutions at sectoral, national and international levels interact with technology. The resultant, mediated effects of new technology are empirical questions that are considered in the following chapters.

3 Manufacturing management
The integration of technical and organizational systems

The manufacturing sector is both a major producer and user of new technology. Product innovations in the manufacturing sector are associated with changes in the structure of manufacturing activity that involve a greater emphasis on medium-high and high technology sectors, and include innovations such as wireless telecommunications (mobile telephony) and the development of new drugs in the pharmaceutical sector. These innovations have resulted in a shift away from low technology manufacturing towards medium-high and high technology sectors such as computer, telecommunications equipment and pharmaceuticals. As we discuss later in the book, there is significant cross-nation variation in the extent to which nations are moving into these growing areas of manufacturing, and the national systems of innovation perspective provides some explanation for the extent to which nations are participating in these knowledge-intensive sectors of manufacturing.

This chapter is concerned with a further dimension of technological change in the manufacturing sector involving the use of new technologies. As well as being major producers of new technological innovations, manufacturing organizations can be understood as key users of new technologies, particularly information and communications technologies, which have been associated with a range of process innovations in the manufacturing sector. Information and Communication Technologies (ICTs) have enabled the manufacturing process to be managed and controlled through computer systems, and associated technological changes have been linked to the introduction of new management techniques such as Just in Time (JIT) management, which involves the elimination of inventories through the use of demand driven production systems, and Total Quality Management (TQM), which is aimed at continuous improvement in organizational processes for the purpose of enhancing customer satisfaction. The first section of the chapter explains the nature of these technological and management changes.

Although there are major new technologies available for use in the manufacturing production process, and a range of new management ideas linked to these new technologies, there appears to be cross-national variation in the extent of implementation of these new technologies and management practices in the manufacturing sector. It would seem that different national institutional environments affect both the extent and nature of uptake of advanced manufacturing technologies

(AMTs), and institutional differences between nations also affect the way in which new management practices are implemented. As the discussion in the second section of the chapter shows, there is some debate as to whether the adoption of these new technologies and management practices will result in the convergence of manufacturing production processes across nations.

There is also contention over the implications of new technologies and management techniques for work, which is the focus of the final section of the chapter. For some, the new era of advanced manufacturing technologies represents an opportunity to eliminate low-skilled and repetitive work through the use of machines, and to adopt more progressive work practices that revolve around high skilled employees who actively participate in the management of production through problem solving in teams or work groups. For others, the new technologies are linked to a process of deskilling of production workers, and are a means for management to adopt new forms of control over the workforce. The final section of the chapter discusses these debates in the context of AMTs and associated management reforms.

New technologies in the manufacturing sector

The adoption of advanced manufacturing technologies by business organizations in the manufacturing sector involves both technological process and organizational process innovations linked to changes in engineering, manufacturing and business techniques. The technological process innovations involve the introduction of engineering technologies such as computer aided design (CAD) and computer aided manufacturing (CAM) as well as technologies in the manufacturing management process such as computer aided planning (CAP). What unites these different technological innovations is that they involve data driven computer integration of the total manufacturing operation (Hunt 1987: 2). Of more recent interest is the use of the Internet and e-commerce to sell manufactured products. New technologies have therefore impacted on the manufacturing process from the design phase through to production and sales.

Organizational process innovations or changes in business practices linked to these technologies include JIT and TQM, which involve changes in the way in which production and work are carried out in the new technological environment. The distinction between the technological and organizational process innovations is difficult to draw because they are closely related: many of the technological process innovations incorporate organizational process innovations, as explained below.

Technology and the manufacturing production process

The introduction of AMTs in the manufacturing sector has involved a shift away from stand-alone machines, towards a manufacturing process that is integrated by computers and communication systems that make use of data to design and control the manufacturing process. Much of the technical discussion in the following material is based on Hunt (1987: 4–52) which provides a comprehensive overview of advanced manufacturing technologies, classifying the technologies according to their contribution to design, manufacturing, management or artificial intelligence.

Computer aided design involves the use of computers by draftspersons and design engineers to develop product specifications as 3D images that are stored electronically. These electronic images can be communicated to computer aided manufacturing equipment, such as NC machine tools, which are used to cut and shape metal, and computer aided engineering which, for example, enables engineers to analyse the functioning and performance of products and their components or elements electronically (Hunt 1987: 6). Advances in CAD in the 1980s have improved the ability of industrial designers to control the design process, because they enable designers to use computer software to model engineering components into their design, reducing the extent to which modifications to the design are necessary during the engineering and production phases. Designers can vary the product design, and the software automatically alters the mechanical features of the product to fit the new design. This technology has both improved the integrity of industrial design and also reduced the length of the design to production phase (Thilmany 2003).

Computer aided manufacturing involves the use of robots, flexible manufacturing cells and systems (FMCs and FMSs), numerically controlled machine tools (NC), and automated material handling system (AMH) and automated storage and retrieval (AS/RS) systems. The overall purpose is to use computers to manage and control the manufacturing process (Hunt 1987:10). CAD and CAM techniques work closely together. In the textile, apparel and furnishings industries, CAD is used to design garments and fabrics and to colour them on screen, along with CAM systems including digitally controlled printers to colour and pattern fabrics and computer aided machines to cut the fabrics (Borland 2003: 53). Particularly important in the metal working industry are NC machine tools which carry out machining operations (such as cutting metal parts) as instructed by a computer numerical control apparatus (Hunt 1987:18, Keefe 1991b: 504).

Industrial robots are an important component of CAM, particularly in the automobile industry. Robots often have the capacity to replace people in the handling of objects, and are usually re-programmable and therefore flexible in the operations that they perform. Typical industrial robots cut and shape metal parts, lift heavy objects, fasten and assemble component parts, move objects between conveyors, stack objects, load machines and spray-paint. As such, it is not surprising that early predictions of the impact of robots anticipated the elimination of dangerous and repetitive work through the increased use of machines in the manufacturing process.

Robots have been used for industrial purposes since the 1960s and were first introduced in General Motors in 1961, where they were used for '3D' purposes – dull, dirty and dangerous work. The performance of robots has improved since, as they progressed from hydraulically controlled to electronically controlled machines driven by microprocessors (Teresko 2002: 25). Robots now not only carry out work that is dirty, difficult or dangerous, they are able to perform functions that are too difficult for human beings, such as semiconductor manufacturing. Further, software advances have impacted on the role of robots in manufacturing. Robots can be taught how to carry out their tasks by software-based simulation programs, which creates possibilities for improved flexibility, as this makes it easier and faster to teach robots new and varied tasks (Dvorak 2000). However, robots have not replaced humans: their limited vision restricts their guidance and positioning capabilities, and their dexterity remains inferior to humans. As such, while computers are capable of training and instructing robots to carry out complex tasks, robot technology is not sufficiently advanced for robots to displace humans, especially in carrying out intricate tasks and tasks requiring detailed vision, space calculations and judgments (Truett 2002).

Robots and numerically controlled machine tools can be incorporated into an overall production system or flexible manufacturing system (FMS) to produce small batches of similar products. In FMSs, the firm's manufacturing system is divided into cells used for the production of a family of related products, which represents a contrast to old techniques that involved the organization of production around machines and their functions (Eckstein and Rohleder 1998: 1199). This is sometimes referred to as cellular manufacturing (CM) or group technology (GT). Manufacturing cells, typically utilizing numerically controlled machine tools, are linked by automated material handling systems (AMHs), such as robots or conveyors, which move components between cells. Computer simulations of the production system allow for the organization of production to maximize efficiency and reduce turn-around time (Hunt 1987: 24). FMSs offer the possibility of producing small batches because, once a part has been produced, the plans for arranging the manufacturing process are in place and can be re-instigated quickly and cheaply for subsequent batches, reducing cost and set-up times. As such, FMSs are superior to dedicated systems because they allow for changes to the products produced with much shorter lead times (Hallman 2003).

Technologically-driven changes in manufacturing production processes have also fed into the processes for the management of production. For example, software advances have improved the possibilities for computer aided planning (CAP). Software packages allow factory planners to model production events within the factory, thereby facilitating the planning of the production process: planners can calculate the potential return on investment in new machinery for the production line. Further, software improves surveillance by allowing camera images of manufacturing cells to be communicated to planning stations where problems can be simulated and solutions developed (Dvorak 2000). Software also allows for the surveillance or computer aided inspection (CAI) of manufactured products, to ensure they comply with original model specifications, and to identify faults.

Management innovations and AMTs

Various management trends have accompanied the introduction of AMTs in the manufacturing sector, the most prominent of which has been just in time (JIT) manufacturing. The JIT system is often referred to as a 'pull' system, because it is based on the idea that customer demand should trigger production. As such, JIT management is related to, and dependent on, advanced manufacturing technologies, because it relies on production systems being sufficiently flexible to cope with small batch sizes and reduced lead times. Being driven by customer demand, production cannot be based on the old mass production techniques of large-scale manufacture of large, standardized batches for inventory stockpile. JIT also depends on suppliers being able to deliver materials and components with short notice after receiving orders from JIT manufacturers (orders which are called 'kanban signals' and are increasingly electronic). The effect of the system is to reduce company inventory levels and operational costs (Jordan 2003: 35–6).

Software packages have been developed to facilitate communication between manufacturing companies and their suppliers. However, the Internet offers improved possibilities for instant communication and faster delivery times. In some companies, such as Dell Computers, the JIT system is referred to as 'pull to order', and allows customers to make specific requests, with the consequence that computers are built according to customer orders (Songini 2000; Sowinski 2001).

JIT management is associated with various other management innovations including total quality management (TQM) and continuous quality improvement (CQI). TQM can be defined quite broadly to encompass an emphasis on quality, or more specifically as a focus on the use of quality production equipment and techniques, and human resource management techniques which allow for employee participation in decision making (Youssef and Al-Ahmady 2002). At one level, TQM is focussed on the customer, emphasizing continual improvement in the level of customer satisfaction with both the product and the process of doing business with an organization, including: ordering and billing processes, the quality of design and production, after-sales services including warranty support, reliability, durability, aesthetics and timeliness. With TQM, the emphasis is on communication with customers for the purpose of linking their needs and preferences to actual changes in the process of doing business (Ahmed and Maddox 1995, 19). TQM is related to the implementation of advanced manufacturing techniques, because flexible manufacturing systems can be designed so that product modifications can take into account customer feedback. Further, TQM techniques which emphasize timeliness in meeting customer demands depend on flexible manufacturing systems that reduce lead times (Youssef and Al-Ahmady 2002).

Finally, much of the literature dealing with the human resource implications of advanced manufacturing systems typically argues that FMSs depend on employee involvement in the process of problem solving. This is because the knowledge of employees in the production process and of different production problems and potential solutions needs to feed into changes in the overall manufacturing system. For example, an important element of TQM is based on employee participation in team-based problem solving. As such, having well trained employees that are 'empowered' is seen as integral to the implementation of flexible manufacturing systems (Gunasekaran 1999). For some, FMSs depend on human flexibility and the capacity of employees to change, which in turn depends on participative management styles and job enrichment opportunities involving task and skill variety, and greater autonomy and control over work functions (Youssef and Al-Ahmady 2002: 888).

The adoption of AMTs and associated management practices from a cross-national perspective

There is patchy evidence on the adoption of advanced manufacturing technologies and associated changes in management practice. The UNECE (2002) report on World Robots in 2002 reveals that there are at least 760,000 robots used in industry worldwide, with around 360,000 in Japan, 220,000 in Europe and 100,000 in North America (figures for Japan are an overestimation, as the definition includes all types of robots and is broader than that used in other countries). Expectations about the growth of robots in industry are strong, as the cost of robots has decreased over time, such that a robot purchased in 2001 cost less than 20 percent of the price of a robot with similar performance in 1990. Much of the growth in robot demand is in the automobile industry, and the highest demand is for robots that carry out spot welding, assembly, material handling and arc welding (Weimer 2000: 65).

The density and complexity of robots in manufacturing and automobiles varies cross-nationally as revealed in Table 3.1. In Germany, there is almost 1 robot per 10 production workers in the automobile industry, or around 1.3 robots per 100 workers in manufacturing. In the United States, the United Kingdom, Australia and France there are fewer robots in automobiles and manufacturing than there are in Germany. However, a higher proportion of new robots in these countries are complex robots with more than five axes. In Sweden, there is almost 1 robot per 100 workers in manufacturing, and around 1 per 20 workers in the motor vehicle industry. A high proportion of new robots in Sweden have more than five axes (91.6 percent). While Italy and Japan have a high density of robots in manufacturing and automobiles, a low proportion of new robots have more than five axes.

In respect of the adoption of integrated manufacturing techniques utilizing advanced technologies in the form of FMSs, it would seem that initial high set-up costs are an impediment, and partly explain why the American automobile industry lags Japanese car manufacturers in their implementation. Ford has recently built a new manufacturing plant at Rouge, south of Detroit in the United States. This plant utilizes flexible manufacturing techniques that allows for the production of nine different car models, and enables the plant to be converted rapidly and cheaply to produce different models in response to changes in consumer demand. Ford is planning to have three-quarters of its factories flexible by 2010 (Mackintosh 2003). While some companies, particularly Japanese and European companies, have had flexible manufacturing systems in place for some time, there have been significant improvements in the systems over time. In 2002, Toyota replaced its previous flexible manufacturing system, called 'flexible body line' with a new system – 'global body line' (GBL) – which increased the number of robots used in the plant from 250 to 350, and resulted in the introduction of more advanced robots. Toyota first introduced the GBL in a plant in Vietnam in

Table 3.1 World robots in manufacturing

	Number of robots[a]	Robot density in manufacturing[b]	Robot density in automobiles[c]	Installation of multipurpose industrial robots with 5 axes or more[d]
Australia	2,963	31	–	81.6[e]
Canada	–	–	–	–
France	22,753	63	540	84.7
Germany	99,013	127	890	63.8
Italy	43,911	102	980	59.1
Japan[f]	361,232	272	1,600	43.0
Netherlands	–	–	–	–
Sweden	6,714	89	550	91.6
UK	13,411	34	520	86.9
USA	97,268	52	700	94.0

Source: United Nations Economic Commission for Europe (UNECE) (2002).

Notes
a   Operational stock of multipurpose industrial robots 2001, number of units.
b   Number of robots per 10,000 persons employed in the manufacturing industry 2001.
c   Number of robots per 10,000 production workers in the motor vehicle industry 2001.
d   Percentage share of industrial robots with 5 axes or more in total number of multipurpose industrial robots installed in 2001.
e   1998.
f   Includes all types of industrial robots.

1996. It is claimed that the new system has improved the flexibility of the plant, resulting in a 70 percent reduction in the time required to undertake a major change in model and a 50 percent reduction in time to switch between models (Visnic 2002: 31).

It is clear that, as with robotics, FMSs have been implemented to different degrees cross-nationally. In the late 1980s, international surveys of manufacturing systems revealed that Western European countries were most advanced in the implementation of FMSs. The United States appeared to be lagging behind Europe in the introduction of flexible manufacturing processes (Darrow 1987). Sweden is regarded as a leading country in the implementation of factory automation. OECD data indicate that at the end of the 1980s, Sweden had 108.1 FMSs per million employees in the engineering industry, while Japan had 31.7, West Germany 19.2 and the United States 17.6 (Carlsson and Jacobsson 1997b: 41). Comparisons of Japan and the United States typically suggest that flexible manufacturing techniques have a Japanese origin (Womack, Jones and Roos 1990) and are utilized to a greater extent in Japan than in the United States (Jaikumar 1986).

However, more recent evidence suggests that the cross-national picture is more complex, in that there appear to be cross-national differences not just in the overall use of AMTs but in the types of AMTs being used in different countries. Kotha and Swamidass' (1998) survey of 260 US firms and 125 Japanese firms revealed that the use of advanced manufacturing technologies differed significantly between US and Japanese enterprises. US firms use certain technologies, such as computers for production scheduling, automated drafting, computers for control of the factory floor and computer aided engineering, more often than Japanese firms. Japanese firms use AMTs on the shop floor itself, including NC machines, computer aided inspection, robots and flexible manufacturing systems, to a greater extent than their US counterparts (Kotha and Swamidass 1998: 3141–2). As such, white-collar workers such as engineers and designers are using more computerized technologies in US firms, while the work of blue-collar workers on the factory floor is less affected by technology changes.

There are various explanations for cross-national variations in the implementation of AMTs. One such explanation concerns the extent to which the policy and institutional environment of companies in a particular country encourages the uptake of AMTs. Carlsson and Jacobbson (1997a) have explained the high level of uptake of AMTs in Sweden with reference to the national system of innovation and its support for factory automation. In Sweden, there was a range of background conditions that created a favourable environment for factory automation, including the facts that unions were supportive and the workforce was highly skilled and highly paid. Further, specific institutions played a key role, including Mekanförbundet (a branch of the Swedish engineering industry) and IVF (the Swedish Institute of Production Engineering Research, which, in collaboration with other government and industry bodies, was responsible for scanning the technology environment and encouraging the diffusion of technology by coordinating information exchange between firms, government and universities. This included on-site visits by IVF representatives to small tool-making firms to demonstrate CAD and CAM technologies (Carlsson and Jacobbson 1997b: 45–7).

A further potential explanation for comparative differences in the extent of factory automation relates to the dominance of particular business strategies amongst business organizations in different countries. Recent research on factory automation in the United States and Japan has linked differences in the extent of the uptake of AMTs in Japan and the United States to the strategic orientation of business organizations in the two countries. Kotha and Swamidass (1998: 3144) explain that US companies may be less willing to introduce technologies on the shop floor than their Japanese counterparts, because they are less interested in the non-cost improvements in the form of quality and flexibility that arise from the introduction of such technologies. In an environment in which blue-collar workers have comparatively low wage levels (as in the United States), there is less incentive to eliminate labour costs through the introduction of new technologies which are expensive in the short term, the main benefit of which is quality improvement.

As with technological changes, the adoption of new management techniques linked to new technologies also appears to vary cross-nationally. JIT management techniques linked to lean manufacturing have a Japanese origin (Womack *et al.* 1990), but there is a dearth of reliable evidence on the extent of implementation of human resource practices such as JIT, TQM and empowerment in manufacturing firms that have adopted FMSs. A 1993 US survey indicated that 41 percent of all US corporations (and 70 percent of corporations with 50 or more employees) had introduced one of the following six practices: worker teams, total quality management, quality circles, peer review of employee performance, worker involvement in purchase decisions, job rotation. Organizations in the manufacturing sector and/or those introducing new technologies were more likely than others to introduce flexible work practices (Gittleman, Horrigan and Joyce 1998). It is clear that variants of the JIT style have been introduced in European countries, although the extent and nature of implementation varies cross-nationally (Berggren 1992; Jürgens 1993).

In explaining the limits and variations in the adoption of FMSs outside Japan, Streeck (1996) has argued that lean production techniques that depend on changes in skills and work may not be easily transferable from the Japanese to the European context. Streeck suggests that there are profound differences between the Japanese and German systems of work and industrial relations that will greatly hinder the full implementation of lean production techniques of the Japanese type in Germany. The German system is characterized by certified occupational skills, apprenticeship training, professional self-regulation, occupational labour markets and co-determination, whereas the Japanese system involves skills development at an organizational level through participation in work teams and job rotation, peer regulation, internal labour markets and traditional forms of organizational obligation through loyalty (Streeck 1996: 144–55). The latter is more conducive to the model of lean production that involves the use of AMTs and management practices such as JIT.

These differences indicate that the introduction of lean production in Germany may not be complete or identical to the Japanese system, mainly because German companies exist in a context where employees have professional loyalties, are part of an external labour market and have existing institutional mechanisms for co-determination that place constraints on the development of company-focussed models of change that are insensitive to the particular characteristics of the German context. This provides a further explanation for cross-national variation in the adoption of management changes linked to AMTs.

Cross-national institutional influences on the work implications of AMTs

As explained above, much of the management literature dealing with the human resource implications of the adoption of advanced manufacturing techniques has suggested that FMSs depend on well-skilled employees with greater control over their work, more rewarding and interesting work involving multi-skilling, less hierarchical forms of business organization that facilitate employee problem solving and input into decision-making, and generally less adversarial relations between management and unions. These management approaches might be regarded as constituting what is referred to as the 'high performance work organization' (HPWO) (Gale, Wojan and Olmsted 2002: 58).

Labour process theorists have cast doubts on the prescriptions of the management literature by showing that there is little evidence that FMSs are necessarily linked to either job enrichment through skill and task variety or worker participation in decision-making, organizational design and organizational change, suggesting the HPWO remains illusive. Some research has shown that there has been a degradation of work following the introduction of AMTs, at least for some occupational categories. At the same time, it is possible to sustain an argument that FMSs and associated management techniques have tended to disguise rather than displace management control over work, and have not necessarily resulted in employee empowerment or enhanced participative democracy within manufacturing organizations. The following discussion summarizes the evidence concerning the implications of AMTs for employee skills and participation in the manufacturing sector. Increasingly, this literature has suggested that institutional and organizational factors mediate the effect of AMTs on skills and participation, which represents a shift away from a position of technological determinism often associated with management and labour-process contributions (Milkman and Pullman 1991).

The debate concerning the implications of technology for skills became prominent in the 1970s when Bell (1973) suggested that technological change demanded a more highly skilled workforce and was resulting in the professionalization of work and the emergence of post-industrial society, while at the same time Braverman (1974) was arguing that technological change was associated with skill degradation and provided management with a new tool for monitoring and controlling workers. Since the 1970s, there have been various empirical studies of the implications of AMTs for skills and the quality of work that have provided support for both of these apparently contradictory positions.

One study (Clark *et al.* 1988) looked at changing skill demands at British Telecom in the 1970s, and considered the impact of the shift from electro-mechanical telephone exchanges to computerized exchanges on the work and skills of maintenance workers whose main job was fault-finding and repair. Whereas the old exchanges demanded that maintenance workers had a good understanding of the principles of electro-mechanical exchanges, combined with manual skills and abilities needed for fault-finding and cleaning, lubricating and adjusting the equipment, the new system demanded skills that were much more analytical and diagnostic. Clark *et al.* (1988) conclude that this study failed to provide unambiguous evidence of either generalized deskilling or upskilling. Rather, some skills (relating to a combination of theoretical knowledge, manual skills and experience) had been lost and some new skills (relating to understanding and interpreting computer-generated diagnostic data) had become critical.

Studies of the effects of the introduction of CAD systems on drafting and design work led to similarly equivocal conclusions on the deskilling/upskilling question. Initial research conducted at Scottish sites in the 1980s indicated that CAD had been used to deskill the work of drafters. Baldry and Connelly (1986) found that drafters reported significant work intensification, less autonomy and discretion, and the work pace being increasingly dictated by the technology. Subsequent research by McLoughlin (1989, 1990; McLoughlin and Clark 1994) revealed, however, a more complex picture in which the deskilling potential of the CAD technology was decisively mediated by the existing division of labour (between, for example, engineering and drafting staff), the nature of the design and drafting work undertaken by the organization (or its 'design profile') and the decisions taken by management at various levels. In general terms, while there was a shift from manual drawing skills associated with manual drafting to a greater emphasis on mouse and keyboard manipulation associated with computer use, the impact on work organization and satisfaction varied considerably between sites. In particular, at sites where centralized and dedicated CAD operator teams where established, deskilling, restrictions on autonomy and work intensification resulted. Conversely, where CAD stations were made available to existing project teams, a degree of multiskilling and, at least for some, upskilling resulted. The cases suggest that realizing the deskilling potential of CAD was very much a matter of organizational characteristics and management decisions, and that those decisions were, over time, often influenced by economic decisions about workplace productivity.

Other studies in manufacturing also confirmed that new technology could lead to varied consequences for the labour process of different workers. At United Biscuits, Buchanan and Boddy (1983) found that new computerized technologies used in the biscuit production process deskilled the work of ingredient mixers while increasing the skills and capacities of bakers. Buchanan and Boddy's (1983) study of the introduction of word processing at a marine engineering consultancy appears to confirm a straightforward case of deskilling the work of typists – not because of the inherent nature of the technology, but because of the social organization of work which led to the separation of word processors from their internal clients. A similar phenomenon seemed apparent in the studies by Dowing (reported by McLoughlin and Clark 1994) of word processors in a US bank. The introduction of word processing here was accompanied by a draconian regime of controlling work breaks and monitoring keystrokes per hour. Again, the research demonstrates that it is the way in which a technology is implemented, rather than the characteristics of the technology itself, which determines the impact of the technology on skills, work discretion, satisfaction and performance.

In the 1980s, Piore and Sabel's (1984) well-known contribution to understandings of post-industrial society was positive regarding the possibilities of technological change for work organization, suggesting that managers could create a flexible organization not just through technology but through a humanization of work and enhanced quality of work life, producing an organizational environment suitable to constant change and innovation akin to the Third Italy. More recently, Womack *et al.* (1990) have made similar claims with reference to flexible employment practices linked to lean manufacturing in Japanese companies that involved the use of teams and multi-skilling. This position was popular in the 1980s as various management and organizational researchers envisaged the emergence of post-industrial work organizations based on high skill employment and participative democracy (Adler 1992; Mathews 1989).

More critical analysis has highlighted problems of intensification, worker stress, management by fear and management by blame linked to AMTs and associated management techniques such as JIT and TQM. Intensification of work and worker stress arise from JIT practices that seek to limit inventories and therefore remove buffers in the production system, with the consequence that problems or delays in one element of the production process impact on all parts of the system. The use of teams creates peer pressure for compliance and intensification of work because workers must compensate for underperformance of their peers. Worker stress is also linked to monitoring procedures associated with TQM and improved management information systems which provide a basis for analysing work procedures and performance, and increase employee responsibility for error (Hampson 1999: 371–5; Sewell and Wilkinson 1992; Taplin 1995; Tomaney 1990).

On the issue of the implication of AMTs for skills, recent evidence is equally divided in support for the labour process or post-industrial positions. Gale *et al.* (2002) report the findings from a 1996 US manufacturing survey which measured employer's perceptions of change in the level of skills required by production workers to carry out their job at an acceptable level. They focussed on reading, mathematical, problem solving, interpersonal/teamwork, computer and technical skills. Over half of employers indicated that computer, interpersonal/teamwork, problem solving and technical skills had increased (either a lot or a little) in the last three years (Gale *et al.* 2002: 56). Their analysis also showed that organizations which used new technologies and forms of work organization were more likely to report an increase in skills levels. In the case of new technologies, this was associated with increases in computer skill, whereas new forms of work organization were associated with increases in problem solving and interpersonal/team work skills (Gale *et al.* 2002: 75).

A contrasting picture is provided by Milkman and Pullman's (1991) study which highlights the differential impact of new technologies on the skills of different segments of the workforce. They undertook a survey of workers and interviews with managers, union officials and workers in the highly automated General Motors assembly plant in New Jersey in the United States. Their research showed that the skills level of skilled trades workers, such as electricians, carpenters and machinists, increased if they were assigned responsibility for working with the more technologically complex-machinery and computer technologies that had been introduced in the automation process. For production workers, the greatest employment effect was the reduction of the total number of workers. For those that remained, their jobs were either unchanged or less skilled because most of the more complex jobs were displaced with the introduction of new technology or, as in the case of repairs, were no longer carried out in the production plant. The overall skill level of the workforce increased because the number of skilled trades workers increased as a proportion of the total number of employees, given the increased demand for skilled workers in the new production regime and the declining demand for production workers. However, the skill differential between these occupational groups continued and was exacerbated. As Milkman and Pullman (1991:144) explain, 'in the aftermath of the changeover, as had been the case historically, production workers remain in many respects subordinated to the equipment, while the role of the skilled trades workers (as it was before) is to maintain and manage the machinery'.

Further evidence of a division between the effects of technology on technical workers and production workers is provided by a recent analysis of four US paper and pulp manufacturing organizations (Vallas 1998; Vallas and Beck 1996). This research has focussed on the conflictual nature of relations between technical and production workers in automated manufacturing firms along three dimensions. First, their analysis showed that both the number of process engineers and their technical importance within the company increased after the process of automation. In particular, their role in supervising production workers and the production process increased. This had the effect of reducing the promotion possibilities of production workers without technical expertise. Second, Vallas and Beck argue that an 'epistemological revolution' has occurred in the firms, with scientific and engineering discourse replacing experience-based craft expertise as the source of legitimate knowledge concerning the production process (1996: 347). Finally, they show that manual workers have reduced discretion regarding the way in which they carry out their work, as job routines were increasingly controlled by management information systems such as Statistics Process Control (SPC) linked to TQM (1996: 348).

Rothschild and Ollilainen (1999) argue that, rather than resulting in higher levels of participative democracy, TQM has the effect of obscuring management control over workers. They argue that the discourse of TQM obscures the underlying meaning and effect of management changes, which depart significantly from more democratic forms of participative democracy that have radical egalitarian roots. They contrast the concepts of TQM, as enunciated in management texts, with the nature of democratic participation in egalitarian workplaces. In particular, they highlight both the divergent practices of TQM and egalitarian participative organizations, and the commonality in language used by these contrasting organizational traditions.

Amongst other things, Rothschild and Ollilainen (1999) show that in the TQM organization, formal processes such as JIT and information systems stipulate and control behaviour as does peer pressure in team situations, while in an egalitarian–democratic organization decisions occur in context, are not pre-stipulated and are subject to control according to widely accepted ethics and normative standards. In the total quality organization, employee knowledge is used for the purpose of optimizing quality and profit for owners who are not the employees themselves, whereas in the democratic egalitarian organization, in which ownership encompasses all employees, the ultimate objective is to allow participation in decision-making by those affected through a process of empowerment (Rothschild and Ollilainen 1999: 601–10). Their overall conclusion is that advocates of TQM use language associated with egalitarian and participative organizations to popularize their reforms with workers, while the actual practice of TQM remains far from the ideal of a democratic organization.

Much of the critical literature highlighting the negative implications of AMTs and associated management reforms for skills and worker participation have focussed on Anglo-Saxon economies such as the United States and United Kingdom. Recent research has suggested that the institutional context may mediate the effects of AMTs, TQM and JIT on work life. It is important to recognize that there are significant cross-national differences in prevailing production regimes that might influence the way in which AMTs and associated management practices are implemented, and the effect they have on worker skill and autonomy.

Lean production, which is associated with AMTs and reformed management and work practices, is usually contrasted with the Fordist system of standardized mass production, involving the division of labour, and the routinization and specialization of tasks closely controlled by management, which was typical of the US model of manufacturing work organization but was never the only means by which production was carried out (Tomaney 1994). Hampson (1999) has argued that the less desirable elements of leanness may be avoided when AMTs are introduced in a context where workers and unions have an existing institutionalized structure for participation in decision-making, both at a broad public policy level within corporatist institutional structures and at an organizational level through legislated co-determination principles. An industrial relations climate of this kind existed in Sweden in the 1980s when Volvo and Saab experimented with alternative production techniques, the most well known of which was Volvo's experiment with the manufacture of complete cars by work teams at its Uddevalla factory. This led to the suggestion that Sweden had developed a humane alternative to lean production (Berggren 1992). As with other aspects of organizational change, the effect of AMTs on worker skill and participative democracy may depend on historical and institutional influences over the role of labour, both within organization and across society more generally.

Future directions

While manufacturing work organization has been affected by the introduction of advanced manufacturing technologies and associated management techniques such as JIT and TQM over the last few decades, work and organization in the manufacturing industry in the future may be influenced to a greater extent by technologies which allow manufacturing firms to outsource large segments of their activities and regulate their relationships with suppliers and distributors. This involves a shift in the focus of management and work organization from internal organizational processes to external enterprise relations.

Supply chain management (SCM) information technologies allow manufacturing firms to communicate with suppliers and distributors in real time. These technologies have facilitated the development of a logistics industry to coordinate the movement of manufacturing products globally, reducing the need for inventories in companies such as Dell and Wal-Mart, which contract out supply chain activities to third parties.

Much of the research on the work implications of the information technologies which have facilitated the introduction of new supply chain management techniques has focussed on the retail sector, in which transportation and warehousing has been outsourced to logistics providers (Lund and Wright 2003). However, we can expect the issues raised in this literature to be of increasing interest in the manufacturing sector in the future, including the concern that dominant firms in the supply chain, increasingly the retailers, may impose human resource management practices involving casualization, work intensification and increased managerial control on dependent firms within the supply chain including manufacturing firms. As Ciscel and Smith (2005: 432) explain, 'supply chain management seeks to squeeze the labor "fat" ... from the logistics process. The business solution – speed with flexibility – requires incessancy ... Cost control comes not just from global outsourcing but also from control of labor scheduling, terms of employment and working conditions through the entire logistics system'.

However, the story is not entirely one of increasing managerial control. As the literature on retail management has indicated, the growth of the significance of supply chains is also a potential source of weakness for firms whose activities may be disrupted by industrial action at any point in the supply chain. Lund and Wright (2003: 103) note the 'potential for a shut-down or stoppage in one enterprise to have a domino-like effect throughout the broader supply chain potentially wreaking havoc within and across industries'. They cite the case of a strike amongst General Motors parts manufacturers leading to the shut down of GM's operations in North America in the late 1990s. Another case of weaknesses in the supply chain causing disruption for firms involved a strike in the distribution and transportation sector in the United States in the late 1990s, in which the International Brotherhood of Teamsters wielded enhanced bargaining power in its strike against United Parcel Service because of the latter's central role in US supply chains (Lund and Wright 2003: 103–4).

These cases indicate that there are significant implications for the organization of work and the relative power of trade unions and employers resulting from the externalization of the employment relation in supply chains. As such, future directions in research on the management of work and organization in the manufacturing sector may be more concerned with cross-enterprise relations than internal organizational structures and processes.

Conclusion

The first section of this chapter outlined the new technologies which are being implemented in the manufacturing sector, and management techniques such as JIT and TQM management which have accompanied the introduction of new technologies. However, the second section of the chapter showed that there are significant differences between countries, both in the nature and implementation of new technologies. The main explanation for these differences concerns the institutional characteristics of nations and the dominant strategic orientation of business organizations from different national contexts. For example, factory automation appears to be fairly wide spread in Sweden and can be explained in terms of the support of government, industry associations and unions for the uptake of new technologies. In the United States, the uptake of new technologies appears to be weak for production work on the factory floor. This might be explained in terms of the strategic orientation of business organizations in the United States towards cost competitiveness. US business might be discouraged from implementing expensive labour saving technology on the factory floor, the main purpose of which would be quality improvement, given that the labour saving benefits are not high, as labour costs are comparatively low in the United States.

It has also been shown that cross-national institutional differences affect the way in which new management techniques linked to these new technologies are implemented within business organizations. The JIT practices typical of Japanese corporations are linked to strong internal labour markets and company-based unionism in Japan, and are not translated intact to countries such as Sweden and Germany, in which traditions of co-determination and strong independent labour organization influence the organization of work and production. This would seem to suggest that there is little possibility of cross-national convergence in manufacturing production and management as a consequence of the introduction of common technologies.

Finally, the chapter has identified the tension between those who see the new technologies and management practices as resulting in an enhanced working life for citizens and those that see the new technologies as the basis of deskilling and increased management control of work and workers. Empirical evidence suggests that the consequences of implementing new technologies and management practices in the manufacturing sector may depend on characteristics of the national institutional environment. In nations such as Germany and Sweden, which have strong protection of workers' interests at an organizational level through co-determination policies and strong union influence over policy, new technologies may have beneficial effects on the overall skill level of workers and on the level of worker participation in decision-making within organizations. In contrast, in countries such as the United States, in which there are stronger traditions of management autonomy and weak union influence over policy, the implications of new technologies for the skills and autonomy of workers may be less positive.

4 Technological innovation and clerical work

Call centres and the reorganization of office and interactive service employment

> … new pieces of office equipment don't simply arrive in peoples' cubicles. What is commonly lumped together as technology – everything from voice mail, through software programs to networks – is specifically designed to fit in with management policies to cut labour costs and speed up processing.
>
> (Greenbaum 1995: 14)

The scope of the office and boundaries of clerical work

The award winning television series *The Office* was a rare example of making clerical work visible in popular culture. Yet 'office' work in itself is something of a misnomer. Work of a huge variety takes place within such contexts, from professional to utterly routine. To some extent this is also true of clerical functions. In C.W. Mill's book *White Collar* (1951), he refers to 'a thousand types of clerks' in the new large-scale private and public sector organizations of the post-war period. But those types were within a narrower band of jobs focussing on 'the processing or maintenance of records or documents which represent the transactions or business of an organization' – which is how US Federal Government defines clerical work. Braverman (1974) described it more eloquently as a paper replica of production, and reminds us that such replication often takes place on the same premises – offices are not always separate 'white collar' workplaces. For example, one survey reported that approximately 50 percent of the staff of high tech manufacturing firms are white-collar workers who make use of IT systems (Kling 1996).

This chapter is primarily concerned with the extent and character of technological shaping of such work. Given its predominance in the occupational structure and the fact that many of us also run home 'offices', it is hardly surprising that we are more familiar with office technology than any other kind. We are also familiar with the seeming rapid pace of change in hardware and software. Many of the changes first associated with 'new technology' are now taken for granted, and others (e.g. the word processor and fax machine) are on their way to being obsolete or marginal. It wasn't always this way. Despite the fact that articles on the 'electronic office' began to appear in the early 1950s, the office has been characterized by a slow pace of technological innovation. It is true that by the

1930s and 1940s many manufacturers had devised electromechanical machines to help manipulate, sort and tally specialized paper records automatically (Kling 1996). But, as Lockwood (1958) pointed out in his seminal study, most of the twentieth century rationalization of the office had not involved mechanization. For example, there was a big gap between the introduction of the typewriter in the 1870s and the word processor in the 1970s, with only a few limited innovations such as the electronic typewriter on the way. The telephone was similarly marked by limited change from its introduction in the Victorian era (Gill 1985: 37–8).

Nevertheless, technology has often been a facilitator or signifier of change. For example, in the 1950s, mechanization made it possible to split front from back office functions – a split that located the more routine tasks behind the scenes, whilst keeping the more complex or more personal tasks at the front. Clerical work is not structured only as a technical, but a social division of labour. The expansion of clerical labour associated with the growing complexity and scale of production pushed employers into drawing on a strata of women previously restricted to a few jobs such as teaching (Fine 1990). With the arrival of the type-writer and the telephone, 'Women were brought into the office to operate the new technology and to do other simple and routine tasks' (Butler 1988: 21), creating new categories of work not in direct competition with men. Considering that the office was formerly an all-male preserve, it was transformed relatively quickly, and was accompanied by ideological shifts that reworked moral concerns about the entry of women into the business world. As the clerical labour force was 'feminized', new legitimations were developed emphasizing the 'naturally' lady-like qualities of obedience and dexterity (Davies 1979: 259). Nevertheless, as Barker and Downing note, 'It was the fact that they were cheaper and more abundant than men which gave that ideological shift its impetus' (1980: 68).

This was not a single or simple trend. As the scale and complexity of the work grew, a double division took place. On the one hand, there was occupational differentiation between men and women, as the former began to move into supervisory or quasi-managerial jobs. On the other, there was an emergent distinction within the ranks of women between the back-office pool proletariat and the ranks of private secretaries or 'office wives' (Butler 1988: 22). Such differences remind us that the social division of labour is also one of class and status. A white collar traditionally marked the practical and symbolic boundaries between the working and middle classes. To an extent, 'technology' was associated with the domain of *manual* work. But as Lockwood (1958 [1966]) notes, even the arrival of the modern and partly 'industrialized' office was not in itself sufficient to move clerks into the ranks of the working class. Resisting Marxist-inspired proletarianization arguments, Lockwood demonstrated that (male) clerical work continued to be characterized by superior conditions and benefits of work, and opportunities for career mobility.

Having outlined some of the issues concerning the scope and boundaries of clerical work, we can turn to a related question – is there an underlying narrative of progress and change, and what is the role of technology within it?

Call centres: disrupting the narrative of change

If we examine one of the best-known accounts of change in clerical work, Giuliano's (1982) depiction of a move from pre-industrial, to industrial and then the information age office, we can see that technology only plays the decisive role in the last stage. The pre-industrial office is characterized as much by the intimacy of relations between boss and employees and limited division of labour, than it is by minimal technology. Though the industrial office has adding and dictating machines, data processing and telephone switchboards, the production lines of clerks and specialized, fragmented tasks were primarily an outcome of administrative rationalization and the application of Taylorism to the office. However, the third stage, it is argued, is based on the convergence of data processing and telecommunications technology. It is 'electronic' because the technology has the capacity to integrate office functions and systems: 'Paper ceases to be needed, as everything is done electronically, and we move from the industrial to information office' (Rowe 1986: 74).

We are still waiting for the disappearance or even decline of paper. Nevertheless, it was long an article of faith that *information* technology not only combined computers and communications in the office, but enabled the (re) combination of tasks and functions previously 'industrialized'. In the 1980s and 1990s, the information age office became the latest staging post in a progressive narrative of change. Popular management writers such as Charles Handy (1995a: 72) predicted the disappearance of the assembly lines of the typing pool and ledger department and their replacement by 'gangs … grouped around sophisticated electronic equipment responsible for the outcome of an entire department'. As we shall see later, even more critical writers such as Baran (1988) and Greenbaum (1995) accepted a sequencing in which information or electronic offices enabled an enhancement of skills and autonomy, at least for many categories of office employees.

Also integrating information/communication, telephone/computer technologies, but with very different outcomes, the arrival of the call centre has disrupted this positive narrative of change. Although exact figures on call centre employment are difficult to come by because of the sheer diversity of services and contexts across industries and countries, there is little dispute that it has been the fastest growing source of jobs in a number of economies, and that this is an increasingly globalized phenomena. A recent report predicted that there would be one million call centre jobs in the UK by 2008 (see OMIS Research 2006), though the government Labour Force Survey of 2005 put the figure at half that.

What kind of jobs are they? A recent wide-ranging examination of trends in European countries begins by stating that: 'Call centres are the area of front-line information work, which most clearly approximates to the model of regimented or Taylorised service work organisation' (Shire, Holtgrewe and Kerst 2002: 1). This is one of the politer descriptions among the full gamut of negativity – electronic sweatshops, battery farms, assembly or production lines, the epitome of panoptic power – that can be found in academic and journalistic accounts. In inverse relation-ship to its public image, the industry has been reinventing the terminology, with an emphasis on customer contact centres and workers as 'consultants'.

That has not stopped the sector from becoming emblematic of poor service to consumers and poor treatment of employees. Not surprisingly this has given some commentators the opportunity to reverse the narrative in classic back-to-the-future mode. Poynter uses the experience to resuscitate the proletarianization thesis once popular in Marxist treatments of office work. Mental labour has become variously Taylorized, de-professionalized, routinized and manual, 'sharing many of the characteristics of the assembly line' (Poynter 2000: 151). Meanwhile in a more detailed and nuanced contribution, Callaghan (2002) argues that there is a direct line from previous models of the industrial office, combining scale with scientific management, to the call centre, though adding a new dimension of engagement with the emotions and social skills of employees.

One problem of interpretation is that call centre work is part office, part inter-active service job, so we cannot draw a direct line from past to present. The rationale for focussing on call centres in this chapter is that we already know a lot about the nature of routinized service work in retail, thanks to studies such as those of Ritzer (1998) and Leidner (1993), and that the sources of routinization and surveillance in call centres, on the surface at least, such as the scripting of interactions, is technological. Nevertheless, as the chapter unfolds we will con-sider the interactive service work dimension. Meanwhile, we return to examining whether such claims of a new or disrupted narrative of office work are justified. To do so, we have to step back from the immediate experience of call centres and look afresh at evidence of previous phases of technology and work organization.

The modern office: a tale of bureaucratic rationalization?

Images of the 'industrial' large-scale office are central to post-war society, par-ticularly associated with corporate head offices, banks, insurance and local gov-ernment. The best available account of those early post-war years is provided by Lockwood. Originally written in 1958, his central concern was 'to study the class consciousness of the clerk' (1958 [1966]: 13), and in doing so counter a simplistic Marxist thesis of proletarianization. Nevertheless, we do get a detailed account of changing work relations as clerical work moved gradually from the nineteenth century counting room to the modern office. Lockwood sticks firmly to a notion of diversity in clerical labour. The concentration of the means of administration has indeed led in some instances to 'office factories characterized by specialization and sub-division, impersonal relations and standardized tasks. Mechanization has played a role in areas such as data processing, but largely to reinforce and support existing clerical functions' (1958: 88), rather than to deter-mine outcomes. In contrast, most clerical work, he argues, is limited by the size of business operations, and remains based on a clustering of tasks, a degree of discretion, close co-operation with managers and internal labour markets with a proliferation of job titles.

Over fifteen years later (Braverman 1974) studied the same territory and reached a different conclusion, referring to 'the conversion of the office routine into a factory-like process in accordance with the precepts of modern management and available technology' (1974: 347). Pursuing a Marxist perspective, this was, perhaps, to be expected. But it is possible that something significant had changed and that the industrial office as exception, in the period Lockwood describes, may have become the norm. Interestingly, Lockwood is one of the few academic studies that Braverman refers to, though he selectively quotes only the evidence consistent with an industrialization argument.

Braverman also shares, though from a different perspective, the view that technology is not the driver of change. The fundamental shape of office work was effected prior to extensive mechanization. Braverman not only argues that clerical labour resembles manual work, but applies and extends his analysis of that work. The story of clerical labour, in other words, is one of the gradual destruction of a craft. Previously, clerical labour had been a relatively small part of production expenses, largely self-supervising and concerned with 'whole' tasks. The complexities of scale required an expansion of administrative and office tasks, and a pressure to cut and control costs. Scientific management became the primary vehicle to transform office work into an administrative labour process in its own right. At this stage, the mechanization of the office lay 'far in the future' (Braverman 1974: 310).

Taylor himself had no doubt that the costs of production could be lowered by sub-dividing mental labour and subjecting it to control and measurement. As early as 1917 the application of scientific management began to lead to the 'breakdown of the arrangement under which each clerk did his or her own work according to traditional methods' (Braverman 1974: 307). Under the control of office managers, all clerical work began to be investigated for the most effective means of standardization and rationalization. Because clerical operations are conducted on paper, this task is easier than in the factory.

Mechanization awaited the introduction of early computer systems that facilitated a new division of labour focussing on data processing, its incipient craft strangled at birth through sub-division. The key-punch operator, Braverman argues, typifies the direction taken by office work. Similarly, typists, receptionists, payroll clerks and other roles are mechanized and subjected to routines, divesting them of the need to understand the wider work process. Microprocessor-based 'new' technology was at its earliest stage when Braverman was writing *Labor and Monopoly Capitalism*. That did not stop him coming to some definitive conclusions. This generation of computers would revolutionize secretarial work, destroying the social office, specialize and sub-divide tasks into word processing and administrative support roles. Interestingly, he comments that: 'There is no disposition on the part of office management to reject the Babbage principle and to have those functionaries who are now assisted by secretaries begin to do their own typing and other chores' (1974: 344).

Given the later emergence of what some now dub the 'clericalization of professional work' and that we now do many of our own chores, it may be that when you are the 'beginning of a revolution', as Braverman admits, it is wise not to pronounce with too much certainty.

The emergence of new technology: from microchips to ICT

With the emergence of microprocessor technology, the electronic or information office finally arrived, albeit a little late. Enthusiasts such as Giuliano (1982) projected this as a move away from mainframe computers, batch systems and rows of operatives doing specialized tasks, towards multifunctional, terminal-based work stations and integrated systems. Rowe (1986: 77) quotes Arthur Andersen LLP: 'With current technology, individuals can now be responsible for an entire job since all the information can be provided at their fingertips'. Clearly this clashes with the arguments of Braverman and his co-thinkers. It became conventional to describe this as a clash between optimists and pessimists, drawing equally determinist conclusions from technological innovation.

As we shall see, this is not wholly accurate. With benefit of a little hindsight, we can observe that it may be better to view developments in terms of a series of 'waves' of technical and managerial changes in the office (Baran 1988; Greenbaum 1995). Drawing on research in the insurance industry, Baran argues that the first 1970s wave increased fragmentation and centralized control, thus corresponding 'to the expectations of the Bravermanists' (1988: 687). This is confirmed by Greenbaum who refers to the 1970s as a period in which large scale offices processed high volumes of data on a factory model.

Certainly, studies influenced by labour process theory (LPT) in that period provided convincing evidence on this score. One of the best known, Glenn and Feldberg (1979) found no evidence of increased autonomy or integration of tasks. Instead, computerized machinery required that information be treated in a standardized and fragmented form. Although clerical workers were less directly supervised, the requirements of the machine replace the directness of an immediate supervision. Furthermore, although some routine jobs such as tabulating are eliminated, other specialized tasks such as keying data into terminals come into being. Once more the creative tasks are located further up the occupational hierarchy, though other studies were similarly sceptical about higher level office computing jobs, referring to the industrialization and sub-division of programming work itself (Kraft 1979).

Other studies of the clerical industries confirm the above trends. Case studies of banking, insurance and local government in the United Kingdom undertaken by Crompton and Jones (1984) found that computerization had led to deskilled tasks, functional specialization and centralized control, with little indication that this would be reversed by on-line systems. Their findings on banking were confirmed by Smith and Wield who argued that automation of branch accounting systems had 'converted tellers who were in effect mini-bankers into "automatons"' (1987: 101).

However, none of these studies claimed the trends were unitary or directions monolithic. Polarization of skills continued to be a central theme, often overlaid by a gender dimension. Crompton and Jones (1984) found that even though computerization had helped to deskill lower-level clerical jobs, the existence of hierarchical career ladders provided an escape route for many male employees. Nor were any of the arguments technologically determinist. Managers have considerable discretion to vary the extent of specialization (Crompton and Jones 1984: 51), and workers find ways to resist the destruction of the social office. Smith and Wield (1987: 101) refer to the Taylorist design values of US technology suppliers and, like a number of radical studies, back their case up by quoting the somewhat injudicious remarks from the managing director of Olivetti that the extension of Taylorism through Electronic Data Processing (EDP) has produced an organizational technology that is both a productive force and control tool for capital.

Economic restructuring, including the introduction of microelectronic technology, was also seen as providing employers with an opportunity to transform traditional structures of skill and control as they affect women. If the typewriter had been a relatively static feature of office technology for many decades, the introduction of the word processor became a pivotal symbol of the transformation of the office. In an influential study from a labour process perspective, Barker and Downing (1980) noted the massive increases in productivity, shedding of labour, and its replacement by staff less trained and less expensive. This, they argued, was aimed at 'squeezing out the lost labour power' untouched even by the application of Taylorist techniques to the office: 'Word processors are an attempt to achieve this by the replacement of patriarchal forms of control by more direct capitalistic forms of control – the move towards the Real Subordination of office workers' (1980: 24).

It is widely held in this and other studies that word processing reinforced or recreated a polarization between top secretarial, administrative jobs on the one hand, and task-specific, machine directed jobs on the other, though the typing pool may become the 'word processing centre' (see Gill 1985: 45–52). Butler (1988) draws on a useful distinction between centralized and distributed forms of organization in her Australian study of secretarial skills. For those at the centralized end, it was almost universally held by a new generation of feminist commentators that the new arrangements led to deskilling (given that previous competencies could be incorporated in the software), work intensification and associated health risks such as repetitive strain injury, and enhanced managerial control as a result of the in-built capacity to monitor performance. The sales pitch of companies dealing in office automation appeared to provide ample evidence of such intent. One reproduced a testimonial from a grateful customer stating that: 'a less experienced typist is able to produce the same quality of work as a really skilled girl and almost as quickly' (quoted in Counter Information Services 1980: 11), whilst a lot can be gleaned from the titles of products such as Timemaster, Mastermind and Thoughtmaster (Callaghan 2002: 12). Amongst the consequences of change were the depersonalization of the relations between managers and secretarial staff, and the decline of the social office with its space for informal self-organization by female employees.

With hindsight, it is clear that this technology was in fact a small resting place on the road to office automation. To be fair, this was recognized by some commentators at the time, Gill (1985) stating that such office technology was at a very early stage of development; the future effects on office jobs must inevitably be somewhat speculative. The labour process debate quickly recognized the existence of considerable constraints to deskilling and enhanced managerial control through technology-facilitated change. Reflecting on the early experience of new technology, Thompson (1989) argued that the technological potential for deskilling had often been stressed at the expense of a more considered analysis of the organizational and other factors which may limit or shape it. In addition, the loss of existing skills has too often been taken as proof of deskilling. Word processing is a good example of the fact that technology contains possibilities for different types of skill. Authors from Braverman onwards made great play of the destruction of old manual skills and increased separation of conception (word originators) from execution in the form of standardized data. However, as Webster's (1990) research shows, the machine can also be used to experiment with different layouts, enhancing judgement and initiative. Indeed, many of the mechanical skills such as centring a heading were regarded by those interviewed as chores. She adds that secretarial work, in many organizational contexts, is inherently varied, and that while typists are subject to mind-numbing routine, that was the case before the advent of the new technology.

Similarly, the fact that technology enhances the potential for managerial control does not mean that it is always used. Butler (1988) found that few of her survey organizations had utilized the possibilities for monitoring and control at all, or at least to the full. Employers may be unable to afford to routinize the labour process beyond a certain point owing to the negative impact this would have on the ability to recruit, high competence staff and avoid excessive labour turnover (Reid 1978). In addition, an employer may not benefit from complete homogenization of the workforce. A uniform mass of low-grade workers may bring problems of control, consent and resistance that are more costly than the cheapening of labour through deskilling.

This kind of objection fuels a wider argument briefly referred to earlier, that the 1980s saw a second wave of office automation. Greenbaum (1995) argues that by the end of the decade the contradictions of office factories in terms of limits to expansion and innovation, as well as employee dissatisfaction, were surfacing. A change of direction called for new hardware and software. This is a theme taken up by Baran (1988) in her study of the American insurance industry. Both authors argue that the high-powered personal computer, often linked to local area networks, allied with more sophisticated, interactive software, facilitated the development of decentralized, dispersed operations and integrated jobs. Computer-mediated work is also accompanied by a shift in design and lay-out, typically towards the open-plan cubicles beloved of Dilbert cartoons.

Baran illustrates this with reference to insurance, detailing the emergence of multi-activity jobs that transfer previously separate tasks such as data entry, rating, routine underwriting and in some cases policy preparation to a skilled clerical worker. All this, as she says, 'is a long way from the typing pool' (1988: 691). In her influential study, Zuboff (1988) argued that informed work would raise clerical labour to semi-professional status, drawing, for example in banking, on knowledge and information management. Meanwhile, Gill (1985: 52) also drew on banking studies to report that job descriptions for tellers were changing from information handling to information marketing – handling queries and promoting services.

It is important to note, however, that such writers should not be simply pigeon-holed into an 'optimistic' category. While identifying changes, they also present a downside and alternative directions. Jobs remain polarized, either because of a bifurcation between high and low value products, or classic front and back office functions. The latter were still characterized by centralized, rationalized activities. Clerical industries were still in pursuit of cost-cutting and economies of scale, and both ends of the spectrum suffered from increased workload and stress levels, and remained subject to bureaucratic, rules-based practices, as well as enhanced capacity of managerial monitoring. On the employment side, the two-track workforce is held together by a further tier of insecure contingent workers, and even the increasingly educated, female labour force was often underpaid, under-valued and faced by reduced career paths.

Within these somewhat contradictory trends, 'the critical question is not the logic of the new technologies but the element of social choice' (Baran 1988: 704). Any optimism about the outcomes of such choices is tempered for Baran by a recognition of the continued orientation of US corporations to short-term profit maxmization. Greenbaum, too, is cautious, noting the possible emergence of a third wave in the 1990s of business reengineering-led rationalization of clerical work and employment. In contrast, Smith and Wield temper their previous argument on the dominance of a Taylorist path by identifying a more 'conservative' software-driven return to higher quality customer contact in banking:

> Personnel would be able to ask the system sensible questions on the nature and spread of customer accounts in order, for example, to get to know about their accountholders and devise marketing strategies … Jobs could then be constructed around 'service' and information. There are no technical reasons why, for example, personal bankers (enhanced enquiry clerks who are usually women) should not be given access to any such system and be allowed to develop 'banking' skills further, thus demonstrating old style 'commitment', 'aptitude' and 'dedication'.
>
> (Smith and Wield 1987: 110)

Such predictions were soon to be put cruelly to the test.

Back to front offices: debating the call centre

Given the tendency for theorists to see what they want to see in new technological and organizational developments, it is useful to set out the product market and technological context to the emergence of call centres before examining the associated debates.

The hype about e-commerce and virtual organization is ironic in that the most concrete manifestation of the latest technological revolution has been the creation of high tech office factories. To the extent that there was a technical logic to these developments, it was present earlier in mail order, travel and directory information operations. However, as Bain and Taylor (2000) note, these lacked the integration of information and communication technologies, facilitated, for example, by the utilization of real-time, interactive networks of workplace PCs that emerged in the early 1980s.

In their most characteristic form, the resultant Automatic Call Distribution (ACD) systems receive inbound calls, automatically allocate them to customer service representatives (CSRs), place calls in a queue and (in conjunction with other software) offer sophisticated management information gathering packages. The technology plays a similar role in outbound call centres, where power-dialling software ensures a constant stream of customers.

Technology in such call centres, therefore, tends to control speed not through running the line at a constant rate but rather through ensuring CSRs know queue numbers and average waiting times. The socio-technical system goes further than pacing and directing work, by assisting management in monitoring.

> The supervisor can be in full control of the daily business within the call centre by closely monitoring all activities through real time windows. Call Centre performance statistics, presented in report format, provide valuable input for short and long-term planning. Business plans based on reliable and accurate information on call centre performance result in better planning, better control and better business ... CCM allows the user to define thresholds and set alarms to signal when these thresholds have been exceeded. The call centre manager will be alerted by the change in colour of the threshold value on the real-time display, a written message and optionally, an alarm will sound and a red bell icon will blink.
>
> (Ericsson Dynamic Network Administration, Call Centre Manager)

As Ellis and Taylor (2006: 108) note, these ICTs not only influenced and standardized work design, they 'collapsed distance', enabling location in regions and towns with lower labour costs. As they observe, however, it is a mistake to focus too much on technology as a driver of change: 'Growth is inexplicable without reference to the broader political and economic environments of neo-liberalism, deregulation, restructuring and financialization of markets' (2006: 110).

The emergence of call centres was also driven by a sectoral logic, reflecting the key role played by strategic choices in the transformation of banking and financial services. The concentration and centralization of customer service operations corresponded to the run down of conventional outlets such as branch banking, with its attendant hierarchical and gendered internal labour markets and occupational structures. As an early and influential study by Marshall and Richardson (1996) noted, this followed a similar pattern to previous centralization and automation of back office administration and data processing. But this time, the front office took centre stage.

They argue against a 'reverse product cycle view' that sees services as proceeding through technical innovation to production efficiencies, improvements in service quality, and *then* a range of new services. This wrongly sees services as passive recipients of innovation. Instead, 'rather than being technologically led, it is better to see technical changes as providing new possibilities for the exploitation of service expertise and skills' (1996: 1846). The industrialization of services is based on new and intensive telemediated links between producer and consumer, with profound consequences for the nature of 'clerical' work.

Outcomes and explanations

Market and technological drivers set the context for the development of a distinctive socio-technical system. As usual, however, what constitutes that distinctiveness is hotly debated. As is typical, the early stages of the debate showed some classic signs of an optimist–pessimist divide.

Given the public image of call centres, it seems appropriate to start with the latter. Early studies of automated telephone systems in the United States described the routinized, scripted and monitored tasks of customer service representatives (CSRs) as an 'electronic sweatshop' (Garson 1988). Later in the United Kingdom the pessimistic territory was colonized by the much-publicized views of Fernie and Metcalf (1998). Appropriating then fashionable Foucauldian imagery and arguments previously applied to the factory (e.g. Sewell 1998), they proclaimed call centres as the 'epitome' of the operation of Foucault's panoptic power. Surveillance technology gives management 'ultimate' or 'total' control. Workers are never sure which call is being listened into by management, with the result that 'the surveillance is permanent in its effects, even if it is discontinuous in its action' (Foucault 1977: 201). The extent and unobtrusive nature of surveillance leads to their well-known formulation that a 'frictionless' workplace regime is established in which direct supervisory power is redundant: 'In call centres the agents are constantly visible and supervisor's power has indeed been "rendered perfect" – via the computer monitoring screen – and therefore its actual use unnecessary'. (Fernie and Metcalf 1998: 29).

Such perspectives focussed largely on control. Others were only too willing to extend the pessimism to skills. Poynter endorses the view that management regimes in call centres have achieved both a qualitatively higher level of control and hegemony over employee hearts and minds. As indicated earlier, he goes on to argue that new forms of service work embody practices once the preserve of the assembly line and manual employees, routinizing and deskilling professional work: 'A form of organisation that was once the preserve of manual labour has rapidly diffused within industries that were previously associated with white collar workers and the exercise of "mental" labour' (2000: 151). Stanworth (1998) too, refers to the creation of a new, deskilled workforce that does not need qualifications and extensive training.

Optimists have a tougher case to make. Those willing to try tend to draw on the new service management literature (Schneider and Bowen 1999), emphasizing trends in service work largely consistent with the official call centre industry image of empowered, semi-professional, highly skilled, and committed employees, delivering customized, quality service. While such accounts were largely confined to the consultancy fringe, some support could be garnered from the influential research of Frenkel *et al.* (1998, 1999) on front line service workers. Criticizing labour process approaches for neglecting such workers and the growth of knowledge work, they point to the general decline of low skill jobs. The need to meet diverse customer requirements places constraints on the extent to which work can be routinized: 'Management will tend to develop policies that enhance employee knowledge and the skills necessary to ensure good customer relations' (Frenkel, Tan, Korcyznski and Shire 1998: 9). Such work is different from the back office precisely because of customer interaction in conditions of intense competition in the service sector.

Admittedly, when they move to more concrete statements on call centres based on comparative cases in Australia, the United States and Hong Kong, the arguments are more circumspect. Management faces contrasting pressures for standardization of process and product, and customization aimed at specific customer demands. Hence, call centres can be found along a spectrum of hybridized mass customized bureaucracies, characterized by 'a form of work organisation that remains primarily bureaucratic but includes elements associated with professional or knowledge-intensive settings' (Frenkel, Korcyznski, Shire and Tan 1999: 958). The result, as expressed elsewhere by one of the research team, Korczynski (2002), is a 'dual logic' of efficiency and bureaucratic standardization versus customer-oriented service quality, whose features vary according to sector and segment.

The possibility of different outcomes within a general hybrid is pointing towards contingent explanations that could locate optimism and pessimism as outcomes of looking at different segments. In other words, against any idea of a deterministic or singular logic, it is necessary to recognize that there is a degree of variety in call centre work. The major determinants of that variety are the extent to which calls are inbound or outbound and therefore responding to requests for information and action or concerned with more demanding telesales and marketing, the complexity and variability of the product, and the depth of the knowledge required to handle the service interactions and the extent to which this knowledge is contextually-bound.

The most sophisticated account of such variation is provided by writers who link product market segments to organizational strategies. Batt (1999) sees a tension between serving and selling, and contrasts mass production strategies that maximize sales and minimize costs with 'relationship management' that seeks to maximize sales by providing good service. Each invokes different patterns of skill and work organization. Batt and Moynihan (2002) argue that work organization and HR practices reflect product market segmentation between high value (professional service model) and low value (mass production) customers. It is accepted that the norm is mass production, but Batt and Moynihan explore the potential for a hybrid mass customization model similar to high involvement and performance practices in manufacturing, one that would facilitate investment in workforce skills.

There are limitations, however, to hybridization and market segmentation arguments. As Taylor and Bain (1999) note, despite these variations there are substantial similarities in the call centre labour process, something that is striking when visiting call centres within and across different countries. In part this is driven by a socio-technical system based on the integration of telephone and computer technologies and the entering and retrieval of data to manage the service interaction. Noting the persistent drift back to strong control and away from progressive HR practices in her case studies, Houlihan states that: 'A key source of this leakage is the very nature of call centre work with its vulnerability to call volume pressures and highly visible, duly quantifiable performance dimensions' (2002: 83). Though she found variations in human resource practices across the four cases, the common theme remained low discretion, routinized customer service. It is important to understand that these uniform rhythms and routines frequently apply to outbound operations. Telemarketing, for example, is likely to be organized through ACD and predictive dialling systems.

Relative homogeneity is also a reflection of the fact that most call centre operations are situated at the low end of the market. While there are high-end activities such as IT help desks or complex financial services, most are focussed on the provision of simple information and standardized products, driven by employee interaction with software systems using encoded knowledge and scripted procedures. Most firms in financial services, mail order, retail and public utilities continue to be oriented towards the economies of scale that derive from centralized, high-volume customer management and the need to extract value from labour where such costs are frequently 60 percent of the total (Callaghan and Thompson 2002: 252).

Such observations cast doubt on the dual logic viewpoint. Whereas it is relatively straightforward to identify an 'efficiency' logic that flows through economies of scale, standardization and surveillance of employees, a customer equivalent appears to lack a mechanism other than a vague inference of a desire for quality and diversity. It is true that there is increasing reference amongst managers and in the marketing literature to customer relationship management (CRM). Software streaming technologies allow the identification of customers with a specific profile or who fit high-value criteria, who can then be cross-sold other products or diverted to more specialist staff. However, in the practice of most customer contact centres, as they are increasingly dubbed, the contact is either initiated by companies and visited on the unaware or unwilling, or customers have no choice but to be targeted, having dialled into the centres to seek information or manage their accounts. For most, it is a frustrating and annoying experience.

With these factors in mind, it may be wiser, in most circumstances, to focus on the management of 'internal' tensions. Hybridity would then be an outcome of those constrained managerial choices. As Taylor and Bain (1999) observe, management is preoccupied by attempting to resolve the quantity versus quality dilemma, and is continually adjusting the balance of controls and rewards. Houlihan extends this kind of argument by developing the idea of a characteristic high commitment, low discretion model of call centre work and management. Use of the term 'high commitment' is an important indicator that something different from the classic low skill, low discretion managerial regime is going on. The next section seeks to break down the typical elements of the characteristic call centre regime, whilst remaining aware of potential variations in the practices of managers and workers.

Characteristics of call centre work and employment

This section draws on some of the key contributions to recent debate, particularly, though not exclusively from a labour process perspective, and tries to draw the threads of evidence together. Four dimensions of work and employment are examined.

A combination of controls

The most appropriate description of the work organization of call centres would appear to be *technical control,* as described by Richard Edwards (1979). The CSR is individually tied to the computer screen, but the workflow is collectively directed by ACD and power dialling software. By adapting the power of a technical control system to single unit production, management overcomes one of the difficulties with continuous flow technical control identified by Edwards. In addition to physically directing calls to workers, technology is also designed to direct specific work tasks within calls. Call centre technical control systems, further enhanced by remote monitoring, therefore not only paces and directs work, but assists management in its monitoring, thus information gathering, measurement and surveillance capacities are much greater. It is important to note that, contrary to the views of commentators such as Fernie and Metcalf, the obtrusiveness of managerial intervention is only too apparent. There is a clear division of labour in most workplaces between people and/or functions involved in collecting and analysing surveillance statistics and activities such as coaching that support skills and performance. Employees can see and appreciate the difference (Callaghan and Thompson 2002).

One of the limitations of early LPT was its tendency to rely on linear, self-contained models of control that fail to demonstrate how different dimensions of control are configured at the same time and place. Callaghan and Thompson (2001) use their Telebank case study to develop a view that call centres operate through integrated systems of technical, bureaucratic and normative controls. The practical process of integrating bureaucratic and technical control systems emerges from the supposedly 'objective' statistical information, which is combined with bureaucratic standards for values and behaviours. Telebank has 19 core standards of behaviour, inherited from the traditional banking structure. These include 'maintaining appropriate standards of behaviour, dress and appearance'; 'pleasant and enthusiastic with customers'; 'welcoming feedback and apologizing when mistakes have been made' and 'acting in an open and honest way'. Under bureaucratic control, then, management specifies values, beliefs and standards. Though such standards are used to evaluate and reward work, it is not obvious that a combination of technical and bureaucratic control is sufficient to handle the complexities of the process. As Deery and Kinnie observe, 'Tightly specified work regimes are not sufficient to secure quality service delivery. Consequently, most organizations have sought to instil values of good customer service in their staff by way of cultural or normative control' (2002: 5).

The most obvious manifestation of such controls in call centres is the considerable attention paid to social and recreational events designed to ameliorate the intense nature of call centre working, both during and after office hours. Fun and surveillance, as Purcell *et al.* (2000) note, go hand in hand. This can be seen most clearly in the widespread use of teams. The call centre labour process clearly does not require teamwork and there is no evidence that teams have any significant decision rights or role in workplace governance. Rather, teams are used as forms of socialization, and as a means of offsetting the negative aspects of an individualized division of labour by providing a focus for social contact, mutual support and the 'autonomy' to design your own work area (Thompson, Callaghan and van den Broek 2004). Sometimes, a team orientation is an explicit part of recruitment criteria and efforts are made to link team output to performance through competitions and pay structures. In such cases the same kind of peer pressure observed in factory settings may be present (Barker 1993). However, teams remain marginal in most call centres. At Telebank, management did not even bother with team meetings, whilst in other cases they are regularly sacrificed to cope with performance pressures. Not surprisingly, the privilege of being able to paint their own area and receive small gifts for particular performance outcomes receives a sceptical response, as this remark from a Telebank employee illustrates:

> Morale is a big thing in here, they try to build morale. We actually have quite low morale in our team at the moment ... You'll see they've decorated, a lot of bright coloured walls, this is all psychology. Once you've been here a long time it's basically bollocks. You come in and do your job. You don't really feel part of a team. In a sense it's a big team, but you're in 12 segments.
>
> (CSR quoted in Thompson *et al.* 2004: 143).

Baldry *et al.* (2007) also report managerial attention to a 'deliberately constructed symbolic environment', with one company even designating a full-time 'Dr Fun' position. So far, a limited scope for normative controls has been considered, but this may underestimate their significance as the emphasis has been largely on indirect mechanisms such as games and competitions. A stronger argument is advanced through Foucauldian-influenced studies that put emphasis on the willing incorporation of employee subjectivity into identification with brands and customers (Knights *et al.* 1999; Alferoff and Knights 2002). Such authors are seeking to put some distance between themselves and what they see as deterministic uses of Foucault that have placed undue emphasis on top-down technology and electronic surveillance. Competitive advantage in call centres is said to rely on the quality of front line staff who can successfully 'impersonate' the corporate brand to meet the expectations of ever more demanding customers. But, management are not always successful in this quest. CSRs resent having to sound like robots, whilst resisting rigid scripting and specification of the service encounter (Alferoff and Knights 2002). There is also the problem that in customer contact centres that serve a variety of corporate clients (and their brands), it is harder to build a distinctive, enduring organizational culture (Baldry *et al.* 2007). We shall return to the question of resistance and service quality later. A partial reliance on normative controls highlights a second distinctive feature of the management of call centres, but this time in the sphere of the identification and development of skills.

Social competencies and skills

In some descriptions of call centre operations a familiar picture of skill and work emerges. Batt's case study of a US telecom's operation describes the skill requirements for a customer service representative as customer interaction skills, keyboard skills, knowledge of procedures, products, services and legal regulations, technical proficiency in programming languages and databases. This reflects both the varied and complex demands of the job, and an institutional context where 'the historic HR practices of the Bell system had created a highly skilled work force with tremendous tacit knowledge of the customers, the telecommunications infrastructure, and the use of information systems' (1999: 557).

However, this is neither typical nor particularly transferable. A more common situation is outlined by Belt.

> Most call centre job advertisements do not specify any distinct requirements in terms of training or qualifications. Instead, the importance of personality characteristics and social competencies such as 'bubbly personalities' and 'customer focus' are emphasised. Managers tend to express very clear ideas about the kinds of people they are looking for, and these requirements are remarkably consistent across different organisations.
>
> (Belt 2002b: 3)

Potential CSRs are largely unqualified but not unskilled; they merely lack the standard indicators of possession of skills. Call centres, like many other services, put considerable emphasis into identifying potential employees who are predisposed to become effective customer service representatives. Managers see themselves as 'recruiting attitude'. As one manager put it,

> You're looking for self-motivated individuals who are prepared to be themselves at work, who really do want to talk to people. You need people who can make conversations, and build rapport and think about what they need to change in themselves in order to build rapport with people.
>
> (quoted in Callaghan and Thompson 2002: 242)

The perceived centrality of social skills and competencies leads management to use rigorous selection and training procedures more usually associated with high discretion jobs. Managers are sifting through life experience and/or experience of previous service work to try and predict the extent to which candidates are willing and capable of internalizing service norms and who have the potential to consciously manipulate their individual characteristics and competencies in order to produce convincing customer service.

Callaghan and Thompson (2002) compared managerial and employee perceptions of the skills necessary to do the job. Interviews revealed some continuity between the groups. In particular, there was common ground that social rather than technical competencies and knowledge are primary. But employees were more likely to emphasize patience, tolerance, empathy and sense of humour, rather than positivity, enthusiasm and passionate belief in customer service.

As Belt (2002a) notes, some of these constructions of social competency are decidedly gendered and it is certainly true that most call centre employees are women. At Telebank, recruitment information sent out to applicants states that: 'running a house and raising children requires many of these skills we are looking for'. Before, however, we accept too close an identification of interactive service work and gender stereotypes, it is worth noting that large minorities of call centre employees are male. The additional presence of numerous students and graduates is a further indication that ultimately what management is looking for are able communicators, regardless of their gender.

There is an interesting tension in managerial attitudes towards those competencies. They often argue that while keyboard and technical skills can be taught, customer service is 'in you'. However, new recruits are not simply let loose on the phones to match their bubbly personalities with discerning customers. Companies also go to great lengths to try and shape attitudes and enhance social competencies. There is considerable emphasis on 'building rapport'. As Houlihan observes,

> Employment begins with a four to six week induction and training programme. During this time, newcomers are heavily socialised to the culture and beliefs of the organisation. Most of the time is spent on systems training, but this is interleaved very skilfully with an imparting process based on apparently informal and spontaneous storytelling which frames norms, values and coping mechanisms.
>
> (Houlihan 2000: 231)

Given the limited role of technical expertise and procedural knowledge, the emphasis is firmly on training in competencies such as managing a conversation (techniques of conversational control) and managing yourself (control over one's energy and enthusiasm). In Telebank, a 'conversation cycle' is used to teach trainees to 'build rapport' with the customer. While 'rapport' evokes images of empathy, the actual focus is on specific techniques of managing the information flow through question prompts and situationally-appropriate answers.

Some product and system navigation skills are required, but they are located firmly within software-framed procedural knowledge. In a number of cases, CSRs have been given reference folders containing details of procedures (known as 'cookery cards') and files for more complex procedures (known as 'added ingredients'). The dominant role of information technology determines the 'what' of the process, while routinized scripts, reinforced by training determine the 'how'

(Becker 2000). CSRs do build up tacit knowledge which they share with each other and sometimes with management, but companies have generally failed to either formalize, transfer and extend this knowledge, or provide any significant space free from the demands of work intensity and surveillance (Houlihan 2000; Alferoff and Knights 2002). Discretion and judgement are largely the province of supervisors, who have knowledge and connections across the various divisions, facilitated by intranet access. Zuboff's (1988) earlier prediction of informating technology that would facilitate intellective skills has not come to pass in the case of call centres.

Despite all this pessimism it would be wrong to use the term deskilling. Not only does this underestimate the importance of those qualities which companies do seek to identify and develop, it is based on a false comparison with traditional white-collar occupations such as those in banking. Interactive service work is distinct from, rather than a debased version of, such work. One key difference is the centrality of emotional labour, which clearly does not fit neatly into the classic manual/mental divide.

The importance of emotional labour and the emotional effort bargain

From an early stage, leading studies, particularly those influenced by LPT, have drawn on and extended Hochschild's (1983) concept of emotional labour as a key explanatory tool (Taylor and Bain 1999; S. Taylor 1998). The latter study of a telephone sales operation of a British airline developed the argument, not only that employees were being encouraged to deep act – actively work on and change their feeling to match the display required by the labour process – but that, in this process of building rapport, CSRs were required to transfer the stress on to themselves. In other words, it was the responsibility of the CSR to absorb, depersonalize and manage impatient, rude or ignorant responses from frequently fed-up customers.

Managing feelings in service sector work was not a new observation, as studies of hospice nurses (James 1989), betting shops (Filby 1992) and supermarkets (Ogbonna and Wilkinson 1990) illustrate. As MacDonald and Sirriani (1996) pointed out, whereas manufacturing and traditional clerical workers could do the job competently and still hate what they do and who they did it with, interactive service employees have to at least pretend to care about and enjoy what they do. Utilized in a call centre context, such arguments were important in moving the debate on from views that the labour process was merely a combination of new technology and old Taylorism. As Taylor and Bain (1999) memorably put it, this time the assembly line was also in the *head*. Returning to the theme of an integrated control model raised earlier, it is the particular combination of physical and mental pressures that make the labour process so demanding and the high turnover rates so unsurprising. This is not merely intelligent observation. Studies such as Deery *et al.* (2002) have found a clear link between emotional exhaustion and various symptoms of employee withdrawal.

Not all critical studies of call centres look favourably on the concept of emotional labour. Alferoff and Knights (2002: 197) argue that the concept is essentialist in its depiction of 'natural' human emotions violated by instrumental management actions. This may have some resonance when applied to Hochschild, but research has moved on since then. Recent studies of call centres (Callaghan and Thompson 2002) have drawn on more sophisticated conceptualizations of emotional labour (Bolton 2005) to demonstrate that, far from being passive providers of management requirements, employees are active and skilled emotion managers in their own right. CSRs manifest a variety of responses, from a small number who appear to deep act, to a larger segment that shut down and go through the motions.

> I work until 7 o'clock at night, and it's the last thing you want to do, be bubbly on the phone, you can't be bothered. So there is a bit of pretence behind it sometimes.
>
> (CSR quoted in Thompson *et al.* 2004: 146).

There is, therefore an emotional effort bargain that constitutes a hidden and con-tested dimension of the call centre labour process. This raises a number of broader issues about the nature and extent of resistance.

The persistence of resistance

Employee resistance and misbehaviour is not in any significant way distinct to call centres. But it has been a significant part of the debate, if only because of the early popularity of images of electronic surveillance, panoptic power, perfect control and self-disciplined subjects. Many of the case studies discussed in this chapter have demonstrated how employees have developed a repertoire of informal and formal means of contesting the technical control aspects of managerial regimes (Houlihan 2000; Bain and Taylor 2000; Callaghan and Thompson 2001; van den Broek 2002; Barnes 2004). Trade union organization and collective forms of resistance have been growing in many countries. However, given relatively low unionization and the difficult conditions for formal action, most of the evidence has been about infor-mal behaviours. Referring to a regular clerical task, a Telebank CSR noted that:

> Some days I won't have any to do but I'll bang in 922 and just sit there and chill. If anyone comes over I say I was just doing an amendment sheet.
>
> (quoted in Callaghan and Thompson 2001: 29)

Such comments illustrate that workers can identify 'blind spots' in the system and use them to influence the pace at which they work. Not all such resistance is indi-vidual. Taylor and Bain's (2003) ethnographic accounts of employee misbehaviour in two call centres show how use of workplace humour can be an important source of collective identity and dissent, and in one case fed into a unionization campaign.

It has also been widely reported that CSRs question the supposed objectivity of surveillance data and performance statistics, even to the point of using the tapes to overturn management claims (Callaghan and Thompson 2001; Ball 2002).

Resistance is not just to electronic surveillance and technical control. What can also be observed is evidence of a degree of employee distance from, disenchantment with, and resistance to, normative controls. Confirming studies in manufacturing settings

(Findlay, McKinlay, Marks and Thompson 2000), many CSRs reveal unhappiness with practices they perceive as 'a cult that wasn't natural in a Western corporate environment', or a 'religious aura where there was no room for dissent'.

> ... a mass brainwashing session where new employees are blinded by the hype that is Servo. Servo was portrayed as a non-conflict company where nobody had differences with each other and all problems could be resolved through discussion. Employees were filled with extravagant hype and expectations of their future with the company.
>
> (quote from van den Broek 2004)

A counter-Foucauldian view is again outlined by Alferoff and Knights who see the management search for quality and the employee desire for the 'beautiful call' as mutually reinforcing: 'In short, they have embraced the identity of serving the customer not just as a compliant response to management demands but as part of an aesthetic project for the self' (2002: 198). It is certainly true that a wide range of studies show that CSRs complain that quantity gets in the way of quality and that they will take longer on the phone to chat with old people or customers that they like.

The arguments may not be as far apart as they may seem. Take the CSR quoted in Callaghan and Thompson: 'They [CSRs] are all different personalities, but they're trying to mould them into a Telebank person. Like robots, and they're always pushing, pushing, and if they keep pushing, I'll be out of the door soon' (2002: 247). Almost identical negative reactions to 'robotization' and 'taking personality out of the job' are reported by Alferoff and Knights. It comes down to how you interpret those behaviours. What the evidence shows is that even in a technology-intensive, normatively scripted environment, CSRs manifest an active agency, aware of managerial demands and capable of inserting their own conceptions of appropriate emotional labour.

All dressed up and nowhere to go: a call centre career?

With most of the research emphasis placed on work organization and control issues, insufficient attention has been paid to managing the employment relationship in general, and issues of careers and broader organizational structures more specifically. In the place of explicit attention and detail has been a widespread view of a flat structure with limited career opportunities that contribute to employee dissatisfaction and low retention rates. This view is not without validity; indeed it can be heard from managers themselves, some of whom believe that two or three years on the phones is the likely maximum for effective performance prior to burn out. Frenkel *et al.* (1998: 965) report that while there were informal career ladders from novice to team leader, there were limited opportunities to progress to supervisor and beyond, either because the positions were scarce or appointed from the external labour market.

Nevertheless, we should recognize that perceptions of employment and career depend on the point of comparison. To a large extent, dominant perceptions have been based on unfavourable comparisons with traditional banking and financial services with their long hierarchies and internal labour markets. This may not be the comparison made by potential employees themselves. There have been recent attempts in Scotland and the North East of England to enhance the access of socially marginalized groups to an 'industry' where looking good and sounding right may be barriers to those with perceived social skill deficits. Belt's (2003: 12) interviews showed that while trainees were aware of the high pressure, routine work, they viewed the prospects positively:

> My friend actually started on the lines last year, and she's worked up to team leader, and last year she made £23,000. You know there's a lot of leeway for promotion, so that interested me.
>
> I think it is better than a factory ... I want to get *dressed* to go to work. [Where I used to work] I used to wear blue overalls, full of resin, black resin ...'

Their points of reference were existing factory or McDonaldized service settings. In earlier work, Belt also qualified the dominant view with reference to the experience of women. Whilst most remained on the bottom rung and were recruited in part because restricted life options gave greater stability to a labour force with high turnover, 'It is important not to characterise call centres as "careerless" ' (2002a: 65). A significant minority of ambitious women did exploit the relative openness and female-friendly nature of the call centre environment to become team leaders, and in a small number of cases managers; though in the latter case evidence of a glass ceiling was still present.

It may also be the case that the flat structure perception is a little more complicated. Whilst most call centres are at the lower, routine end, their activities are located within quite different broader patterns of ownership and sector structure. For example, Watson, Bunzel, Lockyer and Scholarios (2000) compared two Scottish cases, noting that both were drawing on a labour pool that included many younger, well-qualified people. A large proportion had no notion of a career in any traditional sense, yet at 'M' a far greater proportion viewed their jobs as part of a career than at 'T'. This reflected the fact that 'M' is embedded in a market segment of the financial services industry that allows some of its CSRs to acquire formal knowledge, qualifications and mobility within the wider company. In contrast, 'T', though containing some high value operations, is basically an outsourced centre supplying services to a variety of clients. Moss, Salzman and Tilly (2003) also report that some, albeit a minority, of US retail and finance companies that have experienced human resource problems arising from cost-cutting and standardization have changed course and begun to rebuild job and mobility structures in their call centres.

Conclusions on the call centre phenomenon

If the debate really is between optimists and pessimists, the evidence would point to a qualified pessimism. It is qualified in two senses. First, that the technological surveillance and control nightmare projected in some early studies has not come to pass. The managerial hand is still visible and contested, with both voice and exit options being pursued by employees (see Bain and Taylor 2000 for a very effective critique of the electronic panopticon evidence). Second, though the work is heavily routinized and scripted, the emergence of new social competencies, an emotional effort bargain and limited career structure offset any simplistic notion of a deskilled, devalued workforce.

Nevertheless, the picture is still largely a negative one. The call centre 'industry' has constructed a particular form of work organization that inverts the logic of a socio-technical system. As Thompson *et al.* argue,

> Reference to the term socio-technical system normally refers to attempts by management and other actors in the employment relationship to construct mutually supportive and jointly optimised relations between the technical and social dimensions of work systems. Within the dominant pattern of call centre practice management have indeed created a closely aligned set of arrangements, but that integration results in perverse and negative outcomes for employees and to some extent the organisations that employ them.
>
> (Thompson *et al.* 2004: 149)

What such a system creates is a series of tensions and paradoxes: between quantity and quality (Taylor and Bain 1999), fun and surveillance (Purcell *et al.* 2000), investment in human capital through recruitment and training, and standardized, scripted work (Callaghan and Thompson 2002). The prominence of conventional soft human resource management (HRM) practices alongside neo-Taylorist work organization raises considerable doubts about a market segmentation argument that identifies investment in skill, plus high involvement and commitment, with servicing high value customers (see Batt and Moynihan 2002: 15). Of course, diversity and strategic choice will remain, and in some instances it will be shaped by classic, market and institutional factors. This is the conclusion of an authoritative international study of call centres across 17 countries (Holman, Batt and Holtgrewe 2007). The findings qualify assertions of the globalization of service work by highlighting variations in job quality, training, performance monitoring and collective representation. Major drivers of differentiation were the type of market economy, which customer segment was being serviced and whether the operation was in-house or sub-contracted. Not surprisingly, employees were better off in-house, serving business customers under regulated markets.

Cross-national factors are confirmed in qualitative studies such as Collin-Jacques (2003). She demonstrates in her study of the growth of call centres providing telenursing services in the United Kingdom and Canada, that there will always be factors outside the labour process, such as occupational identity, that filter practice and experience. However, it is a characteristic of the call centre 'industry' globally, even in countries with denser institutional frameworks such as Germany, that call centres are devised and operated in ways that allow some distance from those potential impacts compared, for example, to traditional banking operations (Shire *et al.* 2002). Even taking into account the national variations reported by

Holman *et al.* (2007), their report noted the considerable similarities in work and organization in an industry that has emerged, unusually if not uniquely, at the same time in many countries. For example, most agents work in call centres that have 230 employees or more, 75 percent work in mass market segments, 78 percent take inbound calls and job discretion is generally low.

With such trends in mind, there is a double strategic choice, between models constrained by product and labour market conditions, and more significantly *within* the constraints of the dominant mass market, socio-technical system. The most appropriate conceptualization of that choice is provided by Houlihan with her notion of a low discretion, high commitment model. In her four case studies, a variety of HR practices and normative control measures were used to generate commitment and mediate the tensions arising from the organization and control of the labour process. Ultimately the latter outweighed the former: 'The common theme to these cases was low discretion, routinised customer service' (Korczynski 2002: 82). The central role assigned to HRM by a number of key commentators, to cope with the tensions between serving customers and managing employees, has not been consolidated. Rather than a dual logic, as discussed earlier, it is notable that customers are managed through the same technology and management system as employees.

Managing the tensions and trade-offs is less a stable hybrid and more a shifting and precarious set of choices and adjustments. For example, Wallace, Eagelson and Waldersee's (2000) 'sacrificial HR strategy', which resolves the tension by accepting stress and burn out as the price for low cost, high quality service, is only viable if there is a continual supply of the kind of labour force that companies need (Deery and Kinnie 2002: 6–7). As problems become pressing and alternatives more feasible, different options open up. Companies are already beginning to go down the US route of using voice recognition software to automate some of the more routine interactions. At the opposite end, a small number of organizations are moving away from surveillance and soft skills training by dumping scripts and developing more knowledgeable staff (Caulkin 2003). Perhaps most significantly, there is the option of keeping all the advantages of the existing low discretion, high commitment model, but transferring operations to countries such as India who can supply high quality, English speaking, but much cheaper employees. Companies also get the added bonus of holding a threat to outsource over their local workforces. Reality, however, is seldom that simple. It is certainly true that industry estimates of wages 60–80 percent lower has persuaded large numbers of US and UK companies to relocate some of their more routine operations. But as Taylor and Bain (2003, 2005) show, such outsourcing has not been without problems. Labour may be cheaper but it is not necessarily easily substitutable. Cultural and linguistic differences have been exacerbated by the negative effects of night shifts, long hours and the usual consequences of routine, strictly monitored work, particularly for the women who make up over half of the labour force. Stung by such problems, domestic customer dissatisfaction and potential damage to their brands, there have been a growing number of high profile returnees from India.

Final reflections

> Compared to their peers thirty years ago, America's 80 million white-collar employees are working longer hours, for the same pay and fewer benefits, at jobs that are markedly less secure …
>
> (Beatty 2001: 1)

So begins a review of Fraser's (2001) *White Collar Sweatshop*. If pay and employment conditions have worsened for many, the message of this chapter has been the significant elements of continuity in the organization of industrialized office work (Callaghan 2002). If we examine the history of office automation we find that it has played a progressively greater, if not more progressive, role. 'Optimists' seized on the personal computer as the decisive harbinger of the information age office. Writing in the *Financial Times* (14 August, 1996) under a strapline 'Desktop technology that has reshaped the office', Harvey argues that the two distinctive features of the PC era have been that most offices now look the same – neat rows of computers and people – and empowered, autonomous employees: 'We are no longer just bricks on the wall: with PCs, we can redesign the wall ourselves'.

Optimists and pessimists have too often merely been two sides of the same technological determinist coin. New technology in the office has always been at best a facilitator of change, and subordinate to the market and work organization goals of corporate executives and systems designers. Contemporary ICT is versatile and adaptable. The networked workstation can be a source of creative or constrained tasks. The call centre may not be what the 1980s commentators expected the future to be, but neither can it be understood within a simple industrialization narrative. Instead, the growth of the call centre model should be seen as a hybrid of what has traditionally been seen as the front and back office. Back offices have historically been the location of routinized, technology-intensive operations, leaving the front office as the sphere of smaller-scale, personalized work relations. As the outcome of a search for a flexible, low cost, high volume way of dealing with customer interactions, the call centre combines and modernizes these elements.

With this in mind, it is important to remind ourselves that the call centre is not typical of all office, let alone white collar and service, work. Some interactive services, for example in retail or leisure sub-sectors, rely heavily on aesthetic labour, recruited for looking good and sounding right, with technology playing a minimal role (Witz, Warhurst and Nickson 2003). Additionally, we can recognize that something resembling an information office, with a degree of shared access to data and integrated tasks, may be found in small-scale locations servicing professional work in higher education or law. These observations bring us back to the starting point of this chapter, that categories such as white collar tend to confuse rather than clarify. The real subjects of Fraser's *White Collar Sweatshop*, with their 'newly technologized, stressed-out, paranoid and cynical production line of human cogs solely for the benefit of Wall Street', are predominantly professional and managerial employees. It is to them that we now turn in the next chapter.

5 New information and communication technologies, and the organization of managerial and professional work

This chapter is concerned with changes in the working arrangements of managers and professionals brought about by the diffusion of the new information-communication technologies. In this context 'working arrangements' has two meanings: the work such groups undertake to control and coordinate organizations and make them more creative; and the arrangements made to monitor and manage those efforts. Managers and professionals may be both the masters of and subject to new technologies. The key issues to be considered therefore include, on the one hand, the challenge to organization itself, as the new technologies are seen to encourage an increased flexibility of time and place and promote project-focussed collaborative networks characterized by loose amalgamations of autonomous individuals, capital and technology, and on the other hand, the way previously tacit knowledge of professionals is now more likely to be subject to codification and rationalization by technological systems integrated with organizational practices.

Debating managerial work

Many texts continue to bemoan the absence of extensive and detailed knowledge of what managers actually do. This is a well worn but misleading refrain. What is more accurate is that debates about managerial work tend to be stuck in a rut, not so much between optimists and pessimists, as rationalists and realists. The former is predominantly associated with the classical school (Fayol, Barnard and others) and its search for the common characteristics of general management. The work of business historians such as Chandler (1977) emphasize how changes in the nature of markets and the size of organizations re-shape managerial hierarchies as new forms of coordination are required. In turn, managerial capitalism is linked to the growth of an *organization society* encompassed by a technocratic view of an enlightened managerial elite in business, politics and civil society that would use rational expertise and planning to produce growth and social stability (Burris 1993). Such views were promoted by post-war management theorists such as Drucker (1955) and through emergent sub-specialisms such as operations research and management science.

Writers professing a more grounded, 'realist' view of management and its practices eventually challenged such thinking. Picking up on observational and diary-based studies (Lindblom 1959), a new and contrary picture emerged of management practices as piecemeal, incremental, reactive and satisficing. The second element of challenge to rationalism was an emphasis on the heterogeneity and unpredictability of management, particularly in the work of Rosemary Stewart (1967). An appreciation of the diversity of ideologies and practices in different contexts has also been boosted by the growth in the literature on cross-cultural management.

It is not our intention in this chapter to commentate on these debates in any detail, other than to note that it represents something of a false polarity, dependent, in part, on which end of the telescope you are looking down. For example, if you follow middle managers around, you will find a great deal of muddling through and fire-fighting. If you focus on corporate management, you will find more evidence of strategic planning. As Hales argues, the danger of an over-reaction to classical views is that we end up with research strong on description, but weak on explanation: 'a catalogue of disconnected actions, events and encounters' (1999: 336).

Interestingly, this debate was to be repeated in a different form in the 1970s and 1980s. Post-Braverman labour process theorists (LPT) developed alternative models of management strategy, such as technical and bureaucratic control (Edwards 1979) and responsible autonomy and direct control (Friedman 1977). These focussed on how management responded to labour organization and resistance and to competitive pressures by developing new regimes of control, though these could never be wholly successful or separate (see Thompson and McHugh 2002: Chapter 8). Whilst influential, such perspectives were increasingly challenged by those using more contingent explanations of management motives and behaviour. Grint accuses LPT of being, '... locked into assumptions about the rational explanation for managerial behaviour. Managers do what they do because the dynamics of the capitalist market coerce them into such actions' (1995: 51). New contingent studies echo perceptions of management practices as uncoordinated, fragmentary or socially constructed.

What is notable in classical and realist perspectives is the virtual absence of any reference to technology. Even the term 'technocrat' referred to a belief in rational planning rather than technology as such. Admittedly the debate between LPT and its critics did focus on the pertinence of technology, but as a device used to control others rather than something which shaped the actual work of managers.

Given the current emphasis on IT, it is worth noting that the traditional debates on managerial work did focus on the nature and uses of information. This is particularly associated with Mintzberg (1973) and his emphasis on the centrality of different kinds of information processing to the managerial function. In the classical model, access to information is part of the process of reducing uncertainty, enhancing rational planning and accurate prediction (Newman and Newman 1985). Realists are more likely to emphasize that long hours, high pressure and discontinuous interactions result in information handling rather than strategic planning. This is reinforced by Kotter's (1982) and Mintzberg's (1973) research findings of managers heavily reliant on information through what we would now call networking. Information, in other words, is unsystematic and derives from verbal interaction rather than access to centralized technology.

Such orientations offered a remarkable contrast to writings about routine work in the same period, when technological determinist explanations were at their most influential. Such research (e.g. Woodward 1958; Blauner 1964) was not necessarily pessimistic about automation, skill and control, but firmly believed that work design and organizational structure were largely outcomes of specific technologies. The difference can be accounted for in a widespread assumption that the essence of managerial work is its autonomous, self-directing character, though there was some recognition that this partly depends on level and opportunity to exercise choices about role.

While such contrasts do, of course, reflect meaningful differences in discretion and power, it is misleading to present management as wholly free and unconstrained. Hales (1999) argues that managerial action necessarily draws on material and cognitive resources derived from their control over a sub-unit of capital or other organizational system. It is distinctive of the managerial labour process that those resources enable managers both to direct the work of others and to be subject to the constraints of direction from above. For Hales, important components of those resources are technological and informational. The next section of the chapter examines whether those resources have become significantly enhanced, and whether they allow some of the tensions between rival accounts of managerial work to be resolved.

ICT as a means of resolving the tensions?

There are certain commonalities between how popular management theory and some social theorists view technology as a trigger of change. Heller is typical of the former:

> The full powers of IT are essential tools of the technology – including that of management. Thus, synchronous working by multi-disciplinary, semi-autonomous teams becomes indispensable. Old-fangled sequential working, from design to engineering to production to marketing, just takes too long and delivers too little. High-speed efficiency is incompatible with the hierarchy, bureaucracy, due process, turf wars and top-down decision-making beloved by the 'corpocrats'.
>
> (*The Observer* 13 August 2000)

Such writers tend to see the Internet as the final nail in the bureaucratic coffin and as the basis for an information sharing democracy (Malone and Rockart 1993).

From the heights of social theory, Castells (2001) also sees the Internet as a major tool for change – the organizational form of the information age. The Net and ICT more generally are seen as a means of letting go, facilitating new forms of co-ordination and accelerating the growth of professional and creative labour: 'an unprecedented combination of flexibility and task performance, of co-ordinated decision-making and decentralized execution, of individualised expression and global, horizontal communication, which provides a superior organisational form for human action' (2001: 2). This is admittedly a somewhat selective interpretation based on highly optimistic literatures. As ever, there is a pessimistic shadow story based largely on the capacity of management information systems (MIS) for surveillance, audit and inspection in the private and public sectors (Collinson and Collinson 1997; Hood 1995).

Whether either story is accurate, it seems unarguable that new technologies loom considerably larger in contemporary accounts of managerial work. The rest of the chapter will consider the ways in which ICT can resolve some of the analytical and practical tensions in management work and structures. Managerial and professional work is too diverse to consider every group and trend. However, with this analytical framework in mind, this chapter will examine three sets of issues: the role of ICT in co-ordinating contemporary organizations; whether technology plays a greater role in managing managers; and what 'knowledge management' means for the work of key professional groups. The latter category covers a huge range of occupations. So as to focus on a meaningful set of practices and research, we examine the labour of scientific and technical experts, a group sometimes dubbed 'the organized professions'.

ICT and the management of new organizational forms

As we argued earlier, whether ICT is presented as a trigger or tool of changes in organizational structures, there is a widespread view that the outcome is substantively different forms of coordination. A number of writers (e.g. Heckscher and Donnellon 1994) refer to new organizational forms in terms of the 'post-bureaucratic organization', characterized by a decline in hierarchy and high levels of cooperativeness and communication between employees. This argument is made not merely at the level of the individual workplace or organization, but across organizations. The most common term applied to new inter-organizational forms is a network. For many, these are seen as fundamentally different from the traditional large firm. As with the single organization, the imagery is of cooperative alliances held together by trust rather than authority and hierarchy (Thompson 2003). Indeed, some observers have dubbed such decentralized structures as 'heterarchy' (Solvell and Zander 1995).

ICT is central to this process because it can reduce coordination costs and offset the loss of managerial resources if organizations reduce the number of levels of hierarchy – often referred to as de-layering. This also facilitates the development of sub-contracting, outsourcing and other means of disaggregating traditional activities of large, bureaucratic firms. According to the leading US business writers Malone and Rockart, computers are essentially coordination technologies that will allow a return to small organizations, loose, collaborative networks or informal 'ad-hocracies'. Such structures depend on unpredictable lateral communications among constantly shifting project teams, relatively autonomous entrepreneurial groups.

New electronic media, such as electronic mail, videoconferencing, and electronic bulletin boards, enable it to work much more effectively. Computer networks, for example, can be used to find and coordinate people with diverse knowledge and skills from many parts of an organization. New computer-based technologies are particularly useful for this purpose because they can transfer information not only faster and more cheaply, but also more selectively.

(Malone and Rockart 1993: 47)

In such scenarios everybody wins: employees at the bottom can become well informed enough to be included in the decision-making loop, whilst senior managers can monitor the outcomes of those decisions. Meanwhile, IT creates electronic markets that empower consumers with better information, and owners with expanded opportunities to sell to them.

The above arguments have clear overlaps with those put forward by social scientists such as Castells (already discussed in Chapter 1), who says that networks have a new organizing logic in the informational economy. Though Castells allows for different 'trajectories' of organization, a common feature is a shift from vertical bureaucracies to the horizontal corporation. Within such arrangements, information technology allows 'simultaneously for the decentralized retrieval of such information and for its integration into a flexible system of strategy-making' (1996: 165).

However, sociologists tend to be more sceptical of the 'everybody wins' scenario, and to look for the effects of power and inequality in the application of such new technologies. For example, a number of writers have pointed to the negative consequences of de-layering for middle managers (Scase and Goffee 1989; Scarbrough and Burrell 1996; Sennett 1998). These include loss of power, status, authority and job security. Even those that retain their jobs face a 'levelling down', as removal of job gradations also diminishes career prospects. Scarbrough and Burrell place the responsibility firmly at the door of an IT whose 'transparency acts to decompose concentrations of knowledge from flows of information. Managers whose roles are primarily information handling are clearly vulnerable' (1996: 183).

Our main concern in this section is less with the positive and negative consequences for management, but more with the accuracy of this new 'post-bureaucratic' picture of the structure and management of modern organizations. We should start with some common ground. It is undoubtedly true that new organizational forms are emerging and that ICTs are playing a key role in facilitating change. If programmed effectively, IT replaces many of the sequencing, work allocation and coordinating activities that used to be central to the organizational hierarchy. As a result, central coordination activities of the organization can be accomplished with fewer staff. What is at issue, however, is the character and outcomes of such changes.

First, it is important not to lose sight of the continuing role of large organizations in the new patterns of economic coordination. Large firms typically seek to occupy strategic positions within existing networks, by becoming important focal points or 'nodes' within them. Ackroyd (2002) describes such structures as the capital extensive firm or CEF. A CEF typically disaggregates the capital it has at its disposal into relatively small packages. A large multinational manufacturing company, for example, will have hundreds of plants and offices, perhaps in the form of profit centres, in numerous locations, not to mention similar numbers of subsidiary and associated or affiliated companies. In addition, such firms them- selves constitute particular kinds of networks, which Ackroyd and Thompson (2005) call 'directed networks'. Examples would include supermarket chains and retail chains generally, especially in their relations with their outlets, and motor car manufacture in respect of both their suppliers and their outlets. Franchise organizations also tend to be directed networks.

Information flows play a central role in new arrangements, for example, by enabling more sophisticated performance indicators and closer scrutiny of local or dispersed units. The way that strategic control is exercised is different from tradi- tional patterns, but is nonetheless effective in securing adaptation to market changes and consolidating the position of companies within their network of affil- iations. In two extensive reviews of the survey and case study evidence on deci- sion and coordination practices, Alvesson and Thompson (2005) and McSweeney (2005) question the empirical basis of post-bureaucratic perspectives. Integrated computer-based models that can predict yield and return may work through output controls rather than central direction, but taken together with more use of standard- ized, central planning systems still constitutes hierarchical authority.

The point of such arguments is that they put into question the description of new organizational forms as heterarchies or horizontal networks. They are also consistent with the research of other writers such as Bennet Harrison. He argues that networks encompassing the whole value or supply chain can be understood as concentration of capital and power without centralization: 'production may be decen- tralised, while power finance, distribution, and control remain concentrated among the big firms' (1994: 20). Such examples refer primarily to inter-organizational developments, but could also be applied to intra-firm arrangements. Using case study evidence, Hales claims that there are greater continuities in managerial work than much of the business literature gives credit for. Dubbing modified practices as 'bureaucracy-lite', he describes the objectives as:

> ... to retain the tight control over managers' behaviour offered by the combina- tion of rules and vertical reporting relationships, whilst reducing the size, and hence the cost, of the hierarchy through which rules are transmitted and enforced ... In bureaucracy-lite, middle-managers remain individually respon- sible and vertically accountable, to a boss, for the extent to which 'their' orga- nizational sun-unit conforms to centrally-imposed regulations.
>
> (Hales 2002: 62)

Whilst such evidence is persuasive, we should be cautious about attributing changes in organization structure to ICTs and not exaggerate their role as drivers or even facilitators of change. First, many recent changes in managerial roles are the outcome of downsizing and the expansion of responsibilities across the remaining layers. Second, though management information systems are powerful, almost by definition they do not cover every eventuality. Human judgement and action remains necessary for the awareness of emergent problems and opportunities. Paradoxically, such requirements are likely to be greater when IT allows the numbers of managerial layers to be reduced. Given that there will inevitably be gaps in the flow and content of information, particularly when practices and processes have changed, it makes sense for organizations to build human capacity into the system and not regard coordination to be automatically secured through IT. Problem solving or discretion is therefore delegated to an extent to managers and other employees (Davidow and Malone 1992). Houlihan notes that, 'Allusion to management in call centre literature is often framed in terms of Foucaultian or technological determinist arguments about the displacement of management by information technologies' (2001: 211). Yet, even in such highly structured technological environments, human intervention, albeit at a largely micro management level, still plays a key role.

Third, we should not underestimate the capacity for survival of the middle manager. Conventional accounts too often present the managers as a kind of 'relay' in the flow of information, therefore exaggerating the capabilities of IT as a substitute means of coordination (Mutch 2000, 2002). This information processing model confuses and conflates information and knowledge. Using the example of area managers operating electronic point of sales (EPOS) systems to coordinate the work of public house managers, Mutch shows how complex coordination reaches beyond the technical capacity of the systems themselves, with the available knowledge requiring considerable interpretation and manipulation. Though a focus on information neglects the wider structures within which its 'processing' takes place, organizations are also still reliant on personal skills, social capital and political action of managers. We also have to take into consideration the place and functions of managers in the overall corporate power structure. The American economist David Gordon (1996) argued that despite waves of downsizing, occupational statistics show that the number of managers and executives has been increasing. His explanation is that in low trust economies, firms choose to manage through intense supervision. Whether this explanation is accurate or not, other sources such as Storey, Mabey and Thomson's (1997) survey of 904 UK companies, also found that less than one third had fewer tiers of management and a quarter actually had more. One of the potential explanations is that hierarchy tends to re-assert itself, with new layers of management re-emerging, often with different titles. Randle's (1998) study of a large pharmaceutical company found that within six months of a new, slimmer management structure being put into place, there was a 're-layering', partly to fill a coordination void and partly to preserve the career opportunities of staff.

Managing managers: extending the technological reach?

In the above discussion the focus is on the overall structure of the organization and the managerial hierarchy. Sometimes the position and experience of the individual manager can get a little lost in this focus. If the role of ICT as means of coordination is exaggerated, some commentators would argue that it is seriously under-estimated in its capacities for tracking the activities and measuring the performance of managers. When we think about technological surveillance, we tend to think of routine workers, whether that be the factory setting where the performance of production teams are displayed on electronic boards, or the extensive monitoring of the behaviour and performance of call centre workers.

As Collinson and Collinson (1997: 386) note, 'There has been little consideration of time and/or space in relation to management. In the main it has simply been assumed that managers monitor and implement clock time discipline'. The assumption tends to be that this is a one-way street in which the manager directs and controls the process.

Yet such systems are almost always a double-edged sword – the information gathered on others can be used to manage the manager. Take the call centre example. Though the purpose of monitoring the phone conversations of customer service representatives is to monitor time and content, the outcomes can also be used to measure the performance of the team leader or manager. The same observation could be made of many technologies such as the 'informated' systems used to manage paper mills. Zuboff shows how the new systems are used to hold managers to account financially for 'their' operators' performance (1988: 283). Technological systems may also be utilized for surveillance directed solely or primarily at managers themselves. The very technology that was said to create more leisure time and free workers from the office has led to a proliferation of email, broadband Internet facilities, fax machinies and mobile phones at home. Workers are increasingly expected to make a round-the-clock commitment to their employing organization. Companies such as America Online, congratulate themselves for offering their employees an occasional email-free weekend as if having Saturday and Sunday off were a perk of the job.

Fraser's (2001) *White Collar Sweatshop* is full of examples of late nights at the office and the invasion of private time at home facilitated by the new communication technologies. Positive images of a switched-on, high speed future in which unshackled and uncollared workers will be 'as productive working in a T-shirt in the park as they are at the office' abound in the popular management literature (Mandla 2006: 3). One of the few detailed examinations of the enhanced use of time/space surveillance is Collinson and Collinson's (1997) previously-mentioned case study of a large insurance company. Noting the technological basis to the time–space surveillance of managers and salespeople, they too reported how mobile phones, pagers, answer phones and modems created expectations that staff could be contactable at all times. In fact, staff were instructed never to switch off their mobile and car phones. For other managers and professionals, email is the main mechanism of compulsory contactability. For example, many students now regard it as a norm or a right to contact lecturers about their work problems. Whilst some universities leave it up to staff to decide when, whether or how to answer, others are drawing up codes of conduct that specify a time period in which the academic *has* to reply.

Collinson and Collinson rightly draw our attention to a gender dimension, in that male managers were more willing and/or able to conform to such time pressures. The emergence of a serious work–life balance debate is indicative of the clash between employer pressure for 'presenteeism' and extra commitment, and the need for family-friendly employment policies (see Nolan 2002; Pocock 2003). However, the extent to which this can be seen primarily as top-down surveillance is problematic. There is also evidence that few employees take up family-friendly and related policies, whilst this may be conditioned by fears about job security and career advancement, many employees are uninterested in such options because they perceive work, not home, as the less stressful and more emotionally satisfying environment (Hochschild 1997; Trinca and Fox 2004). Put another way, some managers are *choosing* to be electronically available and are hooked by their Blackberrys or 'crackberries' as they have been dubbed.

Examples of time surveillance, whilst potent, are not normally described as management information *systems.* This is much more likely to be observable in the management of *performance*. The increasing transparency of 'decentralized' units in networked organizations and extended hierarchies is, as we noted earlier, dependent on sophisticated ICT systems and regular audits. This kind of emphasis on performance monitoring may help to explain the declining tenure of executives (Armstrong *et al.* 1998). At a less dramatic, but equally significant level, contemporary performance management systems are grounded in highly bureaucratized metrics and measurement. There is a long history of performance management, notably through techniques such as Management by Objectives. Whilst the goal was to establish individual performance objectives that were tangible and verifiable, both mechanism and process were often vague or ineffective. Advocates of new, integrated and sometimes web-based systems, such as 360 degree monitoring and balanced scorecard initiatives, argue that new systems are more strategic and supply quantifiable, usable data that can be assessed at the level of department, division or individual (Lingle and Schiemann 1996). In his study of the introduction of new technology in the air traffic sector, Hallier notes that: 'With this new emphasis on unit performance ... managers were now to be assessed on how well they controlled budgets, increased traffic movements, delivered controller validations, and reduced headcount' (2004: 54). Nevertheless, the study also shows a willingness by middle managers to subvert technical change where it conflicted with their own sectional interests and career prospects.

Resistance is one factor that should make us cautious about the effectiveness of information systems. Nor is technology always the main driver of change. Whilst the emphasis on enhanced performance measurement is virtually universal, the mechanisms are not always technological. This can be seen most clearly in the public sector. There has been a widespread recognition of the growth of a 'new public management' (NPM) associated with public sector reform, one of whose objectives is to subject traditional professional autonomy to greater regulation through external audit and internal general management. As Dent and Barry (2004: 8) observe: 'NPM is becoming primarily concerned with the surveillance (increased "oversight") and regulation of the public sector through mechanisms such as audit and inspection'. Whilst this results in an extensive paper trail that is a long way from the dreams of post-bureaucratic organization, the new controls are primarily through output measures (such as the UK universities' research assessment exercise) or budgetary constraints (such as in health service regimes). Such organizations, like some of their knowledge-intensive equivalents in the private sector, remain more reliant on the professional expertise of their staff, and therefore less likely to use intrusive electronic surveillance of time and performance.

Knowledge management

> Recent years have seen an explosive increase of interest in KM. As well as a massive outpouring of books and articles, many organizations have embarked upon their own KM programmes.
>
> (Scarbrough and Swan 2001: 4)

We have talked about trends in the management of managers. In this section, we shift the emphasis to the regulation of what has traditionally been called 'expert labour' – the scientists, engineers and technical employees who are so vital to innovation in the economy. It is our contention that knowledge management is directed primarily at this group, and that new technology plays a central, though controversial, role in that process.

In many ways, managing the knowledge of expert labour is nothing new. In a recent review of the literature, Barley (2005) notes that in the post-war period, Weberian theorists highlighted the potential conflict between the professional principles that motivated scientists and engineers and the bureaucratic and hierarchical logic that the big firms were bringing to the organization of R&D labs. The tension between autonomy and control has, therefore, long been central to the picture, and many firms adopted mixed forms of control and dual professional and managerial career structures.

Interestingly, the arrival of the first wave of new microprocessor-based technology in the 1970s convinced a further round of researchers, many influenced by Braverman and labour process theory, that this would shift the balance towards loss of skills and enhanced managerial control (Kraft 1979; Cooley 1980). They focussed on the capacity of technologies such as computer aided design systems to fragment skills and reduce job security of drafters and programmers. In practice, it didn't really work out like this. Such arguments tended to confuse the technological capacity of new systems to have such negative effects, and the actual market conditions the technology is operative in. Senior management remain dependent on the skills and knowledge of expert labour, particularly in the context of untested systems in unpredictable and fast changing markets (Thompson 1989: 217; Barley 2005: 384).

As the technology added information and communication dimensions, some social scientists developed a more optimistic vision. In the best known account,

Zuboff draws in intensive case studies to lay out two alternative futures for work and power within a common trend towards the age of the smart machine. Information technology contains a duality that allows companies to automate or informate. Whilst management can accumulate, monitor and analyse comprehensive data about every aspect of production, on the whole, management recognized the need for 'intellective skills' and critical judgement, and therefore for positive motivation and enhanced cognitive abilities. The informated workplace resembles idealized descriptions of the learning organization: an environment based on shared knowledge and collegial relationships, supporting play and experimentation (1988: 308).

Zuboff's descriptions of the informated workplace provide a useful link to contemporary KM literature. Amongst the central themes of writing about the management of 'knowledge workers' is creating 'communities of practice', a concept which suggests high levels of cooperative activity. Originally developed by writers such as Brown and Duguid (1991) and Orr (1997) from observation of craft work and the master-apprentice tradition, the emphasis was on parallel organizational structures in which the formal organization was complemented by informal peer networks generated to solve common problems arising from collective practice.

In contrast with Zuboff, such developments are presented not so much as choice but as a requirement of new conditions. It is the *context* of 'expert labour' that has changed more than its content. For knowledge economy theorists, there has been a qualitative shift towards knowledge as the key economic asset. Knowledge-intensive industries become the drivers of the economy, and the conditions of expert labour are generalized across the occupational spectrum. Knowledge therefore becomes a much more significant form of intellectual capital that must be treated as a managed asset. However, it also has core characteristics that set it apart from traditional factors of production, notably that it 'cannot be separated from the knower' (Despres and Hiltrop 1995). Knowledge workers are presented as highly mobile, powerful and autonomous participants in an increasingly 'free agent nation' (Pink 2001). The scope of expert labour has also been widened. To the conventional cast of scientists and engineers, the array of 'symbolic analysts' – relationship marketers, consultants, designers and strategic managers – identified by Robert Reich (1991) has been added.

In this context, what is the role of new technology? Something of a paradox is apparent in the literature (Hamid 2005). On the one hand, there is recognition that technology has advanced to the point where communication systems and data repositories work in concert to streamline and enhance the capture and flow of an organization's data, ensuring that information is retained and lessons learned. On the other hand, despite the array of electronically-based devices such as knowledge repository databases, most contributors to the debate are explicit in arguing that it is *not* about IT. A distinction is made between information and knowledge management. This ties in with perspectives that emphasize the social process of sharing knowledge through conversation, storytelling and mentoring (Sindell 2001). There is a desire to disabuse the idea that there are tool-based, technological solutions. Instead, the tools are merely 'technological platforms' that can act as enabling devices for the gathering, distribution and sharing of tacit knowledge (Clarke and Rollo 2001).

The real story

If that is the official story, an examination of the evidence reveals a somewhat different one. When most job growth in a contemporary economy is in low skill service work, it is difficult to feel confidence in the idea of a knowledge economy. But this is not the occasion to mount a general critique of this idea (see Thompson, Warhurst and Callaghan 2001; Brown and Hesketh 2004). Our concern is with the knowledge management sub-plot and the role played by new technology.

The context *is* different, but emphasis should be put on the changing conditions of competition in knowledge intensive industries, rather than the emergence of a distinctive knowledge economy. Pharmaceuticals is a typical industry where there are intense pressures to reduce the 'molecule to market time', compress product life cycles and drive a process of perpetual innovation. Case studies by Randle (1996) and McKinlay (2002) show that this leads to requirements for greater control of expert labour. As McKinlay notes: 'Stretching management control back through the development phase and deepening control in the documentation process has become critical to corporate competitiveness' (2002: 78). This observation is consistent with Randle's studies of R&D labs in the same sector. The strategy of reducing development time leads to a greater emphasis on the management of the R&D process. Perhaps this is one reason why the sharpest fall in task discretion reported in the recent UK skills survey was among technical and professional employees (Felstead, Gallie and Green 2004). With this in mind, the language of knowledge management is revealing: capturing, converting, leveraging and codifying know-how from employees. As the idea of communities of practice has become more popular, the emphasis has shifted to actually 'cultivating' such communities, with explicit design principles for appropriate social structures suitable for developing and sharing knowledge in the organization (Wenger, McDermott and Synder 2002). As McKinlay (2004: 250–3) notes, the communities of practice idea has been appropriated for managerialist purposes that are a long way from its origins in the craft tradition.

Unsurprisingly, the role of new technology is more central than mainstream accounts acknowledge. Information not only reduces uncertainty, it can offset the danger of loss of knowledge when experts exit the organization. There is a conceptual distinction between information and knowledge. However, management writers from a knowledge engineering background identify a long list of IT/MIS devices – from intranets, groupware and knowledge repositories to data mining tools – that can play a central role in the 'leveraging' process (Shadbolt and Milton 1999).

It would be wrong to give the impression that everything can be reduced to tools and techniques. The actual practice of knowledge management in organizations is not only heavily dependent on information systems, it is driven by the expertise and occupational interests of IT specialists and engineers. Though agreeing that technology alone will not allow effective management of knowledge assets, Shadbolt and Milton argue that:

> Some might say that cultural problems are insurmountable using knowledge technology. We disagree. We believe that with further modification and adaptation our techniques and tools can be used to capture the ways in which behavioural, cultural and organizational change takes place, and how it can be managed best.
>
> (Shadbolt and Milton 1999: 392)

A number of studies show how IT specialists have tried to turn knowledge management to their own occupational advantage. Scarbrough and Swan spell this out clearly:

> KM has been enthusiastically embraced by communities of IT specialists and practitioners. The focus among this community is on developing tools and systems for KM. The concept of KM, then, has helped IS specialists to legitimate and mobilize management support for organizational change programmes aimed at using IT to capture and codify knowledge.
>
> (Scarbrough and Swan 2001: 10)

In this context, information system (IS) specialists may not be the mothers of invention, but they are at least the midwives of implementation. If knowledge management can be conceived of as a new occupational strategy, there is a longer history. When complex IT systems were first installed in many large organizations in the 1980s, information systems experts and managers used their monopoly possession of specialist knowledge and technique to control and mobilize organizational rules and resources (Orlikowski 1988; Knights and Murray 1994). This pathway has been further facilitated by the reliance of many firms on outsourcing such expertise, as well as the prominence of large IT projects that bring technical and business staff together (Fincham 2000).

There are, however, inherent limits. Despite the inexhaustible demand for new IT specialisms, Fincham notes that the collective strategies pursued via the British Computer Society and the Institute of Electrical Engineers have a weak basis for professionalization, and that neither group has managed to impose significant control over occupational practices or the supply of qualified labour. In addition, IT specialists have competitors amongst other managerial groups. Large consultancy firms have been at the forefront of KM, investing heavily in their own internal systems and using that expertise as a basis for promoting a variety of packages on the external market (McKinlay 2004: 247–50). Meanwhile, human resource specialists, initially sidelined by the emphasis on hard systems, have been busily trying to re-position KM as the 'creation of intellectual capital through the development of employees and the management of organizational culture' (Scarbrough and Swan 2001: 10).

There are also inherent limits to technological mechanisms and expertise. Knowledge work has not suddenly become routinized or easily manageable. Given its tacit character and the high level of expertise, it cannot be an unproblematic Taylorist-like extraction of knowledge from the knower. We should think of the process instead as about managing the tension between creativity and control, and the boundaries between tacit and explicit knowledge. This is clearly illustrated in McKinlay's (2002, 2004) 'WorldDrug' case studies. One the one hand, the company tried to enforce enhanced technical means for tracking projects and formally recording their lessons through a computerized database. On the other, they experimented with 'Electronic Café' – a series of linked websites– to provide spaces for learning and reflection on drug development programmes. MIS have no inherent character. In the context of the management of knowledge, they inevitably play such dual roles.

ICT-based industries and their patterns of management and organization

It would be inappropriate to examine trends in ICT, management and organization without looking at the industries in which the specialist expertise of many new ICT professionals is located. There has been considerable attention paid in recent years to what are sometimes called new media industries and web-based work such as graphic design, programming and illustration/graphics. Many commentators believe that this is where new patterns of non-hierarchical forms of management and work organization are said to be developing. Whilst such discussion is connected to the role of the Internet and the 'new economy', the conceptual focus has been most commonly associated with a debate about the distinctive properties of creative work and industries.

Such industries are increasingly recognized as an important contribution to wealth generation and employment opportunities. Many countries, including the United Kingdom, have developed policy objectives to identify, grow and support creative industries. Creativity is seen to rest in the nature of work itself. Echoing themes of knowledge economy theories, a dominant theme is the assumption that highly mobile, creative workers' search for autonomy and the intangible nature of their intellectual assets requires an abandonment of traditional, hierarchical structures and practices (Scase and Davis 2001).

One of the most influential books of the past decade in the business and social literatures is Richard Florida's (2002) *The Rise of the Creative Class*. Florida argues that in the 'no-collar' workplace the emphasis is on informality, collegiality, high autonomy and self-managing teams. A link is made to the previously-discussed 'communities of practice' model, whereby small groups collaborate horizontally in a process of exploration and discovery (2002: 41). 'Technology plus talent' are the essential ingredients for creativity at work.

There are two problems with this analysis. First, the discussion is extremely speculative. Most of the evidence presented concerns orientations to work, and we gain little sense of how creative work is organized and managed, though there is a lot of very general material on the workspace environment and on the characteristics of labour markets (Thompson *et al.* 2007). Second, there are problems in how creative work is identified and classified. Florida defines a creative economy through commonality amongst a set of occupations in which people 'add economic value through their creativity' (2002: 68).

This approach produces a two-strata class corresponding to 30 percent of the US labour force, but divided by the extent to which individuals and occupations create meaningful new forms. The 'super-creative core' consists of scientists, engineers, university professors, poets, actors and architects, whilst the secondary group is based on creative professionals in knowledge-intensive industries such as financial services and healthcare, who draw on complex bodies of knowledge to solve more particular problems.

Standard Occupational Classification codes inevitably aggregate different types of work, some of whom, for example Computer Support Specialists, would be very difficult to classify as creative, super or otherwise. The list of occupations covered is possibly even more diverse. The creative class is a chaotic concept. It is, for example, difficult to see the logic of any grouping that includes scientists and poets other than they are both (in Florida's words) 'purveyors of creativity'.

As a result of failing to focus on actual work relations, and by conflating occupational categories, such arguments inflate the scope of creativity and neglect tensions in management of creative ICT-based labour. As Terranova notes, much of the shine has gone out of the new economy:

> Working in the digital media industry is not as much fun as it is made out to be. The 'Net Slaves' of the eponymous Webzine are becoming increasingly vociferous about the shamelessly exploitative nature of the job, its punishing work rhythms, and its ruthless casualization.
>
> (Terranova 2000: 33)

The reference to Net Slaves refers to a website that aimed to show what life is really like for many workers in the new, high-tech workplace. Lessard and Baldwin (*c.* 2000) have now turned this into a book whose chapters describe different castes of 'net slave'. Behind conventional roles, such as tech support assistant, HTML author and programmer, are more exotic labels, such as the 'Fry Cooks' (who organize the 'get it done at all costs' projects) and the 'Cab Drivers' (who have to constantly hustle for work such as website design). Terranova also makes the point that one of the distinctive things about work and organization for the Internet is that the creativity on which the medium depends needs large amounts of free labour from the likes of AOL community leaders, open source programmers and mailing list editors. This can be a very different 'community of practice' than we find in conventional work and employment relations.

Florida (2002: 68) dismisses issues of ownership because creative capacity is intangible and the property of individual 'creatives'. Yet rendering ownership and control invisible in analyses of the 'creative economy' raises the question: where is the industry in the creative industries? This problem is partially avoided if, like some leading commentators (Howkins 2001), creativity is classified by sector. He identifies fifteen sectors ranging from R&D, through to software, film, video games, architecture and art, linked in part by their products falling within the framework of intellectual property law (copyright, patents, trademarks and designs). The list drawn up by the UK Creative Industries Task Force is broadly similar. Whilst this does avoid some of the problems of using occupational data, many of the same categorization problems reappear. Sectors include a wide variety of economic inputs and outputs, forms of labour and their management.

Nevertheless, the distinctive characteristics of creative labour *are* best understood within particular sectoral and market contexts. As Pratt (2003: 6) argues, 'Most definitions of the new economy are so wide and all-encompassing that even if there were anything going on it is likely that it would be swamped by the noise of contradictory activity. Thus, we have to begin from the bottom-up, with detailed analyses of what is going on in emergent economic sectors'. In concrete terms, new media industries and web-based work need to be disaggregated from more general ideas of a 'creative economy'.

There is a paucity of evidence on these emergent sectors, but there are a small number of useful studies (Batt, Christopherson, Rughtor and van Jaarveld 2001; Pratt 2002; Sandberg and Augustsson 2002; Lash and Wittel 2002; Abel and Pries 2007; Mayer-Ahuja and Wolf 2007). There a number of main findings.

- In the early, entrepreneurial phase, many such smaller new media firms were indeed highly entrepreneurial, relied on a mixture of charismatic authority and direct control, and had largely decentralized structures and horizontal forms of coordination. Work is essentially project-based and work levels vary considerably. This variation contributes to the wider use of freelancers and alliances with other firms to complete projects. Typically, projects involve a number of different creative and/or professional activities.

- In some economies, notably the United States (Batt *et al.* 2001), this industrial structure suggests that the emerging patterns of employment for recognized creative industries feature a high proportion of freelancers, more frequent job changes and more employment insecurity: a self-managed career, with more responsibility on the individual to maintain and update skills and creative abilities, and more importance placed on networks (formal and informal) to access jobs.

- As the sector/s matured and the new economy boom ended, there was a period of contraction, rationalization and concentration. Whilst still less bureaucratic than many of their counterparts in other sectors, there was a clearer formalization of roles and centralization of authority. Research on 12 German companies by Mayer-Ahuja and Wolf (2007) suggests that its work-flow can be further disaggregated into conception, design and implantation tasks, all of which are undertaken by different workers using different skills and competencies. The collapse of the dotcom bubble in 2001 is the point where control over the creative labour process in the German companies tightens. Previous egalitarian relations within these companies decreased, replaced by increased hierarchy: 'collective muddling through' replaced by 'clearer distribution of functions' and a 'deepening gap' emerged between employees and managers. The trend towards newly established hierarchies and stricter controls is confirmed in the case studies of Lash and Wittel (2002) and Barrett (2004). In the latter – a study of Webboyz, an Australian Internet software company – the company started small and employed younger, 'nerdy' creative staff. But as the company grew and became listed on the stock market, new senior mangers were employed and controls over time and through technology were developed.

- With respect to employment patterns, the United States may not be typical. For example, there is only limited evidence of the sector developing a distinctive new model in the use of non-standard or freelance labour or new industrial relations practices. The dominant pattern is the one we would expect from traditional research: new media firms largely adapted to their institutional environment rather than enacting a new one, particularly in Germany and Austria where they are 'dense' institutional networks. Swedish findings also contradict what might be expected from the US model. Unlike the United States, there is little 'hire and fire' driven flexibility. Instead jobs are more stable, and flexibility is achieved by inter-firm collaboration (Sandberg and Augustsson, 2002). This finding would seem to undermine any technological determinacy and suggest that the model of production is shaped by the variety of national business systems.

Conclusions

We have discussed two types of issues in this chapter: the role played by new technologies in the reshaping of how organizations are coordinated and in how managers and experts are themselves managed. With respect to the former, our view is that the contemporary economy has not suddenly become populated by heterarchies and collaborative networks. As environments and organizational structures become more complex, so there has been a tendency for diversification of types of control and coordination. Hierarchies continue to co-exist with markets and more horizontal forms of coordination and large firms continue to be central players. In essence, ICT facilitates that diversity and experimentation.

The central problem with mainstream accounts of management and ICT is the tendency to remove power and the market from the equation. It is as if new technology has a direct and unmediated role in reshaping work and organization. This runs counter to a core argument of this book: that technology is a facilitator rather than a driver of change. Markets drive the changes, and power relations inside the organization constrain and filter the uses of new technologies. Mainstream accounts miss this not only because of what they don't look at, but what they do. By primarily focussing on the micro level, where computer systems undoubtedly do allow for greater access to and manipulation of information in the management process, they over-estimate its participative and transformational qualities. If we look further up the scale at macro and strategic developments, we still see the central significance of ICT, but also its capacity to reinforce or even enhance centralized relations of power and control.

With respect to managing managers, experts and professionals, as we have argued, there has always been a tension between 'creatives' and 'the suits' or 'bean counters'. This has intensified as organizations seek quicker and more effective ways of harnessing the tacit knowledge of such employees in more competitive environments. Similarly managers are by definition caught in the middle between controlling the work of subordinates and having their own work managed. The difference today is that the means for the former often enhance the latter. In other words, MIS are a double-edged sword that has led to the rise of enhanced technological surveillance.

Whether one takes a pessimistic or optimistic view of the promotion of new technologies as a means of addressing the tensions, neither of these processes can be resolved in any fundamental way. We can change the boundaries and shape the choices within those tensions, but they are inherent to the labour processes of managerial and expert labour.

6 New forms of work organization and the technological revolution

Distributed work arrangements and telework

There is near unanimous agreement in the management literature that new forms of work organization are emerging, and that these have been facilitated by the application of new information and communication technologies. Emergent and rapidly increasing forms of production based on telework and virtual teams have created fundamental challenges for the organization of work and its application to the enterprise. This chapter provides a framework for understanding the political, social and economic forces that have mediated the impact of new technology on the contemporary workplace. The first section raises some key issues about the spread of telework and its impact on occupations and work organization. The second section reviews the contradictory implications for organizational design and governance of computer mediated communication and distributed work settings. These assessments are intended to provide a more measured approach to the costs and benefits of the new virtual organization for the innovative capacity of both workers and the enterprise.

Telework, or the conduct of paid work at a distance from the normal workplace through the use of computer and telecommunications technologies, has the potential to impact significantly on traditional organizational structures and hierarchical management practices. The framework of modern work organization has been developed and maintained within the physical boundaries of the workplace, enabling trust and control to be embedded in organizational structure. That is, the production of goods and services, controls over productivity and the rate of output are formally and informally determined by organizational systems such as hierarchical structures and the coordination of discrete tasks. However, teleworkers generally work outside and across organizational boundaries, commonly in what has been perceived to be the extra-organizational space of the home. Many teleworkers also have potentially greater autonomy in time management and are removed from the pace and rhythms of the workplace.

Telework is clearly a rapidly emerging pattern of employment, potentially independent of time and place and physical networks of communication. Telework confronts managers, employees and unions with new issues of work discipline and control, but it would be a significant exaggeration to view these as fundamental challenges to the nature of organization (Davidow and Malone 1992; Brigham and Corbett 1996; Harris 1998) or to work itself (Armstrong 1999;

Rifkin 2000; Bridges 1995). While changes in organizational structure and work processes are facilitated by the availability and application of technologies, there is no causal relationship between technological change, the nature of work and organizational restructuring. The adoption of information and communication technologies and the purposes to which they are directed need to be understood as a set of social and political processes. Employers, managers and employees actively shape new technologies to their own ends, rather than passively adapting to pre-determined technological systems (Jackson and van der Wielen 1998a).

Telework may be utilized by management to achieve a variety of corporate strategies and managerial goals. These goals may range from a focus on short term profitability by cost reduction in areas such as training, employee benefits and permanent skilled staff on the one hand, through to a long term focus on productive capacity by increasing training, concentration on a high wage, high skilled workforce engaged in high value added production on the other (Boreham, Hall and Harley 1996). The latter strategy seeks to cultivate greater commitment and productivity from employees through the provision of relatively secure employment, job enrichment strategies, skill development, functional flexibility and the extension of various decision-making rights to individual employees and work teams. The former approach emphasizes the imperatives of 'flexibility' customarily associated with an increasingly volatile and global economic environment. Increased labour flexibility can be achieved through a 'neo-liberal' strategy of returning the regulation of labour relations to the bare contract of employment which facilitates casual and temporary staffing, deskilling and Taylorist forms of work organization. In many countries, changing frameworks of industrial relations and labour law have created opportunities for cost reduction by facilitating a change of worker status from that of employee to independent contractor or sub-contractor.

Telework is part of an employment relationship and is therefore characterized by expectations and obligations. The context in which these relationships are manifest may be characterized by relatively high degrees of trust and autonomy, as is often the case for managerial and professional work, or by low trust and a panoply of organizational control processes, which is likely to be the case for clerical employment. For these reasons, conceptual issues cloud any analysis of the data purporting to show the social and organizational impact of telework. The diffusion of telework does not correlate with any particular vision of the workplace of the future or its management.

Nevertheless, there is now substantial evidence to suggest that there is a considerable potential for the growth of telework with a commensurate effect on labour markets, especially among groups who are presently under-represented in the contemporary workforce. The data discussed below allows us to come to some preliminary conclusions about the dispersion of telework in the advanced economies, the profile of employment on which telework is currently focussed, and the implications for organizational restructuring that might flow from this extension of time and place in work organization.

The diffusion of telework in the advanced economies

Current assessments of the extent and growth of telework need to be viewed in the light of the adequacy of the data collection on which they are based. Quite inconsistent definitions of the concept have been employed in several major studies and in official country statistical collections. For example, it is not always evident from studies reporting survey data whether the concept embraces only those working from home using information and communications technologies or whether it embraces a much broader category of 'mobile telework' and work undertaken in 'telecottages' and neighbourhood offices. Other significant data problems surround the working time devoted to telework and the status of teleworkers as employees or self-employed. Nor do most studies collect information on the motivation for introducing telework.

These data issues assume a great deal of importance when hypotheses are introduced about the challenges telework poses for organizations. Clearly, some of the most substantial elements of contemporary teleworking practice, such as self-employment and call centres, will not pose organizational issues of an order similar to those presented by the minority of professional 'knowledge workers' associated with the 'virtual organization' so enthusiastically endorsed and promoted by many organizational analysts (see Reich 1991). This is not intended to deny the potential significance on work organization of the utilization of information and communications technologies, but simply to voice some caution about assuming the prevalence of virtual organization in modern advanced economies. The following review of the data on the diffusion of categories of telework in the advanced economies is intended to illuminate these observations.

Environmental, financial and management initiatives have provided the impetus for the promotion of telework in the United States. In 1996, the federal government implemented the national telecommunications initiative with the objective of increasing the number of teleworkers in federal employment and in other key areas of economic activity. Data provided for the United States by WorldatWork, who are a part of the International Telework Association and Council (ITAC) show that the number of teleworkers (defined as those who telework at least one day per month) has increased from 8.5 million in 1995 to almost 23 million in 2000, to 28.7 million or 20 percent of the employed population in 2006. Substantial growth has also been exhibited in the number of US enterprises allowing telework, from 7.6 million in 2004 (30 percent of all enterprises) to 12.4 million in 2006 (WorldatWork 2006; see also Kominski 2000; Riley, Mandavilli and Heino 2000).

In Europe, telework is considered to have great potential for allowing access to previously excluded labour pools, and to increase work options to attract and retain talented workers. In 1994, the European Commission set a goal that 10 million telework places were to be created by 2000. The Commission supported this objective with a substantial programme of policy and information measures. In 1999, the European Electronic Commerce and Telework Trends (ECaTT) project generated representative information on the prevalence and spread of telework across Europe. Data collection involved an interview survey of a sample of 7,500 members of the EU population covering attitudes to and practice of telework, and an interview survey of decision-makers in 4,000 EU establishments covering current practice and plans to introduce the various forms of new ways of working. Both surveys involved ten EU member states: Germany, the United Kingdom, France, Italy, Spain, Sweden, Finland, Denmark, the Netherlands and Ireland.

The ECaTT project data indicated that 36 percent of all establishments practised some form of telework (ECaTT 2000b). Moreover, compared with data from a similar survey completed in 1994, there was a rapid expansion in the number of telework establishments with an annual growth rate between 22 percent (France) and 31 percent (United Kingdom) (ECaTT 2000a). More recently, the Information Society program of the European Commission, Statistical Indicators Benchmarking the Information Society (SIBIS) estimated that, taking into account all types of telework, 13 percent of all employed persons were teleworking in the 15 EU countries surveyed in 2002, an increase from 6.1 percent in 1999 (SIBIS 2003; Gareis 2002). This rate of growth appears set to continue, and projections estimated from the ECaTT survey data suggest that there will be in excess of 20 million teleworkers in the European Union in 2006 (see Gareis and Kordey 2000). Similar patterns of telework manifest themselves in other developed economies, with estimates for teleworkers at about 8 percent of the workforce for Japan in 2000 (Higa and Wijayanayake 1998) and 7 percent of employed persons in Australia in 2000 (ABS 2001).

Impressive as these data are, they need to be disaggregated with some care before interpreting the rise of telework as a fundamental challenge to contemporary work organization. The first point revealed by the SIBIS data for the European Union and the United States, summarized in Table 6.1, is that regular (at least one day per week), home-based teleworkers constitute only 2.1 percent of the labour force. Of these regular, home-based teleworkers only 3 percent are described as permanent (at least 75 percent of their working time is home based). While the trend is for telework to increase, there is presently insufficient evidence to suggest that this group confronts the architecture of contemporary work organization with an irresolvable dilemma.

The second issue to be addressed throws further light on the nature of telework. It concerns the background characteristics of those who regularly telework. The data presented in Table 6.2 shows that, compared with the non-teleworking working population, teleworkers are overwhelmingly likely to be male, predominantly in the 30–49 age category, and to come from significantly higher educational backgrounds. They are disproportionately drawn from the Financial and Business Services sector and are much more likely to work for large organizations. These data do not suggest that telework has become the characteristic mode of employment for a broad stratum of the workforce. On the contrary, regular teleworkers tend to be representative of an elite group of experienced, male, professional-managerial employees who might be expected to exhibit a relatively high degree of autonomy in enterprise decision-making.

Some important questions about the spread of individual teleworkers are suggested by data from a survey of establishments carried out by ECaTT in 1999 and

Table 6.1 Forms of telework in the European Union and United States, 2002, as a percentage of the labour force[a]

	Home-based telework – alternating or permanent[b]	Mobile telework[c]	Self-employed telework[d]	Home based telework – supplementary[e]	All – excluding overlaps
France	(2.2)	2.1	(0.8)	(2.3)	(6.3)
Germany	1.6	5.7	5.2	6.3	16.6
Italy	(0.8)	5.5	(2.6)	(1.7)	(9.5)
Netherlands	9.0	4.1	(5.0)	11.6	(26.4)
Sweden	5.3	4.9	(2.0)	(9.5)	(18.7)
United Kingdom	2.4	4.7	4.5	8.5	17.3
European Union	2.1	4.0	3.4	5.3	13.0
United States	5.1	5.9	6.3	12.2	24.6

Source: Statistical Indicators Benchmarking the Information Society (SIBIS) (2003).

Notes
a   Figures in brackets have limited validity due to low absolute numbers of response to the respective question.
b   Working at home for at least one full day per week. Alternating: Central office plus home for at least one day per week. Permanent: 75% of working time at home.
c   Ten or more hours per week from a mobile workplace using on-line links.
d   Self-employed, working from a home office using email/Internet connections.
e   Less than one day per week. Additional or preparatory work in office/central workplace.

Table 6.2 Characteristics of regular teleworkers compared with those of the non-teleworking workforce, Europe 1999

	Percent of regular teleworkers	Percent of those in paid work but not teleworking
Male	81.3	53.9
Age 30–49	68.2	56.3
High education levels	58.9	27.2
Low education levels	4.1	21.3
Financial and business services sector	23.5	10.7
Public administration and education sector	9.7	18.4
Size of employing organization (1,000 and above employees)	36.4	16.0

Source: European Electronic Commerce and Telework Trends (ECaTT) (2000a).

set out in Table 6.3. While as many as one third of establishments practised some form of telework, only a little over 5 percent of enterprises employed permanent teleworkers. More significantly, the number of teleworkers in each teleworking enterprise was quite low, with a median of only six employees teleworking (all forms of telework including supplementary but excluding mobile). Moreover, as the ECaTT report notes, while the diffusion of telework to new establishments

Table 6.3 Spread of different types of telework within establishments in 10 EU countries, as a percentage of all establishments, 1999

Any regular telework	29.7%
Home based telework	13.9%
Permanent telework	5.4%
Alternating telework	11.8%
Self-employed telework	9.2%
Mobile telework	20.0%
Supplementary telework	21.4%
Median number of teleworkers per establishment practising telework[a]	6
Areas in which telework is practised[b]	
Professional	48.4%
Managerial	44.8%

Source: European Electronic Commerce and Telework Trends (ECaTT) (2000b).

Notes
a   Includes supplementary, excludes mobile teleworkers.
b   Of these establishments practising telework.

was quite high, the internal diffusion, or the expansion of telework in each tele-working establishment, has only proceeded very slowly (ECaTT 2000b: 18).

The data from teleworking establishments reported in Table 6.3 also confirms the assessment made earlier, on the basis of the survey of teleworkers, that the two most common fields of activity in which teleworking establishments are engaged are professional, qualified tasks and managerial work. Secretarial and clerical duties are the least often practised activities in the form of telework.

The assessment of telework trends presented above has largely drawn on European data because of its conceptual clarity. Data from the United States (Edwards and Field-Hendrey 1996; Helling 2000; Van Horn and Storen 2000; Kominski 2000; Pratt 1999) presents a broadly similar picture, albeit with higher diffusion rates because of the greater penetration of home office technology, a pattern repeated in comparative assessments of telework in individual European countries (ECaTT 2000a, 2000b; Gareis and Kordey 2000; Mitchell 2000). The main thrust of this assessment has been to suggest a degree of caution in inter-preting data concerning the rapid expansion of telework. What is particularly evi-dent in the data is that telework, despite confident assessments as to its applicability (Nilles 1998), has not extended into lower skilled, less knowledge intensive occupational areas commensurate with its adoption in professional-managerial domains. This suggests that advocates of the view that the principles underlying traditional management practices may need to give way to principles based on remote management (Nilles 1998; Pratt 2000; Baffour and Betsey 2000) are, at best, premature in their assessment and, at worst, adopting a view that management principles are determined by technological imperatives detached from the political, social and economic context in which management operates.

With these caveats in mind, it is important not to lose sight of the opportuni-ties and challenges that have been created within those more specific domains in which telework has established a presence. Some of the key questions that arise concern the capacity of new forms of organizing: to provide a balanced response to increased competitive pressures on the one hand, and to positive employment relationships on the other; to integrate workers and workplaces across less stable organizational boundaries and distributed work settings; and to balance trust relationships with all employees with management's perceived needs for the control of work in a new technological and regulatory environment. The remaining sections of this chapter turn to an assessment of these issues.

Management strategies, new technologies and the reorganization of work

Organizations typically implement a variety of managerial practices and work processes to ensure that production is achieved in compliance with organizational goals and values, and conforms with established plans, schedules and quality standards. These arrangements facilitate the coordinated action of individuals in the labour process, while embodying mechanisms that control the manner in which tasks are executed and the pace and quantity of output. In practice, the multifaceted patterns of control in organizations are given effect through a process of formal and informal negotiation mediated by the organizational, industrial or political power of employees. In the context of providing a clearer understanding of the challenges and opportunities that telework and distributed work arrangements are alleged to pose for the management of the modern organization, the following brief section provides a disaggregation of the categories of control that are generally conceived to manifest themselves at the contemporary workplace (see Clegg, Boreham and Dow 1986; Thompson 1989).

Management of the modern workplace generally involves an emphasis on various combinations of a number of broad categories of organizational control. These managerial practices will range from direct personal control by managers and supervisors, through to strategies in which control is embedded in the social and organizational structure of the workplace. In the latter circumstances, control may be embedded in the technical infrastructure of the production process. That is, the sequence, nature and pace of work tasks are controlled by technologies built into the production process by systems engineers and managers. This is exemplified by production lines in manufacturing, but also by any system in which production protocols are structured by designs incorporated into computer software.

A second form of control is that embedded in the bureaucratic structures and procedures of the firm. Through these structures, production techniques and standards are maintained through formal rules, processes and policies which must be adhered to by employees responding to the incentives of career pathways and employment status. A related form of control is that embodied in organizational cultures. This is the process through which a system of norms and values congruent with those espoused by the organization is internalized by employees. Widely held organizational perceptions and attitudes concerning appropriate behaviour at work thus obviate the need to maintain extensive bureaucratic rules (see Coombs, Knights and Willmott 1992; Sackmann 1992; Robey and Azevedo 1994).

Finally, control over work practices and skill may have its origins in institutions external to the organization. Professional, scientific and other expert employees may be expected to have been formally inculcated with knowledge, skills and dimensions of ethical practice during lengthy periods of professional training and higher education. Control is thus delegated, in part, to the professional schools and occupational associations. In these instances, authority is vested in the individual on the basis of credentialled skills applied to complex organizational problems.

As noted above, it is common for control mechanisms to complement and supplement one another, and for different mechanisms to be emphasized as strategic responses to particular economic, social and political contingencies in the firm's operating environment. Employees located in particular organizational strata will also be surrounded by divergent forms of control embedded in quite distinct organizational structures that comprise the architecture for different levels of the workplace. It is argued, for example, that key employees are required to acquire and develop a diversity of skills appropriate to constant changes in the production priorities of firms responding to more immediate global market pressures. These trends have been associated with processes of disaggregation and delayering to restructure corporations into a small group of core employees, with other non-core services provided by networks of smaller, more versatile organizational forms including independent profit centres, partnerships, licensing arrangements, franchises and sub-contractors (Reich 1991; Ackroyd and Lawrenson 1996; Heery and Salmon 2000).

Many enterprises have begun to experiment with these new organizational forms as they respond to increased political and economic pressures in their competitive environment. The environment in which modern organizations operate is a very complex terrain whose key orienting features – 'globalization', 'flexibilization' and 'new technology' – have created a powerful symbolic discourse influencing business strategies and structures. However, this discourse is one that often portrays a coherent package of imperatives for organizational change that are somewhat at odds with the variability of workplace practices. The following set of observations concerns the variable dimensions of the political, economic and technological forces at work that constrain and facilitate workplace change.

Globalization

Globalization is portrayed as an irresistible imperative combining with technological innovation to establish a domain of employment organization beyond the reach of traditional regulatory institutions and practices (Giddens 1998). Advances in communications and information technologies during the past two decades are said to have 'sustained the progress of globalization by making possible the rapid transfer of goods, money, ideas and information' (Keating 2000: 15). Globalization is a complex array of processes propelled by political, economic and technological influences and promoted by political and corporate actors. The salient features of the globalization process appear to be:

- the production and distribution of an increasing fraction of value and wealth worldwide through a system of interlinking international networks;
- the international integration of national economies manifested by a major growth in world trade;
- the linkage of the world's financial institutions and the creation of immense financial exchange transactions across international borders not primarily directed at trade;
- an increase in the proportion of international trade in intermediate or semi-finished goods and services, a large proportion of which take the form of inter- and intra-firm transfers;
- the internationalization of research and development and the global sourcing of scientific and technical knowledge;
- the internationalization of the division of labour in which different components of the production process are located in different countries and regions to take advantage of labour conditions;
- the creation of new demands for governance or new forms of administrative and regulatory capacities from both governments and autonomous non-state agencies.

Globalization fuels more intense competition in capital and product markets which places pressure on management continuously to reduce costs. This will often result in employment restructuring and changes in work processes entailing more flexible working arrangements and lower labour costs.

Flexibilization and deregulation

The process of globalization has been facilitated by the broad adoption of flexibility embedded in neo-liberal market principles as foundational elements of economic policy in most of the advanced economies (Castells 2000). The prescriptions of this regime have required a comprehensive retreat from the extensive regulation of social and economic activity that prevailed for half a century until the early 1980s. The new orthodoxy has targeted prevailing institutional and regulatory structures as obstacles and rigidities to be overcome. The common trend has been towards flexible production processes mirrored by flexible labour market practices (see Kalleberg 2001; Wood 1999a). In the interests of imposing criteria determined by the market as the primary signal for economic activity, governments have sought to roll back collective and protective regulations in labour markets and to dismantle the institutions of industrial relations and employment regulation (Boreham 2002; Cousins 1999; Godard and Delaney 2000). The task for government under such a policy regime is to withdraw its involvement in regulating the macro-economy in any comprehensive manner, and to concentrate more narrowly on increasing the ability of corporations in both the private and public sectors to respond 'flexibly' to volatile markets. Governments have tended to support a variety of specific strategies which involve:

- Reducing the 'regulatory burden' on business in matters such as anti-discrimination legislation, termination and redundancy provisions and training.
- Pursuing the decentralization of industrial relations and facilitating the authority of management at the level of the enterprise.
- Shifting regulatory control from a centralized institutional level to the level of enterprise management on specific matters to enable firms:
  - to adjust the number of workers employed more rapidly to changes in demand;
  - to adjust the number of working hours and the time hours are worked to meet changes in demand and in patterns of work activity;
  - to replace employment contracts with commercial contracts to facilitate sub-contacting and other forms of outsourcing.

- Reducing the jurisdiction and coverage of the institutions of industrial relations.
- Promoting legislative intervention to diminish trade union power.

The direction and pace of these changes will be influenced by the form and capacity of worker representation. Emergent employment conditions and labour standards will be contingent on the ability of trade unions to maintain their representative status and to formulate appropriate policies and strategies to resist or accommodate them. Yet trade unions themselves and the institutions that provide them with a voice in national, social, economic and industrial policies are also under challenge by the new political ideologies that give prominence to individualism and the market.

Responding to the 'flexibility imperative' new divisions have become entrenched in the labour market. Cost reduction measures are ubiquitous, resulting in greater workloads, longer hours and irregular employment. The pressures for outsourcing, contracting-out and resulting 'self employment' have removed the expectation of career paths from the lexicon of employment benefits in large organizations (Boreham 2003). Enterprises now place much greater emphasis on flexible or non-standard forms of labour contract as compared with the traditional full-time employment contract with no specified time duration. The main trend has been the spread of temporary or what has been termed precarious employment (see Burgess and Campbell 1998). As a consequence, there is now an established and rapidly growing pattern of casual workers, part-time workers, contract labour, outworkers and teleworkers in most industrial sectors. These new divisions – more horizontal and locational – have been further enabled by new information technologies, and particularly networked software that has the potential to coordinate horizontally divided labour market segments (Greenbaum 1995).

New technologies, management and organizational design

Technology does not determine organizational structure but it facilitates managerial strategic choice in the face of external contingencies or powerful discourses about the pervasive features of such contingencies (see Grint and Woolgar 1997; MacKenzie and Wajcman 1999). It is to these issues that this chapter now turns. By the 1990s, new information and communication technologies enabled computer system specifications to reflect the requirements of management systems that sought to take advantage of new approaches to national economic management. The new emphasis on labour market deregulation and decentralization discussed above served as a catalyst for the creation of a growing peripheral group of flexible workers and work arrangements, with services formerly provided in-house now outsourced or delivered by autonomous networked providers (see Thompson and Warhurst 1998). The consequent decentralization of production envisaged information technology systems designed to support distributed work settings and sophisticated communications functions within and between organizations. Greenbaum (1998) correctly summarizes the design focus for new computer systems as shifting from 'systems that automated flows of products produced under one roof to systems that needed to co-ordinate and control workers and information spread out over time and place' (1998: 131–2).

Communications and information technologies focussed on the coordination of horizontally divided labour are manifest in networked software as well as in the hardware and software links underlying Internet and intranet applications. Both vertical and horizontal coordination in software design are also evident in email, scheduling and mobile communications applications. New communications and information technologies, in fostering collaboration across time and space, permit a combination of decentralized decision-making and centralized monitoring which have formed the basis of the new occupations such as teleworkers and call centre operatives discussed earlier in this chapter (see also Jackson 1999). These information technology systems also reduce the transaction costs associated with communications and contract agreements between distributed work settings, and thus facilitate the outsourcing of services.

The consulting operations of multinational computer firms witnessed a diffusion of these technical systems which, in turn, influenced organizational design in diverse areas of production (Archibugi and Michie 1995; 1997b). Specialized computer systems developed for large financial institutions and telecommunications organizations have been tailored not only for integrating and coordinating distributed labour but also to arrange the data about tasks into monitoring reports and statistical analyses for senior management. As Greenbaum (1998: 137) notes, the implementation of these communications and information technologies has also provided senior management with direct access to pre-processed information without the middle-management intermediary functions of compilation and analysis. Finally, by embedding technology with informational and communication properties that generate analytically based knowledge, system designers have encouraged the development of restructured management decision-making systems and new forms of work organization (Frenkel *et al.* 1999).

'Business process re-engineering' is the rubric under which senior managers were provided with strategies for work redesign integrated with supportive technical systems (Conti and Warner 1994). Management systems thus accelerated the development of communications and information technologies designed to replace existing technical systems. One objective was to facilitate *communication* between geographically dispersed or distributed units of production on the one hand, and between vertically and horizontally structured workplace divisions on the other. To some degree this posed a direct alternative to the routinized operations, centralized control and hierarchical structures that characterized many workplaces in the 1980s. A second goal in the design of new technical systems was concerned with facilitating the re-integration of divided labour processes through more *cooperative* data sharing and decision-making arrangements (Boddy and Gunson 1997). In summary, the design of computer systems was predicated on the need to support non-routine work practices, within an organizational context characterized to a greater extent by cooperative and distributed working arrangements (Cooper and Rousseau 1999).

The interlinked processes of increasing competitive pressures from globalization, the deregulation of employment relations and labour markets under the auspices of new economic policies promoting flexibility and the impact of new technologies have provided the impetus for changes in the organization of work in all of the advanced societies. A great deal of the popular management literature on these new organizational forms has emphasized their democratic potential. The groundswell for radical changes in the workplace promoting new organization structures and work practices has captured the imagination of both management practitioners and the social science academic community. Drawing their initial impetus from the work of Piore and Sabel (1984), the architects of the new 'high performance' workplace credit it with raising productivity, while at the same time promoting various participatory and skill-enhancing schemes for employees. Indeed Zuboff (1988) asserts that productivity enhancement from the new technology may only be realized if organizational processes involve a transfer of decision-making power from managers to workers. The form of management required by the new organization is said to be collegial rather than supervisory, providing encouragement of communication across all dimensions of the enterprise.

Many authors who have endeavoured to specify the criteria that will characterize successful organizational and employment models for firms at the forefront of technological change have identified a number of dimensions which would amount to a radical revision of the structures of organizational control that characterize the modern workplace. In this assessment, the old coordination and control functions of middle management are no longer required, and the occupants of these positions are in the process of disappearing from corporate hierarchies.

Coordination of the labour process is predicted to be based on semi-autonomous teams with hierarchical control giving way to the management of ideas. The future of these organizations will be in the hands of 'knowledge workers' who will be assessed and rewarded according to credentials, competencies and individual performance rather than experience or seniority. These workers will see the profession or occupation rather than the work organization as their community of reference. This group will be accorded high status and given considerable discretion to access company computer networks both nationally and globally. They are expected to have high trust relationships with senior management and considerable autonomy about where and when they work. Most would be afforded the opportunity to work both in an office and at home as teleworkers (Harris 1998). Performance targets would generally be expressed in qualitative terms within overall budgetary constraints rather than specified quantitative criteria. It is argued that, for such employees, work will provide new possibilities for creativity, learning and personal growth.

Other contributors to the literature have focussed on the implications for organizational culture of the diffusion of technological knowledge within the enterprise (Tether 1997; Pavitt 1999). The process that has been identified involves the codification of technical knowledge and the subsequent absorption of such codified knowledge in both the technological infrastructure and the organizational culture (or cultures, where potentially disparate values may be espoused by different, potentially conflicting sub-cultures within the organization: see Robey and Azevedo 1994). This knowledge becomes tacit or taken for granted and leads to commonly perceived realities within the broader organization. This human embodied expertise of managers and employees, together with the organizational interactions between organizational members and technologies as they evolve over time, will determine the firm's capabilities in product and process innovation (Granstrand, Patel and Pavitt 1999: 87–103).

The literature offers little consensus concerning the material dimensions of the work organization of the future, but the following broad features of emergent changes in work organization have been widely described and promulgated:

- New information and communications technologies foster collaboration between colleagues in time and space, and thus the firm's boundaries become blurred, enabling the emergence of the 'virtual organization' (Handy 1995b; Cooper and Rousseau 1999; Jackson and van der Wielen 1998b).

- New technologies and market pressures promote the development within and between large corporations of networks of smaller, more versatile organizational forms, including independent profit centres, partnerships, licensing arrangements and franchises (Reich 1991).

- Disaggregation is combined with delayering and downsizing to restructure corporations into a small group of core employees, with other services outsourced or provided by autonomous networked providers (Ackroyd and Lawrenson 1996; Heery and Salmon 2000).

- Communications technologies facilitate outsourcing and thus alter the relationship between a small core directly employed by the organization and a growing peripheral group of flexible workers and work arrangements (Jackson 1999).

- Changes in the organizational structure of large corporations promote the replacement of centralized hierarchical structures with flatter, more decentralized and flexible networks (Zuboff 1988; Womack *et al.* 1990; Kochan and Osterman 1994).

- Information technologies encourage decentralized decision-making in distributed enterprises, and thus require management to delegate responsibility, share information, and encourage upward and horizontal communication (Despres and Hiltrop 1995; Greenbaum 1995; Whitfield and Poole 1997: 749).

• The utilization of information and communications technologies provides access to new analytically based knowledge, and contributes to worker empowerment as coordination is based on collaboration between professional and technical groups who maintain authority over their own work (Zuboff 1988).

• Organizations place greater responsibility on workers with professional and technical credentials relying on internalized rules and norms of behaviour rather than on external bureaucratic rules and decision criteria (Adami 1999: 147).

• There is a 'technologically driven decline in demand for unskilled labour and the need for educational upgrading to produce future generations of workers capable of functioning in the factory and office of the computer age' (Milkman 1998: 29).

• Organizations witness the demise of long-term, stable career paths as core knowledge workers obtain status and power as part of occupational rather than organizational communities (Greenbaum 1995).

• There is an absorption of knowledge into the organizational culture defined by Hofstede (1991) as the collective programming of the mind which distinguishes the innovative capacity of firms (Pavitt 1999).

These dimensions of the new organization, reflecting the impact of new technology and the new competitive environment, are based on claims in the literature that have achieved very wide circulation. There is no doubt that the availability and efficiency of new technologies combined with the forces of deregulation and decentralization and the accessibility of global networks have had a significant impact on the organization of work, employment relations and the labour market. These are the features that frame the rapidly emerging pattern of distributed work arrangements and telework described earlier in this chapter. But how realistic is the picture of the new workplace of the computer age that has been proclaimed in the literature? The remainder of this chapter is devoted to an examination of how the development of communications and information technologies changes the nature and role of organizations, as manifested in the mechanisms through which organizations control the application of telework and distributed work arrangements to the production of goods and services.

Telework and organizational transformation: the contradictory implications of new technologies at work

This chapter has been devoted to an assessment of the relationship of organizational change to major transformations in the social, economic and technological context in which work takes place. The views that we have canvassed have become quite pervasive in the social science literature. They portray a scenario in which organizations are required to 're-engineer' themselves to react flexibly to a globalized market place which is neither predictable nor subject to many of the conventions upon which production has been based in the past. It is argued that responding to these conditions will require a retreat from many of the aspects of traditional bureaucratic forms of organization, and an embrace of new forms for organizing work activities. Such forms of organization call for the abandonment of hierarchical structures in many areas of the workplace, an increase in the autonomy of workers and work teams, and a much greater reliance on temporary and often distributed networks of expertise and of production itself (Hughes, O'Brien, Randall, Rouncefield and Tolmie 2001). Information and communication technologies provide the technical structure and telework provides the employment framework which underpin these 'virtual organizations' (Castells 1996; Cooper and Rousseau 1999; Hinds and Kiesler 2002; Jackson 1999; Igbaria and Tan 1998; Woolgar 2002a).

Trust and control in the virtual workplace

It is not necessary to accept the entire package of claims about information and communications technologies and the new virtual workplace to recognize that management has been placed under considerable pressure to improve labour productivity and quality. A substantial restructuring of the labour process focussed on innovation and continuous improvement has led many companies to modify aspects of the traditional Fordist production regime (Callaghan and Thompson 2001; Osterman 1994). This has manifested itself in practices such as quality circles, employee involvement and teamworking which require a work process geared towards group decision-making, problem solving and multi-skilling (Warhurst and Thompson 1998: 6). Employees are required to be integrated into the management of production at the workplace level (Milkman 1998: 31).

However, it is essential to emphasize that the changes to work organization of which technologies are capable are largely a factor of the strategic decisions of those who deploy them. In other words, technologies can be advantageous in furthering significantly different approaches to workplace organization. What is most unlikely is that management will adopt a new system of workplace relations simply on the basis of an improved technical capacity to do so. By far the greatest determinants of change or resistance to change are existing ideas and assumptions about the management of the workplace and the organization of work. This is particularly the case for the new 'high performance' workplace with its emphasis on new participative relationships (Whitfield and Poole 1997; Wood 1999b).

As Milkman (1997) indicates, while some firms have successfully implemented reforms to traditional workplace practices, in many others a major discrepancy has emerged between the rhetoric of high performance and participation and the reality of conditions on the office or factory floor. She concludes that, despite the pervasive celebration of re-engineering and 'high road' organization, most management practices use technologies to monitor and evaluate employees through processes such as internal benchmarking or financial targeting, and thus to intensify supervision (see also Ackroyd and Procter 1998; Orlikowski 1991).

The proponents of the high performance workplace, with horizontal and vertical communication and high levels of employee involvement, seriously underestimate the social and political issues involved in establishing a corporate environment that is based on trust between employees and managers (Jones 1997). Indeed, most of the research reported in the 1990s indicates that, for ideological reasons, managers are much more likely to suppress rather than encourage the empowering potential of new technologies, and most companies remain traditionally managed, committed to authoritarian forms of management, anti-union practices, and low trust dynamics in employee relations (Gordon 1996; Milkman 1997; Stanworth 1998; Zuboff 1988).

Technological developments have been used to build on and reinforce many existing employment practices. System design and application is a process of social contention and politics as much as technical determination (Beirne *et al.* 1998). Information-communication technologies and market strengthening government policies have been used to facilitate organizational flexibility by creating new peripheral labour markets for routine and repetitive 'back-office work' usually undertaken by females. Such practices are generally driven by short-term cost reduction strategies, and are undoubtedly successful in reducing labour costs (Tomaskovic-Devey and Risman 1993: 382). But there is little evidence to be found in most workplaces of the emergence of the virtual organization using knowledge based technological applications and 'high road' employment practices to develop new processes and new products.

It appears that new horizontal forms of coordination have complemented rather than replaced more traditional vertical hierarchies (Harris 1998). Increased financial accountability and easily calculated quantitative targets provide an added dimension of complexity to coordination, but the vertical division of labour remains at the core of the organizational command structure (Ackroyd and Procter 1998).

What needs to be recognized is that workplaces exhibit characteristics that place them on a continuum of management practices from those focussed on the fusion of technology and knowledge work driven by concerns with project focussed, collaborative networks uninhibited by time and space, to 'computerized Taylorism' focussed on the routinization and deskilling of clerical and administrative work with no advantages for discretionary commitment or innovation. While the location of enterprises on such a continuum is not an *ad hoc* or random process, the deployment of new technologies in the workplace appears not to be significant in determining forms of work organization, and may characterize firms at either end of the continuum. The major forces at work may be characterized as follows:

- Management ideologies and practices and the level of trust relationships existing at the workplace will strongly influence the use of technologies and their integration with forms of work organization.
- Public policy approaches to labour market flexibility and business regulation will determine the parameters within which enterprises have the capacity to develop new management practices.
- National institutional factors supporting industrial relations systems will determine those aspects of labour market processes that are subject to regulatory oversight and those that may be imposed at the level of the workplace.

- The power of trade unions to influence workplace change through industrial relations institutions or workplace negotiation will impact on the interests and ability of management to develop participative practices or impose authoritarian structures.

In summary, the liberalization of systems of economic governance and developments in information and communications technologies have made the world of work vulnerable to systemic change (Castells 1996, 1997, 1998; Sinden 1996). However, change has not manifested itself in a conceptually coherent workplace of the future. Continuity and intensification of existing structures and processes have been just as evident as change (Taylor and Bain 1999; Wright and Lund 1996). While there has been a piecemeal adoption of workplace reform, there is little evidence from the studies reported in the international literature that the information age has greatly transformed the employment landscape (Conti and Warner 1994; Hughes *et al.* 2001). On the contrary, there has been a remarkable stability in the structure of modern workplaces. As Frenkel *et al.* express it, 'the bureaucratic tendency remains powerful in the face of alternative, gradually-emerging arrangements' (1998: 958).

Management and innovation in the virtual organization

The discussion in the previous section suggests that we need to develop a more sceptical response to the implications of new technologies in the workplace, not only for their promotion of more participative practices, but also for the reorganization of collaborative work across space and time. It is to this latter issue that we now turn.

Virtual organization involves an impermanent network of individuals, capital and technologies that operates as an amalgamated organizational form loosely structured by organizational boundaries and hierarchies (Sparrow and Daniels 1999: 46–7). Virtual organization tends to be based on specific projects that require a diversity of differentiated but interdependent competencies that are both spatially distributed and not bound by contemporaneous timing. It is also important to emphasize the point made earlier in this chapter that, currently, this generally applies only to knowledge intensive, specialist occupational areas involving professional discretion and managerial innovation (Maglen and Shah 1999). In this context, Reich refers to work performed by 'symbolic analysts' whom he defines as:

> ... those involved in the manipulation of symbols – numerical visual, scientific, musical and electronic. They include problem-identifying, problem solving, and strategic broking activities which can be traded globally.
>
> (Reich 1991: 174).

The 'virtual organization' of distributed work settings in these occupations has both its staunch advocates and its critical antagonists (see Harris 1998; May 2002). On the positive side, there are three issues that recur in the management literature. First, the application of computer mediated communications technologies to the work of 'symbolic analysts' is said to involve interactions that are more egalitarian and democratic than face-to-face interactions in structured organizational settings (Tapscott 1998). This is said to have positive consequences for innovation, as status and power differentials are less inhibitive of open communication and critical reflection. This environment is considered to engender a renewed force for empowerment, commitment and collective responsibility (Casey 1995; Zuboff 1988).

The second aspect of virtual organization that has attracted positive evaluations concerns the capacity provided to enterprises to create networks of smaller, more versatile organizational forms that are able to respond flexibly for innovative, knowledge-based projects. This obviates the need to withdraw key personnel from core organizational functions for such projects or to develop in-house skills in new areas of activity. A third issue is the use of virtual teams as a conduit for the transmission of specialized knowledge held by individuals or groups external to the organization. To the extent that intellectual property can be absorbed into the core organization, virtual teams create an inexpensive pathway to organizational innovation that can subsequently be reproduced in similar contingencies. The following section provides an assessment of the veracity of these assessments.

The much touted virtual organization with an emphasis on telework appears to have its major application across only two major categories of work: first, professional knowledge workers operating as consultants on a self-employed basis; and second, core management employees with considerable autonomy over work location and working hours. From the perspective of these workers, status and material rewards reflected in job titles are somewhat likely to be replaced by a series of contracts that refer to individual portfolios of knowledge that are, in turn, sustained by status dependent on their role in virtual networks of project based programmes. In these circumstances, as Dawson, Drinkwater, Gunson, and Atkins point out, knowledge workers are likely to be 'far more active in protecting and developing their own personal career portfolios … in order to sell their expertise within the virtual marketplace' (2000: 33). Questions about organizational commitment and compliance with corporate norms come to prominence in these circumstances.

This raises an important issue concerning the place of trust in organizational management. Trust is intimately associated with particular forms of regulation and control. Dimensions of trust and control may be vested in interpersonal relationships between professionals, or may be embedded in institutional or technological mechanisms. In professional and managerial locales where commitment to organizational values (rather than just compliance with enterprise goals set elsewhere) has assumed importance, then much greater emphasis will be placed on what Fox (1974) referred to as 'high trust' organizational culture. That is, there may be some potential for managerial control to eschew a hierarchical structure of reporting and command relationships, and to rely instead on professional self-regulatory protocols and contract relationships (see MacKenzie 2002).

Trust and the decision-making autonomy that goes with it are elements which are always likely to be in tension with managerial regulation of the work process (see Reed 2001 for an overview of these arguments). While high trust arrangements have provided the context of the labour process for professional employees for some time, the virtual organization further removes control over skill and knowledge from within the confines of traditional organizational boundaries and processes of management. In these circumstances, tensions are likely to come to the fore, as new technologies provide an alternative means for management to more directly monitor the performance outcomes of employees in distributed work settings. In light of these observations, it would be reasonable to conclude that the increased capacity of remote electronic surveillance and the increased pressure on individual achievement and self-interest is unlikely to support the notion of a high trust, empowered workforce.

While the capacity to monitor performance outcomes has been enhanced by new technologies, the infusion of management goals and organizational norms into the decision-making process of virtual teams is likely to become a more difficult issue. It has been partly addressed by the provision of auditable data on the basis of which it is hoped that individuals in such teams might be inculcated with appropriate group norms (see Mason, Button, Lankshear and Coates 2002). However, it is not evident how such mechanisms replace the social processes of organizational socialization. A similar issue arises in the tendency of individuated, computer mediated communications to devalue authority based on experience or access to wider organizational knowledge networks. Effectively, organizational histories and accumulated knowledge are lost, to be replaced by the limited capacity of dispersed networks to reconstruct the strategic contingencies which formed the background to past decisions and practices. In general, the evidence cited in the literature suggests that behaviour in the virtual organization is situated and constrained by the social and technical context in which decisions are made, and especially the relationship between these factors (see e.g. Woolgar 2002b; Watt, Lea and Spears 2002: 76). As yet, the ability to manipulate or manage these interactions remains at best underdeveloped.

A second area of critical concern involves the limits placed on social structural norms of behaviour in 'virtual' forms of communication. That is, the positive effects of social interaction such as social regulation and accountability are likely to be significantly diminished in circumstances of computer mediated communication (Watt *et al.* 2002). For example, cultural and linguistic barriers to communication may be more evident to co-located teams, and appropriate compensatory norms developed in ways that are likely to escape the attention of distributed work groups. Such matters can have an important effect on communication efficiency, participative behaviour and group decision-making in dispersed teams (Watt *et al.* 2002: 67). Assumptions based on long established organizational processes and protocols developed on the basis of co-location have been co-opted while more flexible practices of decision-making based on more egalitarian and democratic virtual structures have been assumed to develop vicariously through the supposed liberating effects of new technologies. Indeed, virtual organizations are often sites for micro-political contests for power between different organizational status groups who have fewer media for establishing their status and authority than in traditional organizations. This can lead to significant additions to communications costs that are much less likely to prevail in co-located groups.

Virtual organization almost always involves cooperative work across distributed work settings, where communication and information sharing is provided by advanced technological systems. It is the *combination* of these three elements that poses unique problems for the regulation of virtual teams. Similarly, problems for organizational governance emerge, as the experience of managing virtual teams is lost in a discontinuous process of team development across different projects. The management of distributed work and virtual teams has been the subject of sanguine assertion in the virtual organizations literature. However, much less has been said about protocols for cooperation or, as Hughes, Rouncefield and Tolmie (2002: 263) have argued, the notion of virtual *teamwork* has been paid altogether less attention.

Cooperative work, as Lyytinen and Ngwenyama (1992) put it, 'relies heavily on the reciprocity of practices among networks of agents, and routinization (the development of a vast reservoir of taken-for-granted activities) which enable frictionless encounters, effective and efficient social interaction' (1992: 25). That is, cooperation requires a stock of tacitly agreed, shared interpretive rules that have been built up over time. The question remains how these tacit and informal stocks of knowledge for interpreting and coordinating the actions of co-workers can be established outside of conditions of co-presence.

Virtual organization may place substantial impediments in the way of one of the primary vehicles for organizational innovation. There is a considerable body of research that places organizational knowledge at the core of the firm's ability to innovate. As Thompson *et al.* point out, this is not a new phenomenon associated with knowledge work. Workers have always relied on tacit skills grounded in informal and practical knowledge of the work they do (2001: 929). Workers' tacit knowledge manifests itself as informal working practices, techniques and 'know how' transmitted through and embedded in social networks at the workplace (Lam 2000; Ambrosini and Bowman 2001). These networks have both individual and organizational properties (Blackler 1995), and are shaped by 'the social structure of coordination and the behavioural routines and work roles of organizational members' (Lam 2000: 489).

In contrast with what might be termed technical knowledge, which may be codified, formulated and abstracted for use by any organization that purchases it, tacit knowledge can only be transferred in the context of close interaction and the development of shared understanding and trust. There is no clear mechanism through which the tacit knowledge and knowledge transfer within virtual teams can be drawn into a culture of innovation within the core organization (Sparrow and Daniels 1999: 47). Innovation is most likely where work organizations constitute an enduring milieu in which technical and tacit forms of knowledge interact and become embedded in decision-making processes (Howells 1996).

Innovative organizations are dominated by networks of social relations (Lam 1997). However this social embeddedness (Granovetter 1985) is unlikely to be nurtured in the communicative practices of non-co-located or virtual teams.

The issues raised in this section are broadly concerned with the realities of establishing working practices relevant to distributed work settings reliant on information and communications technologies. This is particularly so for the 'virtual teams' that have captured the attention of management and organization theorists. The dilemma centres on the absence of the often taken-for-granted organizational resources that have been developed on the assumption of co-presence. There has clearly been a lack of attention paid to the organizational processes that provide the context of distributed work. Where formal, theoretical accounts have been proposed, they have not generally been guided by empirical observations of the actual work practices of virtual teams, such as those provided by Hughes *et al.* (2001) and Hinds and Kiesler (2002). There is presently a highly developed set of procedural rules and organizational practices for maintaining the efficacy of co-located teams. Most of these working practices have been borrowed in a modified way by virtual teams in distributed work settings. However, practices that depend to a great extent on co-location, such as tacit understandings about how work is embedded in clearly specified corporate goals, shared organizational vision and relevant normative orientations, pose a substantial challenge to the 'organization' of distributed work (see Cramton 2002).

Knowledge work and its organization: a summary

During the past three decades, complex organizations have been faced with accelerating competitive pressures in a turbulent global economic environment. National regulatory regimes have not been immune from these forces, and have tended to facilitate an array of flexible labour market and employment practices that have acted as a catalyst for workplace change. These changes have coincided with the advent of new and sophisticated information and communications technologies that have allowed corporate management to take advantage of their new operating environment to make profound changes to the architecture of work organization. The key dimensions of the new workplace in the knowledge-based economy are said to involve the replacement of centralized hierarchical structures with flatter, more decentralized and flexible networks, where services are provided to the core organization by autonomous networked providers with distributed work arrangements. These dimensions of the new organization are based on claims in the management literature that have achieved very wide circulation.

The analysis presented in this chapter suggests a much more cautionary approach needs to be adopted toward some of the more sanguine approaches to the benefits of telework, distributed work arrangements and virtual organization. First, it should be emphasized that while much has been written about the future development of virtual organization, concrete examples of its widespread adoption or accomplishments are somewhat less evident. What *is* particularly evident in the data is that telework, despite confident assessments as to its applicability, has not extended into lower skilled, less knowledge intensive occupational areas commensurate with its adoption in professional-technical and managerial domains. Even in these areas, the take up of telework has proven to be much more piecemeal than many analysts propose.

The architecture of the new workplace has also proved to be resistant to fundamental organizational change. Assumptions based on long established organizational processes and protocols developed on the basis of co-location have been co-opted, while more flexible practices of decision-making based on more egalitarian and democratic virtual structures have simply been assumed to develop vicariously through the supposed liberating effects of new technologies. This account significantly underestimates the social aspects of communicative behaviour. What seems clear is that workers' tacit knowledge of the processes of innovation manifests itself as informal working practices, techniques and 'know how' transmitted through and embedded in social networks at the workplace. Innovative organizations are dominated by networks of social relations. However this social embeddedness is unlikely to be nurtured in the communicative practices of non-co-located or virtual teams.

Finally, a great deal of the popular management literature on these new organizational forms has emphasized their democratic potential. However, studies of the application of new technology indicate that managers and system developers tend to implement information technology that embodies existing institutionalized practices, forms of control and authority relationships. While new technologies have the potential to facilitate democratic or participatory employment practices, those who assume that these arrangements are a necessary component of the new workplace seriously underestimate the social and political issues involved in establishing a corporate environment that is based on trust between employees and managers. Trust and the decision-making autonomy that goes with it are elements which are always likely to be in tension with managerial regulation of the work process. There is simply no reason to believe that management principles are likely to be determined by technological imperatives detached from the political, social and economic context in which management operates. Workplace change has not manifested itself in a conceptually coherent workplace of the future. Continuity and intensification of existing structures and processes have been just as evident as change.

7 New technologies and new patterns of institutional relationships in the global economy

Over the last several decades there has been a liberalization of global markets for the exchange of goods, services and labour, allowing for higher levels of global economic interaction. During the 'Golden Age' of post-war growth in the 1950s and 1960s, capitalism was conceptualized within a national framework, and governments were regarded as having the capacity to manage national economic outcomes to achieve particular social and economic goals, including full employment and social protection. Social scientists are now grappling to understand the implications of economic globalization for national political–institutional frameworks and varieties of capitalism (Axtmann 2004; Howell 2003; Putzell 2005; Radice 2000).

The technological and political liberalization of global capital markets and the growth of cross-border activities by multinational corporations challenge autonomous state strategies and distinctive national varieties of capitalism (Cerny 1996; Frieden 1991; Goodman and Pauly 1993; Moses 1994; Radice 1998; Strange 1997; Webb 1991). However, there is contention regarding the implications of globalization for national political autonomy in areas such as fiscal policy, monetary policy, labour market policy and social policy, with some researchers highlighting continuing possibilities for national economic management, the critical role of politics in the 'global corporate economy' and continuing variety in models of capitalism (Axtmann 2004: 274; Boyer and Drache 1996; Garrett and Lange 1991; Garrett 1998; Lowi 2001; Wade 1996; Weiss 1998; Whitley 1998).

A further dimension of economic change is associated with the acceleration of technological advance and the changing structure of economic activity towards industries and services characterized by rapid technological transformation. Information and communication technologies (ICTs) have played a critical role in this process of economic change, partly because they impact on productivity in a range of manufacturing and service industries. In addition, the ICT sector itself now constitutes an increasing component of total economic activity amongst the OECD countries, with its share of value added increasing from around 8 to 9.6 percent between 1995 and 2001. The ICT sector therefore accounts for almost 10 percent of business sector value added in the OECD countries, and an increasing component of international trade (OECD 2005a: 122–4). In addition, there has been a shift in the structure of value added and trade amongst OECD countries involving a decline in the share of low and medium-low technology industries, and an increase in the share of high technology industries. Medium-high and high technology industries now account for over two thirds of total OECD manufacturing exports, and their share of domestic value added is now 7.5 percent amongst the OECD countries. High technology sectors, such as pharmaceuticals, medical and optical instruments and communications equipment, are some of the fastest growing sectors in international trade (OECD 2005a: 172–9 and 166, 207). Finally, there has been a growth in knowledge-intensive services activities, such that knowledge-based services, which include telecommunications services, computer services, Research and Development (R&D), legal, accounting and management consultancy, architectural and engineering services, now account for around 20 percent of business value added in the OECD countries (OECD 2005a: 166, 204). Further indicators of the importance of knowledge-intensive activities include the acceleration of patenting activity, especially in molecular biology and semiconductors, and the growth of the science and engineering workforce (Powell and Snellman 2004).

This chapter explores the interplay between technology change and globalization, and examines debates concerning the implications of these trends for work and employment. The capacity of governments to mediate the influence of technological change and globalization on national outcomes is a central concern of the chapter. The first section outlines the key debates concerning the globalization of economic activity and its relationship to technological change, and interrogates the concept of 'techno-globalism', which emphasizes the role of technology in driving the globalization of economic activity. The second section canvasses new patterns of interaction in the international economy in the areas of international finance, trade, the activities of multinational corporations and the development and diffusion of technology. The third section of the chapter examines the implications of the globalized knowledge economy, with its emphasis on technology and global exchange, for work and employment, and the possibility for governments to influence the outcomes of the globalized knowledge economy within a national context. The chapter concludes with the argument that in the context of the globalized knowledge economy, governments remain important in mediating the effect of globalization and technological transformation on work and employment.

Contemporary changes and current issues

Contemporary developments are often portrayed within the discourse of techno-globalism or hyperglobalization (Hay 2004) that emphasizes the close interplay between global economic developments and technological transformation. The techno-globalist perspective incorporates three core propositions. First, the globalization of economic activity has been driven by technological advances and is beyond the control of national governments. Second, the current level of global economic exchange is massive and unprecedented. Third, national governments have a reduced power to influence the outcomes of globalization, including the implications for work and employment (Radice 1998; Strange 1997).

Techno-globalists suggest that it is advances in information, communications and media technologies that have facilitated new forms of economic interaction in the global economy (Dicken 1992: 103–10; McMahon 2001). Massive techno-logical advances in the last twenty years have facilitated information transfer and improved communications (OECD 1999a). As Baily (2000) explains:

> The evolution in computing technology has certainly been dramatic. In 1944, the Mark I computer could carry out 3 instructions per second compared to more than 400 million instructions per second today. In 1970 a state of the art computer cost about [US] $4.7 million, an amount equal to 15 times the life-time wages of the average American worker. Now, a personal computer with more than 10 times as much computing power costs only $1,000, or less than 2 weeks of the average worker's pay. Microprocessors, the fundamental build-ing block of the new technology, have made products better, cheaper, and more efficient. A single memory chip now holds 250,000 times as much data as one from the early 1970s. This is like cramming 1600 books onto one page. The cost of storing one megabit of information – the equivalent of a 320-page book – fell $5,275 in less than 25 years from $5,275 in 1975 to $0.17 in 1999.
>
> (Baily 2000: 99)

These technological advances have fed into the process of globalization in all its dimensions, by removing time and spatial limitations on market activity. As large quantities of information can be stored and transmitted instantaneously, market participants can engage in transactions without the limitations associated with distance or time zone. International economic interaction is perceived to be on a scale that is unprecedented in the history of capitalist society. The new global economic system places constraints on welfare policy, taxation policy and labour market policy, as global economic players, such as financial markets and multi-national corporations (MNCs), view government policy intervention suspiciously. As a consequence, 'room for independent or deviant policy decisions is heavily curtailed' (Went 2004: 339). Hay identifies the major source of this view as the 'airport lounge/business school globalization literature' (2004: 233). According to this perspective, technological advances have empowered MNCs and financial markets through enhanced mobility and fluidity, and this is thought to create an inevitable and uncontrollable bias in the international system towards liberal markets.

In contrast, sceptics of techno-globalism argue that technology alone cannot explain the growth of the global economy. Critics of techno-globalism point to the influence of political choices which have resulted in the adoption of neo-liberal economic policies, particularly in the area of trade, foreign investment and currency exchange, and which have encouraged international economic expansion. The rapid technological change of the last three decades has been accompanied by a dominant political ideology in the international arena which has favoured reduced political interference in market transactions. The prevailing market ideology is based on a belief that market mechanisms, including the price mechanism, allocate scarce resources most efficiently and therefore maximize wealth. This ideology favours impersonal or arm's length interactions between isolated individuals working in competition with each other and discourages social and political allocation of resources. The globalization of economic activity is closely linked to the re-emergence of market ideology, because governments influenced by neo-liberal economic philosophy have sought to reduce political obstacles to international market activity, such as barriers to trade or restrictions on currency exchange (Barrow 2005; Helleiner 1995; Hutton 1995).

Sceptics also cast doubt on the techno-globalism thesis by questioning whether globalization is as massive or as unprecedented as the techno-globalists would suggest. It is possible to identify a high level of international interaction at the turn of the last century, or even trends towards cross-cultural interconnectedness between civilizations spanning back several centuries, if an exclusive focus on the West and economic aspects of globalization is abandoned (Hirst and Thompson 1999; Holton 1998: 24–33). Those who doubt the globalization thesis argue that, while in some areas of international exchange, such as trade and financial interaction, there has been significant growth, in other areas, such as the activities of MNCs and the processes of technological development and diffusion, internationalization is less extensive than the techno-globalism perspective would suggest.

A further point of contention between techno-globalists and their sceptics concerns the capacity of government to intervene in the process of technological development and international economic exchange, in order to pursue social objectives or secure outcomes which benefit workers within particular national or regional contexts (Braithwaite and Drahos 2000). Opponents of the view that government has become impotent in the face of global economic pressures highlight continuing differences in national policies and institutions that appear to influence both the capacity of a nation to capture the benefits of technology and globalization, and the way in which those benefits are shared between different social groups and regions.

This chapter develops three core arguments in response to these contemporary issues and debates. First, a review of the literature suggests that it is both technological change and neo-liberal economic policies that have facilitated an expansion of international economic interaction. It is not technology alone, but also political developments that lie behind the globalization of economic activity. Second, the latest research indicates that the globalization of economic activity is patchy, with some areas of activity remaining regional and national in character. Finally, the implications of globalization and technological progress within different national contexts appear to depend on nationally specific mechanisms, both for capturing the advantages of knowledge industries and global exchange, and for distributing these advantages within society. National governments continue to play a role in influencing the process and outcome of technological change and globalization.

New patterns of global interaction

The concept of globalization encompasses a broad range of economic developments including the proliferation of international financial transactions from the 1970s, the postwar growth in international trade, increases in the size, number and strategic importance of MNCs and the globalization of technology. While there is no doubt that there has been massive change in the global economy in the post-World War II period, and particularly in the period from the early 1970s, much debate remains both about its long term historical significance and about the forces that have driven global transformation. As indicated in the introduction to the chapter, techno-globalists argue that we are currently experiencing a fundamentally different era of global economic interaction which has no forerunner in the history of human society. This epochal transformation, according to the techno-globalists, is a consequence of a range of technological developments, particularly revolutions in telecommunications and information technologies, which have eliminated spatial and time barriers to international exchange and driven the process of globalization. The following discussion examines these propositions by analysing both the causes and extent of the globalization of finance, trade, production and technology.

Finance and financialization

A prominent feature of the contemporary global economy is the massive quantity of international financial exchange, which Radice has called 'international monetary anarchy' (1984: 127) and Strange has called 'casino capitalism' (Strange 1998). Increases in cross-border capital flows, foreign exchange trading and the globalization of banking and financial facilities are elements of a new global order characterized by the technologically facilitated interdependence of the world's financial markets. Improvements in information and communications technology have contributed to the growth in international financial transactions by reducing the cost and improving the speed of information transfer necessary for global financial decisions and transactions.

Money flows across boundaries instantaneously, seemingly in search of the most profitable location for investment. This development has, in part, resulted from advances in technology in the fields of telecommunications and computing. A plethora of information about markets is transmitted instantly via advanced telecommunication facilities, allowing investors to respond to *all* market developments instantly – thus multiplying the occasions on which capital reacts to new information and potentially relocates. The capacity to move investments from one location to another, or from one currency to another, is also attributed to advances in computer and telecommunication technologies, particularly satellite and fibre optics which are responsible for the linkage of computer technologies with information technologies in major economies (Dicken 1992: 103–10; McMahon 2001).

Exchange and Euromarkets are critical components of this new global financial order. The growth of Euromarkets has its origin in the 1960s when a Eurodollar market emerged, wherein US dollars were deposited in banks outside the United States, particularly in London. While cold war politics played a role in their growth, as Russian banks sought to deposit US dollars outside US territory, the market also developed out of the desire of US banks to avoid domestic banking regulations. Similar markets emerged in other currencies. Technology facilitated the massive expansion of the markets during the 1980s. A related development was the advent of the Eurobond – a bond issued in a currency other than the currency of the market in which it was sold. Eurobond markets also arose out of the desire of corporations to escape domestic regulations (Coleman and Porter 1994: 194).

Dealings in foreign currency increased dramatically from the 1980s. Between 1998 and 2001 there was a decline in traditional foreign exchange trading from 1,490 billion to 1,200 billion US dollars per day. Despite the fall from 1998 to 2001, was significant long term growth in foreign exchange markets, such that foreign exchange markets in 2001 were more than double their size in 1989 (Bank for International Settlements 2002). The International Monetary Fund (IMF) reported the value of world exports of goods and services for the whole of the year 2001 as amounting to 7,487 billion US dollars (on average, 20.5 billion per day) (IMF 2002). This would indicate that foreign exchange trading is around 60 times the value of world trade (or that world trade accounts for the value of about six days of foreign currency trading). These measures indicate that a large proportion of activity in foreign currency markets is speculative and unassociated with international trade in goods and services.

These data are consistent with estimations that over 90 percent of currency transactions are now unrelated to trade or productive investment (Wachtel 1995). The term 'casino capitalism' has been used to describe speculative international financial activity (Henwood 1997). Much of this activity is associated with the derivatives markets that include swaps, options, futures and hedge markets. These various financial instruments provide a means for financial players to speculate on future interest rates, currency values and commodity prices. Volatility in international financial markets has created the imperative for exporters to hedge against the risk associated with international transactions, the value of which often depends on future prices and currency values (Bryan and Rafferty 1999: 225–7).

Although financial market activity has increased dramatically as a result of communications and information technologies that allow financial transactions to take place rapidly without spatial limitations, government policy has also played a critical role in facilitating international economic exchange. In order to understand the role of government in the internationalization of finance, it is necessary to understand the financial regime which prevailed in the post-World War II period and which collapsed in the early 1970s. The internationalization of financial markets occurred subsequent to the demise of the international currency regime established at the Bretton Woods conference in 1944. The Bretton Woods conference was concerned with post-war reconstruction and the development of a stable regime for the settlement of international transactions. The US dollar was the central currency in the international system and the dollar had a fixed value in relation to gold. All other currencies had values fixed in relation to the dollar and were therefore indirectly tied to gold and to each other. This regime was designed to stabilize the value of currencies, not just to facilitate international transactions, but also to control cross-national imbalances. National governments sought to maintain stability in financial markets by controlling the flow of capital into and out of their borders through exchange controls (Block 1977).

This system broke down in the early 1970s when the US government declared that the US dollar was no longer convertible into gold. Over the following two decades, national governments responded by floating their currencies and abandoning exchange controls. These regulatory changes, combined with communications and information technologies, facilitated the massive expansion of international capital flows (Helleiner 1995). Government policy decisions which resulted in currency deregulation and the lifting of financial controls are therefore important in explaining developments in international markets.

The tendency to give undue primacy to technology as the driving force in the globalization of financial markets is identified by Hirst and Thompson, who argue that there is only a difference in degree between information transmitted by sailing ship and electricity:

> Financial and other major markets were closely integrated once the system of international submarine telegraph cables was in place and in a way not fundamentally different from the satellite-linked and computer controlled markets of today.
>
> (Hirst and Thompson 1992: 366)

As Karl Polanyi noted, from 1879 'short term money moved at an hour's notice from any point of the globe to another' (1944: 205). The removal of policy and institutional constraints on international economic interaction has reinforced the effect of technological developments, and has therefore contributed to the internationalization of economic activity (Grassman 1980: 124). The growth of international markets cannot be seen as a result of technological developments alone, but as the combined result of technology and political choice.

Trade

While it is in relation to financial markets that the most dramatic changes linked to technological advances and globalization can be observed, there has also been an acceleration of international trade in the preceding several decades. The key trends in international trade in the second half of the twentieth century are referred to by techno-globalists as evidence of a changing international economic order. First, the growth of world trade in the post-World War II period constitutes an important component of economic globalization. International trade has increased faster than industrial production, indicating that firms sell products in different markets to those in which production takes place. Since 1950, the volume of world merchandise trade has increased faster than world output. Between 1950 and the turn of the century, the volume of merchandise trade multiplied by 15.8 and world

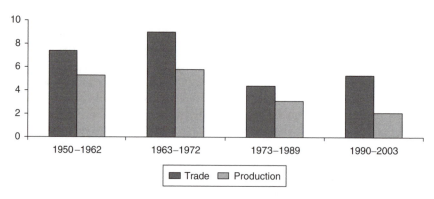

Figure 7.1 World merchandise trade and output, 1950–2003. Average annual percentage
change in volume terms.

Source: Adapted from World Trade Organization (2004) International Trade Statistics, Geneva:
World Trade Organization, Table II.1, page 29.

output by 6.7 (World Trade Organization (WTO) 2000: II.1; 27). The gap
between output and trade was quite dramatic in the final decade of the twentieth
century, during which time the average growth rate in world trade was more than
double that in output (see Figure 7.1).

At an individual country level, the continuing but gradual growth of international trade amongst the advanced economies since the mid 1980s is revealed in
Table 7.1. These data show an increase in the level of imports and exports as a
percentage of GDP in most advanced economies throughout the 1990s, with the
exception of Japan. The data also reveal continuing differences in the level of
exposure to international markets between countries such as the Netherlands,
which has high exposure, and Japan, which has a relatively closed economy.

The second critical trend in international trade concerns the increasing importance of technology intensive products in international markets. The share of high
technology industries in the trade of OECD countries was 25 percent in 2003
(OECD 2005a: 207). As explained above, this data indicates the increasing importance
of high technology industries such as electronics, pharmaceuticals and telecommunications equipment in international trade.

Third, an important element of the globalization of international trade is the
increasing orientation towards intra-industry trade, in which the imports and
exports of a nation occur in the same category. International trade does not necessarily occur because nations specialize in the production and export of goods in
industry sectors different from those in which they import goods. There is a growing tendency for the imports and exports of a nation to fall within the same industry sector. This involves trade in differentiated finished products – similar goods
of different qualities. Table 7.2 shows that manufacturing intra-industry trade
constitutes two thirds or more of total manufacturing trade for most OECD countries, although it is much lower for countries such as Australia and Japan.

Table 7.1 Ratio of trade to GDP, 1985–2000: average of imports and exports as a percentage of total nominal GDP

	Goods				Services				Total			
	1985	1990	1995	2000	1985	1990	1995	2000	1985	1990	1995	2000
Australia	14.1	12.8	15.3	17.5	3.6	3.9	4.6	4.8	17.7	16.7	19.9	22.3
Canada	23.6	21.5	30.5	37.2	3.3	4.1	5.0	5.6	26.9	25.6	35.5	42.8
France	18.7	17.7	17.6	22.8	5.8	5.0	4.6	5.5	24.5	22.7	22.2	28.3
Germany	26.4	24.3	20.0	27.9	5.1	4.7	4.3	5.9	31.5	29.0	24.3	33.8
Italy	18.6	15.5	19.6	21.9	4.2	4.1	5.0	5.2	22.8	19.6	24.6	27.1
Japan	10.8	8.1	6.9	8.4	1.9	2.1	1.8	2.0	12.7	10.2	8.7	10.4
Netherlands	48.7	41.9	44.3	53.3	10.8	10.0	11.2	14.5	59.5	51.9	55.5	67.8
Sweden	27.9	23.1	30.2	34.8	6.2	6.4	6.9	9.7	34.1	29.5	37.1	44.5
United Kingdom	22.6	20.0	22.2	21.5	5.8	5.3	6.4	7.5	28.4	25.3	28.6	29.0
United States	6.6	7.6	8.9	10.1	1.7	2.3	2.4	2.6	8.3	9.9	11.3	12.7

Source: OECD (2002a): ADB database, May 2001.

Table 7.2 Manufacturing intra-industry trade as a percentage of total manufacturing trade

	1988–1991	*1992–1995*	*1996–2000*	*Change*
Australia	28.6	29.8	29.8	1.2
Canada	73.5	74.7	76.2	2.7
France	75.9	77.6	77.5	1.6
Germany	67.1	72.0	72.0	5.0
Italy	61.6	64.0	64.7	3.1
Japan	37.6	40.8	47.6	10.0
Netherlands	69.2	70.4	68.9	−0.3
Sweden	64.2	64.6	66.6	2.4
United Kingdom	70.1	73.1	73.7	3.6
United States	63.5	65.3	68.5	5.0

Source: OECD (2002a), page 161.

As with other dimensions of globalization, there is contention over the relative importance of policy decisions and technological advances as explanations for the changes in the level and structure of international trade as depicted in these trends. Governments have played a role in encouraging growth in international trade. At an international level, free trade policies have been pursued with vigour in a range of international forums, most notably through the WTO, previously the General Agreement on Tariffs and Trade (GATT). These institutions have their origin in the 1944 meeting in New Hampshire (Connecticut), in which representatives of wealthy nations met at the Bretton Woods conference with the explicit intention of establishing international rules for the reduction of barriers to trade. The principal concern of nations was to avoid the 'beggar thy neighbour' protectionist policies that had resulted in a dramatic slump in world trade in the period between World War I and World War II. Eventually this international system of free trade evolved into a legalistic body of rules overseen by an international organization (the WTO), with dispute settlement provisions allowing for enforcement through sanctioned retaliation. Various trading regions have also formed the basis for public policy initiatives in support of free trade – the European Union (EU), the North American Free Trade Agreement (NAFTA) and the Asia Pacific Economic Co-operation forum (APEC). Although these international arrangements have had varying degress of success, combined they represent a dominant paradigm in the international arena in favour of free international exchange.

Public policy has therefore facilitiated the growth of international trade as part of an international paradigm in support of free trade. At the same time, technological advances have played a role in facilitating increased international trade and changes in the structure of export and import industries by reducing the cost of international transportation and communication and increasing the speed of global communication. As Yarbrough and Yarbrough (1997: 92) explain:

These improvements facilitate not just increased *quantitites* of trade, but different *kinds* of trade with different partners. Assembling a Ford Escort from components produced in 15 different countries – a process requiring a substantial level of coordination – becomes not just technically feasible, but profitable. American Airlines can perform the data-entry operations to process its tickets and boarding passes in Barbados. Israel and Colombia can export fresh cut flowers to the United States. Programmers in Bangalore, India, can design computer software and transmit it back to Texas Instruments via satellite.

(Yarbrough and Yarbrough 1997: 92)

Thus while there was the technological capacity in the mid nineteenth century to render international trade *possible* (Hirst and Thompson 1999: 9), improvements in transportation and communications technologies have improved the profitability of international trade, and facilitiated a different kind of trade, in which production is divided geographically and coordinated internationally by multinational corporations (MNCs) (Streeten 1996). As such, corporations are playing a greater role in the global economy as they coordinate and manage global workforces and the international exchange of goods.

Production and multinational corporations

The globalization of production is an important component of the techno-globalism thesis. MNCs are portrayed as mobile and flexible, locating around the globe in response to market criteria in search of the highest profits. Techno-globalists argue that large MNCs have become extremely powerful in relation to national governments, because they are dissociated from national economies and are willing to relocate in protest against unsatisfactory national policy developments in the area of welfare provision, taxation and labour market regulation. These firms are thought to have become 'nationality-less' – beyond the sphere of influence of national governments. They are sometimes referred to as 'transnational corporations' to emphasize their disconnectedness from individual nations (Ohmae 1990). These global corporations are thought to be taking advantage of the opportunities created through technological advances that have enhanced the profitability of global production and trade (Hedley 2002).

The following discussion draws out the key issues associated with the role of MNCs in the international economy. The first concerns the global division of labour. In its early stages, much of the discussion of MNCs was linked to conjecture about the internationalization of production and theories of the new international division of labour (NIDL). Most often attributed to the work of Folker Fröbel, Jürgen Heinrichs and Otto Kreye, the NIDL thesis asserted that production was being relocated from the industrialized countries to the developing countries as the only option available to capital in the competitive pursuit of higher profits.

The development of the world economy has increasingly created conditions (forcing the development of the new international division of labour) in which the survival of more and more companies can only be assured through the relocation of production to new industrial sites, where labour-power is cheap to buy, abundant and well-disciplined; in short, through the transnational reorganization of production.

(Fröbel, Heinrichs and Kreye 1980: 15)

Table 7.3 Foreign direct investment inflows, selected years, percentage of world total

	1970	1975	1980	1985	1990	1995	2000	2001
Developed countries	75.3	63.8	84.7	74.1	81.2	61.5	82.3	68.4
Developing countries	24.7	36.2	15.3	25.8	18.5	34.0	15.9	27.9

Source: United Nations Conference on Trade and Development (UNCTAD) (2002).

The intra-firm division of labour associated with Fordism was expected to expand towards a global division of labour. Fordism allowed for a global division of labour because it involved an intra-firm division of labour based on hierarchy, in which there were high skilled knowledge intensive activities, medium skilled production operations and low skilled standardized production activities. These characteristics of the Fordist mode of production were expected to lead to a geographical re-division of activity according to skill levels, with low-wage developing countries becoming more attractive for unskilled activities (Schoenberger 1988a: 107). Measures of foreign direct investment (FDI) provide some indication of the extent to which corporations are investing in developing countries, because FDI statistics measure investment associated with the attainment of lasting management interests. Recent empirical evidence suggests that, over the last 30 years, there has been no consistent pattern of increase in foreign investment flows to developing countries (Table 7.3). Most foreign investment activity takes place between wealthy countries. As a consequence, early predictions regarding the activities of MNCs seem to have overstated the likelihood of MNCs relocating to developing economies in the pursuit of lower wages and taxes or less organized labour.

The second area in which MNCs are regarded as playing a critical role is international trade. The increase in intra-firm trade – trade between subsidiaries of MNCs – is regarded as a dimension of the globalization of production. Intra-firm trade is often said to be dependent on the executive decisions of MNCs and the global production strategies of these corporations, further emphasizing the reduced influence of government on the economy. There are problems documenting the level of intra-firm trade, as standard measures of levels of trade do not reveal intra-firm trade components. However, available data show that intra-firm trade constitutes around one third of the exports of goods from the United States and Japan, around one third of US importation of goods and one quarter of Japanese goods imports (OECD 2002a: 164). When intra-firm trade occurs between wealthy countries, if is often associated with marketing and distribution, as affiliates in wealthy countries are not often involved in the further manufacture of products that they import. In contrast, intra-firm trade between wealthy and developing countries is more likely to be associated with the further manufacture of goods. The growth of intra-firm trade indicates that the strategic decisions of MNCs are of increasing importance in the international economy. It would seem that international trade may depend to a significant extent on the strategic decisions of corporations.

The third dimension of the analysis of the role of MNCs relates to their significance in employment and production within national borders. Available data on foreign control of output in the manufacturing sector is reported in Figure 7.2.

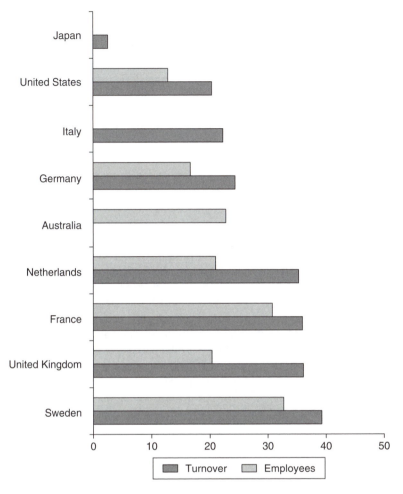

Figure 7.2 Share of affiliates under foreign control in manufacturing employment and turnover, 2002 or nearest year.

Source: Adapted from OECD (2005a), Table E.6, page 202.

These data indicate that the level of foreign control of domestic employment and production within the manufacturing sector differs significant across the wealthy countries. The data show that in Canada foreign affiliates account for around half of production in the manufacturing sector, while in Japan the figure is less than 2 percent. This would indicate that in countries such as Canada, foreign corporations have a significant influence over domestic employment and production in the manufacturing sector.

The fourth point of contention concerning the role of MNCs is the degree of influence of the nation of origin on the activities of MNCs. The significance of this issue relates to the extent of influence of national policies and institutions on the behaviour of global corporations. Hirst and Thompson (1999) provide evidence that undermines the view that MNCs operate independently of a nation of origin and have no substantial or ongoing connection with their home country. Hirst and Thompson examine recent data on the activities of MNCs in order to determine the relative importance of the home and foreign activities of MNCs (Hirst and Thompson 1999: 79). The data relate to the sales patterns, asset distributions, declaration of profits and distribution of affiliates and subsidiaries of MNCs for a variety of countries, including Canada, France, Germany, Japan, the Netherlands, the United Kingdom and the United States. Hirst and Thompson (1999: 84) conclude that 'as much as between two thirds and three quarters of MNC aggregate business activity remains centred on the home region'. The data reveal limitations to the view that MNCs have become disassociated from their nation of origin. MNCs appear to continue to conduct a large proportion of their activities in home and regional markets.

Evidence concerning the motivations for MNCs to carry out activities abroad, such as for the purpose of technological development, provides further support for the enduring influence of the nation of origin. According to Patel and Vega (1999), firms do not carry out international technological activities abroad for the purpose of compensating for weakness in technological competence in their home nation. A study of the foreign activities of 220 of the most internationalized US firms showed that the international technological activities of 75 percent of firms were associated with their home-based technological strengths. Firms scan new technological developments abroad for the purpose of acquiring information that can be used to further develop their own home-based technological competencies. Foreign technological activities are also aimed at supporting foreign production activities and adapting products to suit foreign markets (Patel and Vega 1999: 149, 154). Patel and Vega (1999: 154) therefore conclude that:

> ... far from being irrelevant, what happens in home countries is still very important in the creation of global technological advantage for even the most internationalised firms. Thus for policy analysis it becomes important to understand the nature of the country-specific factors that have an influence in creating national technological advantage, including the competitive climate, the financial system, and education, training and basic research institutions.
>
> (Patel and Vega 1999: 154)

Further evidence of the enduring influence of nations in the activities of MNCs is provided by Pauly and Reich (1997), who show that MNCs from the United States, Japan and Germany continue to be influenced by both ideological and institutional forces that are distinctively national in origin. Their research indicates that MNCs from different national origins have distinctive structures and corporate strategies. The manner in which MNCs adapt to the global economy has specific historical roots. For example, Japanese MNCs investing in the United States tend to invest in wholesale and distribution facilities, while US MNCs investing in Japan tend to invest in manufacturing facilities. Japanese MNCs therefore invest in the United States with the purpose of facilitating trade from Japan to the United States, while US MNCs invest in Japan in order to produce for the local market, therefore replacing trade (Pauly and Reich 1997).

In the area of corporate governance and financing, US shareholdings in MNCs are primarily held by individuals, pension funds and mutual funds. In Japan and Germany, banks and non-financial institutions account for a much higher proportion of shareholdings. This creates a stronger short term orientation in US MNCs, which are subject to capital market pressure from mobile and widely dispersed share holdings. Further, banks play a greater role in financing the activities of corporations in Japan and particularly Germany than in the United States. The centrality of banks in corporate groups in Japan, and the role of banks in the supervisory boards of major corporations in Germany, reinforces a bank-based system of industrial finance (Deeg 1997). This facilitates longer term strategic planning and more diverse corporate goals, that may incorporate concerns with quality or market share rather than short term returns on investment alone (Jürgens, Naumann and Rupp 2000). As Pauly and Reich (1997) highlight, within Japanese industrial groups, there is pressure on banks and companies not to sell significant share holdings, thus avoiding capital market pressures, particularly in times of crisis and restructuring. The different strategic behaviour of MNCs from different countries suggests that the national context continues to influence the global behaviour of major corporations, further rebutting the view that MNCs have become nationality-less.

The preceding analysis suggests that a somewhat cautious approach is needed in analysing the role of MNCs in the global economy. In particular the data suggest that, while foreign investment in developing countries is increasing, most MNC activity occurs within the advanced economies, and does not seem to represent any consistent pattern of relocation to developing countries in the pursuit of lower wages or less regulated market conditions. Further, the data show national variations in the role of MNCs in international trade and domestic employment and production as well as the continuing influence of the nation of origin on the activities of MNCs.

Technology

The above discussion has higlighted changes in the international economy since the end of World War II. It has shown that in some areas, such as international finance, there has been significant change but in other areas, such as the globalization of production, the evidence is more patchy. The above discussion has also revealed national variations in the level of international economic integration, and has identified both political and technological influences over the globalization of economic activity. This section of the chapter examines technology itself – because technology has not only fuelled an internationalization of production, sales and financial exchange, the development of technology has itself become globalized. The extent to which technological development has become international in character is an important issue for modern economies, because technology is increasingly important for economic competitiveness, given the growth of high technology sectors and the importance of knowledge industries. If technology development has become global in nature, this would suggest a further erosion of the capacity of national governments to influence economic outcomes within their borders. On the other hand, if technology development remains largely national in orientation, this would suggest there is a contuing role for national governments in influencing the technological trajectory of national industry bases.

Archibugi and Michie (1997a), and Archibugi and Immarino (2002) have examined the nature and extent of the globalization of technology and provide a taxonomy which can form a useful conceptual basis for the analysis of recent OECD statistics on the globalization of technology. They develop a three dimensional taxonomy of technological globalization. The first dimension is concerned with the exploitation of technological innovations in international markets – 'the global exploitation of technology'. This may involve technology embodied in products which are exported, or disembodied technological innovations such as licences or know-how which are transferred internationally. Technological collaboration between actors such as universities, firms and governments in more than one country constitutes the second dimension of Archibugi and Michie's taxonomy – 'global technological collaboration'. Third, the 'global generation of technology' is the component of the taxonomy which is focussed on the role of MNCs whose R&D or technological generation activities are coordinated across nations (1997a: 176–88).

The growing trade in high technology products revealed in OECD statistics presented earlier is some indication of growth in the exploitation of embodied technology in international markets – a component of Archibugi and Michie's (1997a) first dimension of technological globalization. Further, Immarino and Michie (1998: 344–35) examine the international exploitation of technology longitudinally, and show that it has increased significantly between 1981 and 1993. This is revealed in patent statistics that show a much faster growth in foreign and external patents compared with domestic patents. Thus, in most countries, the number of patent applications from foreigners has been increasing as has the number of external patent applications made by inventors within the country – indicating some intention on the part of inventors to exploit inventions in international markets. Small economies contribute disproportionately to the global exploitation of technology, as their domestic markets are too small to provide a sufficient return on technological investment and, as a result, their external patenting activity is high. The evidence indicates high and growing levels of the global exploitation of technology.

Global technological collaboration, the second dimension of Archibugi and Michie's taxonomy (1997a), appears to be driven by the desire of firms to exploit technological competencies in other countries (Patel and Pavitt 1991). The new technology fields of biotechnology, information technology and new materials account for a large proportion of total growth in international collaboration, which may be explained by the high knowledge intensity of these new technologies creating an imperative for greater collaboration to gain technical know-how (Archibugi

Table 7.4 Technological alliances[a] between firms, 1992–1995

	National	*International*	*Ratio international/national*
United States	3,377	2,067	0.61
Japan	320	908	2.84
Canada	82	386	4.71
Germany	47	383	8.15
France	34	242	7.12
Italy	5	107	21.40
Netherlands	6	136	22.67
Australia	29	84	2.90

Source: OECD (1999c), page 76.

Note
a 'Alliances can take a variety of forms, ranging from simple partnerships (cross-licensing) to the establishment of common research subsidiaries' (OECD 1999c: 76).

and Michie 1997a: 181). National and international technological alliances between firms are reported in Table 7.4. All countries other than the United States have a larger number of international than national technological alliances. These data indicate the importance of global technological collaboration.

Further evidence of global technological collaboration is provided in Table 7.5. While cross-border co-authorship of scientific publications is around 20 percent in Japan and the United States, it is closer to 40 percent in most countries listed in Table 7.5, providing further evidence of the importance of international collaboration in technology development. The percentage of patents with foreign co-inventors is also a measure of cross-border technological collaboration. As reported in Table 7.5, the percentage of patents with foreign co-inventors remains below a total of 10 percent for the OECD countries. While these data reveal the importance of international collaboration in the co-authorship of scientific publications and through international technological alliances, international collaboration between inventors appears to be lower. The data show definite cross-national differences in the extent of internationalization of technology collaboration.

The final component of Archibugi and Michie's taxonomy is the global generation of technology which is closely associated with the activities of MNCs. This dimension of the taxonomy is concerned with the extent to which MNCs carry out technological development activities abroad. Pauly and Reich (1997) show that expenditure by US, German, and Japanese MNCs on R&D abroad is quite small; MNCs tend to locate basic R&D activity in the home country. Table 7.6 reports the share of research and development activity of different countries that is carried out by foreign affiliates in the country. The figure ranges from around 3 percent in Japan to around 40 per cent in Australia, Sweden and the United Kingdom.

Patent statistics also provide some indication of global trends in the generation of technology. Table 7.7 reports data on the cross-border ownership of inventions for a range of OECD countries. Foreign ownership of domestic inventions is indicative of the extent to which foreign firms control domestic inventions (inventor in nation and patent applicant outside nation). At the end of the 1990s, around

Table 7.5 International cooperation in science and technology

	Share of scientific publications with a foreign co-author (%), 2001	Share of patents with foreign co-inventors (%), 1999–2001
Canada	38.4	30.4
United States	23.2	11.6
Australia	36.3	18.6
Japan	19.7	2.9
France	43.3	15.0
Germany	41.7	11.3
Italy	39.7	9.6
Netherlands	44.9	14.9
Sweden	46.3	16.4
United Kingdom	36.9	21.5
Total OECD	–	6.8

Sources: National Science Foundation, Science and Engineering Indicators 2004, Appendix table 5–44 (www.nsf.gov/statistics/seind04, accessed 19 October, 2005) for scientific publications, OECD Patent Database, March 2005 (http://dx.doi/org/10/1787/622567751004, accessed 19 October, 2005) for patents.

Table 7.6 Share of foreign affiliates in manufacturing R&D, 1996–2002

	1996	2002
Canada	31.8	33.6
United States	12.4	15.4
Australia[a]	–	41.8
Japan[b]	0.9	3.4
France	16.7	19.4
Germany[c]	17.2	24.8
Italy[b]	–	33.0
Netherlands[c]	20.6	19.6
Sweden[b]	18.7	38.2
United Kingdom	29.1	38.0

Source: OECD (2005b) Table 64, page 50.

Notes
a　1999 instead of 2002.
b　2001 instead of 2002.
c　1997 instead of 1996, 2001 instead of 2002.

15 percent of patent applications made in OECD countries were owned by a foreign resident. OECD statistics reveal some increase in a relatively low level of foreign ownership of domestic inventions, indicating the relatively weak role of MNCs in national research activities.

Patents covering ownership of inventions made abroad for a particular nation as a percentage of total patented inventions of the nation – where the patent applicant firm is in the nation and the inventor is outside the nation – was highest in small countries such as Canada and the Netherlands (30.4, 30.5) and lowest in

Table 7.7 Cross-border ownership of inventions, 1999–2001, percentages

	Foreign ownership of inventions[a]	*Domestic ownership of foreign inventions*[b]
Canada	34.4	30.4
United States	12.1	17.4
Australia	24.4	12.2
Japan	3.7	3.7
France	21.8	17.9
Germany	13.4	12.0
Italy	18.1	5.9
Netherlands	20.5	30.5
Sweden	18.2	27.5
United Kingdom	37.5	18.4
Total OECD	14.7	15.0

Source: OECD Patent Database (http://dx.doi.org/10/1787/285308278247 and http://dx.doi.org/10/1787/267150665256, accessed 19 October 2005).

Notes
a Share of patent applications to the EPO owned by foreign residents in total patents invented domestically.
b Share of patent applications to the EPO invented abroad in total patents owned by country residents.

Japan (3.7), indicating the less internationalized nature of technology development in Japan than the small open economies. This shows that a significant proportion of the technological activities of Dutch firms take place outside the Netherlands, while in Japan technology development remains principally within the nation. Patent data therefore indicate that cross-border ownership of inventions remains low for most countries.

This overview of the globalization of technology has examined the extent to which technology development can be regarded as a global phenomenon. There is some evidence of the growing importance of global technological exploitation in the form of trade in high technology products and foreign patenting activities, indicating some intention on the part of inventors to exploit inventions in international markets. There is also evidence of international collaboration in technology development in the form of technological alliances and cross-border collaboration in scientific publications, although evidence on collaboration for patented inventions is weaker. Finally, using Archibugi and Michie's (1997a) taxonomy, it would seem that there is evidence of the globalization of innovation, although it varies across the different dimensions of technological globalization and there remains significant cross-national variation.

The implications of technological change and globalization

The above discussion has developed two propositions concerning new forms of international interaction in the global economy. First, it has suggested that it is both technological change and the influence of economic liberal policies that have fuelled the growth of the international economy. Global economic developments cannot be attributed to technological change alone, governments have played a role in the process. Second, the discussion has highlighted the massive growth in international financial market activity and the significant growth in international trade as key components of globalization. However, caution has been expressed about the extent of the globalization of production as indicated by the activities of MNCs, whose pattern of commercial activity seems to have continuing connection with nations and regions. Further, evidence on the globalization of technology itself is quite patchy. It seems that, while there has been a growth in the international exploitation of technology, the development of technology retains a distinctive national orientation in key OECD countries.

As the discussion above has highlighted, there is significant debate concerning the causes and extent of globalization, in particular, the importance of technology – both in facilitating global exchange and as a component of globalization. Similarly, there is contention over the effects of change associated with the globalized knowledge economy, particularly for work and employment. The following discussion deals with a variety of perspectives on the globalized knowledge economy, and examines the capacity of governments to intervene in the process to mediate the effects of change on work and employment.

Three perspectives on the globalized knowledge economy will be highlighted in the following discussion. The first suggests that globalization and technological change are positive developments. It is not of concern to advocates of this perspective that governments may be impotent to resist the process of technologically driven globalization. This is because global market freedom is thought to provide a superior mechanism for the allocation of global resources, therefore resulting in social benefits, improvements in work and employment, as well as enhanced profitability for corporations and global investors (Friedman 1999: 87; Shipman 2002). The second and contrasting view emerges from a concern that the state and labour movements are rendered impotent in the face of technological change and globalization, with significant negative effects for work and employment (Hedley 2002). The third and final perspective has emerged from the analysis of differences between countries that continue in the face of common trends associated with technology and globalization. This view suggests that the outcomes of the globalized knowledge economy are contingent, and depend on specific national conditions over which governments remain influential. This is the view of scholars engaged in comparative institutional analysis, and can probably be described as the dominant view in the field of comparative political economy (Radice 2000: 721).

The first perspective embraces the globalized knowledge economy and is associated with the views of orthodox economists and the populist business literature (Hay 2004: 233) that reasons that international economic liberalization enhances economic performance by facilitating the efficient allocation of resources across the globe. The orthodox approach is sometimes associated with the views of international institutions such as GATT, the IMF, the World Bank, the International Institute of Management Development (IMD) and the OECD, whose policy recommendations typically favour the removal of remaining barriers to international trade and capital mobility with the promise of enhanced economic performance for all. In this view, governments are impotent to intervene in the process of globalization. However, the political constraints imposed by globalization are embraced by this perspective because markets are regarded as more efficient in the allocation of resources than governments (Ohmae 1990) and globalization is believed to contribute to increased economic wealth (Shipman 2002).

Another version of this view of technological change and globalization suggests that the globalized knowledge economy provides the opportunity for growth in high skilled professional and autonomous work, and enhanced flexibility in working hours and location of employment. Technology is seen as the mechanism for reducing low skilled factory work, which is now performed by computers and robots. In this scenario, productivity improvements resulting from technological advances provide the basis for shorter working hours and increased leisure (Mathews 1989; Piore and Sabel 1984). Several of the earlier chapters in this book have interrogated this perspective.

The second and contrasting perspective focusses on the potentially destructive impact of globalization and technological change. This version of the debate is concerned with the heightened power imbalance of technologically-driven global capitalism relative to national governments and labour movements. The suggestion is that the existence and potential for international capital mobility has enhanced the power of business relative to labour. This has meant that business can use the threat of relocation to extract policy concessions from national governments – including lower taxation, less rigid environmental, health and safety regulations, wage and employment flexibility, privatization, welfare state cutbacks and deregulation of the economy more generally (Cox 1994; Fröbel *et al.* 1980; Wilks 1996). Increasingly, national governments will sacrifice employment conditions and wage protection in an effort to enhance the profitability of capital and to attract capital to their borders (Bryan 1992; Holloway 1994). From the critic's viewpoint, international volatility and competitiveness is expected to worsen economic outcomes and to alter the relative power of labour and business in favour of the latter. The possibility of working class mobilization or state intervention being directed to improved economic outcomes for the nation or labour is viewed suspiciously (Moses 1994).

In this view, financial markets, or the expectations and pronouncements of their participants, now exert considerable influence over the policy choices of national governments (Goodman and Pauly 1993). The transnationalization of financial structures and instruments has created a pool of mobile financial capital that poses a significant obstacle to national governments seeking to depart from the austerity measures favoured by international financial players (Cerny 1996; Strange 1998). This has created significant pressure on national governments to adopt a range of neo-liberal policies including privatization, industrial relations decentralization, cut-backs to the welfare state and reduced government spending (Milner and Keohane 1996). Jonathon Moses (1994) has argued that traditional social democratic programmes for full employment are no longer possible because, with the internationalization of economic activity, states, must now prioritize the attainment of external balance. Hugo Radice (1984) has argued that the national economy is a Keynesian myth. Keynesian macroeconomic management and autonomous national economic strategies cannot exist with the extensive integration of national economies in the post-Bretton Woods period. The liberalization of the international market has impinged on the monetary and fiscal capacity of the state, resulting in high levels of convergence of economic policy (Goodman and Pauly 1993; Webb 1991).

A recent focus of the analysis of the negative implications of global economic change is the ascendancy of financial criteria in modern economies (Krippner 2005; Went 2004: 342). The growth of foreign exchange and equity markets are part of a process of financialization – a term which has been used to represent the imperative for modern management to maximize returns on investment or shareholder value. The growth of financial markets and stockholdings is regarded as having created a financially-driven capitalism in which there is an imperative to achieve returns on capital employed of at least 13 percent across all industry sectors (Williams 2000: 6). According to Lazonick and O'Sullivan (2000), American managers over the last two decades have adopted a strategy that emphasizes distribution of earnings to shareholders. Corporate dividends as a percentage of corporate after-tax profits in the United States was 42.4 percent in the 1960s, 42.3 percent in the 1970s, 49.3 percent in the 1980s and 49.6 percent between 1990 and 1998 (Lazonick and O'Sullivan 2000: 22). This was combined with a strategy of share buy-backs, also designed to maximize share value. The system of shareholder capitalism, typical of the Anglo-Saxon economies, is spreading to countries such as France, whose financial systems have not previously allowed for stock exchange pressure to drive managerial decision-making. Foreign institutional investors of US origin have acquired ownership of a significant proportion of French shares, creating the possibility for an extension of financialization internationally (Morrin 2000).

It would seem that the rewards of financialization have been unevenly distributed. Benefits have gone to CEOs, whose salaries have increased massively (and have often included share bonuses), and long term stock values have increased significantly, although it must be remembered that 80 percent of US households own less than 2 per cent of corporate equities (Lazonick and O'Sullivan 2000: 29). During the 1980s and 1990s, major American corporations also undertook a programme of extensive downsizing of their labour force and corporate restructuring. Managers were motivated to reduce the size of their workforce and physical assets in the pursuit of higher shareholder value. This has created a significant loss of well-paid and secure jobs in America's largest firms (Lazonick and O'Sullivan 2000: 18–20).

The less positive depiction of the changes associated with technological transformation and globalization highlights: the increased gap between the rich and poor in modern society; the intensification of work; high unemployment; increased insecurity; and casualization of the workforce. Researchers concerned with the negative implications of change draw attention to: the growing discontent amongst workers displaced from traditional manufacturing industries and unable to acquire the skills necessary for employment in the growing services economy; extended working hours for professional workers; the intensification of work; and the broader disillusionment within modern society (Thurow 1999). The erosion of a sense of collective identity associated with participation in trade unions, churches, community and sporting clubs are further facets of an increasingly mobile workforce with reduced family and community ties (Sandel 1996). Negative conceptions of the globalized knowledge economy focus on the absence of many of the promised rewards of the information revolution, which included shorter working hours, home work, expanded political participation and improved social and community interaction (Lynon 1988).

The negative conception of the new economy points to the divide in the workforce between those who benefit from the changes of the last three decades and those who have born the costs of change. Particular groups within the workforce have reaped the rewards of the globalized knowledge economy and others have suffered the burden of structural change and the decline of traditional employment opportunities. Some authors have suggested that inequality in the labour market is a consequence of differential access to information resources in a global economy. This is conceptualized as a divide between the information rich and the information poor, the different life chances of those who do and don't have knowledge and access to on-going education, information and telecommunications resources.

Castells (1998) has conceptualized the differential impact of the globalized knowledge economy or the information economy on different segments of the labour force with reference to the concepts of generic labour and self-programming labour. The term generic labour refers to the portion of the workforce which lacks the capacity to acquire new skills when technological and structural change renders their existing skills obsolete. In contrast, self-programming labour has access to education and information, which is necessary for re-skilling on an on-going basis in a constantly changing environment. Generic labour changes jobs on a regular basis and tends to be employed in occasional part-time or casual work. This group experiences significant periods outside the paid workforce, resulting in regular life crises associated with employment instability and job loss. These include both personal and financial crises which are often linked to insecure, low paid and irregular employment activities. For Castells, generic labour comprises those unable to update their skills on a regular basis; they therefore fall behind in an environment where competitiveness matters. Everyday existence becomes a struggle, resulting in growing insecurity and social exclusion (Castells 1998).

The plight of generic labour is exacerbated by the decline in collective bargaining and decentralization of industrial relations systems world-wide. Structural change in industry has partially contributed to a decline in trade union membership and centralized wage bargaining, which were linked to traditional manufacturing industries. The new services and information industries are characterized by low levels of trade union membership and individual negotiation of contracts. This process of restructuring has been accompanied by changes in industrial relations and wage negotiation systems which have shifted away from highly organized and centralized processes towards more decentralized and flexible models (Traxler 1998).

These developments suggest that, on the one hand, a part of the workforce has experienced real benefits from technological developments and globalization. This group is experiencing high growth in real wages and the benefits of high quality, high skilled, usually interesting, employment in growing industries. On the other hand, a low skilled segment is increasingly insecure in employment, regularly experiences layoffs as a consequence of downsizing, and lacks the capacity to reskill for new industries. This group is unprotected in the contemporary environment because of the declining influence of trade unions and pressure to deregulate labour markets, where trade unions and labour market regulation have traditionally protected the wages and conditions of low skilled employees. Their protection has been further eroded by the contemporary attack on the welfare state, which has lowered protection for income loss and reduced access to public services except on a 'user pays' basis.

There is a third perspective on the implications of the globalized knowledge economy which is less concerned with the positive or negative effects of globalization than with the importance of the state and political conflict in influencing the outcomes of global economic change. The empirical evidence presented in the first part of the chapter provides a sound basis on which to suggest that the outcomes of globalization are contingent on historical, cultural, institutional and political phenomena. The empirical evidence has shown that technology has not been the only force driving internationalization – government policy decisions have also played an important role. Second, data show that there are limits to the extent of globalization, with national and regional activity remaining important. Third, differences between countries continue, both in the extent and nature of global economic exchange, for example in the area of global technological collaboration, exploitation and development, and in the pattern of activity and strategic behaviour of MNCs from different national origins. All of these factors allude to the continuing importance of the national context, and suggest possibilities for national institutional influences over economic outcomes.

As early as 1985, Peter Katzenstein provided a comprehensive analysis of the way in which international market forces are filtered through domestic political processes in small open economies. Katzenstein argued that the small European states have adopted a distinctive mix of international openness and domestic intervention, and this combination explains their relatively successful performance in comparison to other industrialized nations. Katzenstein's analysis showed that openness to international market forces need not necessarily result in poor social outcomes, provided national political institutions were established and a range of policy tools, including labour market, incomes policies, industry policy and investment policy, were utilized in order to establish political influences over the economy. Katzenstein also revealed that relative openness did not necessarily require the adoption of laissez faire policies at the national level. The small European states were clear exceptions to the generalization that liberalism in the international economy and interventionism in the domestic economy were incompatible

(Katzenstein 1985: 57). The underlying theme in this approach was that the impact of internationalization in different countries was mediated by domestic political and institutional factors (Bienefeld 1994; Milner and Keohane, 1996: 8–10).

The field of comparative political economy sought to contribute to debates about globalization by investigating measurable economic outcomes with reference to international transactions and domestic policies and institutions. Alvarez, Garrett and Lange (1991) showed that domestic political factors (labour organization and left party in government) remained significant determinants of national economic performance even after controlling for trade dependency. While acknowledging limitations to state autonomy resulting from globalization, particularly in the areas of fiscal and monetary policy, research in this field has also sought to identify continuing political capacities in areas such as income policy, social policy and labour market policy (Garrett and Lange 1991).

Recent contributions suggest that the outcomes of globalization are influenced to some extent by national characteristics. Garrett (1998) has shown that government spending, public sector deficits and levels of corporate taxation continue to vary significantly between countries in the current era. Similarly, the level of exposure of a national economy to international markets is not strongly correlated with domestic policy variables, suggesting that the constraints imposed by the international economy may be less than is suggested by the hyperglobalization perspective. Boyer (2005) has argued that social and political conflict remain important influences over the evolution of institutional regimes in different countries, such that it is possible to identify continuing differences in types of capitalism across the OECD countries.

Further, the national systems of innovation and technological systems approaches, discussed in detail in the next chapter of the book, highlight the importance of national institutions in influencing technology development and diffusion. Studies of technological systems and national systems of innovation are solidly grounded in comparative institutional analysis. This literature seeks to explain the varying technological capabilities of firms and industries within different countries by reference to institutional configurations. Innovation is increasingly seen as a cumulative process (rather than an event) resulting from the activities and interactions of a range of players within the national institutional framework (Nelson and Rosenberg 1993).

Studies of innovation incorporate an analysis of organizational characteristics of a nation's firms as well as inter-firm and inter-industry relationships, including relationships between users and suppliers of technology and between upstream and downstream industries (Carlsson and Stankiewicz 1991; Marceau and Manley 2001). The national system of education and training, as well as public and private investment in research and development and the institutional configuration of research laboratories in the private and public sectors, together form the institutional framework for learning and knowledge creation which is critical to the national system of innovation (Lundvall 1992: 15; Zysman 1996).

This research indicates that globalization and technological change manifest themselves in unique ways in individual national economies. National politics already appears to have played an important role in determining the effects of globalization and technological change. This suggests that it is impossible to examine technological change and globalization independently of an analysis of the institutional characteristics of nations.

Conclusion

This chapter has developed three core propositions in response to debates associated with techno-globalism. It has shown that while the globalization of economic activity has been driven by technological advances which have led to improvements in information storage, communications and transportation it has also resulted from policy changes that are associated with neo-liberal ideology and which have had a broad influence on domestic politics across the globe. Second, the chapter has reviewed evidence on the globalization of economic activity which has shown that, while there has been significant change in financial markets and international trade, there remains variation between countries. The evidence on the globalization of production and technology remains patchy and tends to indicate the continuing importance of national variations associated with different institutional contexts. Third, while a number of perspectives highlight the positive and negative implications of globalization, it appears that the outcomes of these processes depend to an extent on the outcomes of political struggles.

8 The evolution and development of national technological systems

The term 'the new economy' is used in public debate to refer to the changed nature of modern economies resulting from globalization and the commercial application of technological advances. In the context of the new economy, there is an increased awareness of the importance of knowledge resources and learning (Lundvall 1992: 1); growth and employment appear to be linked to the capacity of firms to innovate, through the introduction of new organizational processes and, particularly, new products (Edquist, Hommen and McKelvey 2001). Investment in knowledge and learning and the ability to innovate seem to be closely associated with high-quality, high-skilled employment growth. Therefore it is not surprising, that the study of work and employment is also concerned with the processes of technology development and diffusion, and the innovative capacities of firms and industries (Michie and Reati 1998).

An enhanced awareness of the value of knowledge resources and the pressures of global economic competition has caused policy makers to develop institutions and policy approaches that will improve the innovative capacity of the nation's industries. As this chapter will explain, different nations are characterized by very different institutional contexts for learning and innovation. The purpose of the chapter is to explore the impact that those different institutional contexts have on the structure of economic activity within a nation and, in particular, the extent of participation in knowledge intensive activities or new economy industries. In explaining the continuing relevance of national institutions in structuring economic activity and explaining differences in the mix of industries within a nation, the chapter provides an important critique of the idea that national institutions and policies or local economic environments have become ineffective or unimportant in the context of global economic exchange. As such, the chapter does not accord with those elements of the techno-globalism debate, described in the previous chapter, that suggest that national institutions have become ineffectual or irrelevant in a technologically-driven global economy.

The chapter is principally concerned with innovation, which can be defined broadly to include the development and uptake of technology, the introduction of new products or processes, the introduction of different forms of work organization or management structures and approaches, and the utilization of new market opportunities. All of these various forms of innovation appear to be important for growth, productivity and competitiveness. Technology and product innovation are often given central attention in innovation research (Edquist 1997: 22), however, organizational and managerial change has been recognized as critical (Freeman 1995: 24). It would seem that technological product innovation is the form of innovation which is crucial for the generation of high-skilled employment and, as such, is the focus of this chapter (Edquist *et al.* 1998).

The first section of the chapter describes the institutional context of learning and innovation in different countries. The national systems of innovation (NSI) and technological systems (TS) approaches provide a useful framework for understanding the institutions and behaviours that impact on the generation and utilization of knowledge resources, and these literatures are discussed in the first section of the chapter. In comparing innovation systems across countries, a broad distinction can be drawn between coordinated and competitive economies, which represent quite different business environments and are associated with distinctive innovative capacities. The second part of the chapter will explore the link between these different institutional contexts and the industrial structure of advanced economies, particularly the extent to which they are engaged in knowledge intensive activity.

National and technological systems of innovation

The NSI and TS approaches provide a useful conceptual framework for understanding technological development and uptake, or innovation, within particular national institutional contexts. The first key contribution of this literature is its adoption of a systems approach to innovation. Both the NSI and TS approaches have pursued an analysis of innovation on the understanding that firms are not isolated actors, they are part of a *system* of institutions and behavioural patterns or norms. The various interactions within that system affect the innovative activities of firms (Lundvall 1992).

It is this emphasis on systems which makes the NSI and TS approaches different from orthodox accounts of innovation. The NSI accepts that economic actors are embedded in a complex system of institutions and behaviours or social structures and relations, as Granovetter (1985) understood it. These social structures and relations become an important basis for understanding the innovative behaviour of firms, as does culture – the shared beliefs, ideologies or codes of behaviour in a particular social context (Swedberg 1997: 168). The NSI approach has emphasized the importance of social incentives and constraints in understanding the innovative behaviour of firms, highlighting limitations of the orthodox explanation of economic behaviour that adopts a universal conception of rationality as profit maximization. Edquist (1997: 6) explains that many of the important institutions in the innovation system (such as public research institutions) are not profit-maximizing organizations. Further, 'legal conditions, rules and norms' and institutional arrangements create incentives and constraints for certain types of innovative behaviour, creating a more complex basis of behavioural patterns than simple profit maximization.

The second contribution of the TS and NSI research is its identification of the key institutions which impact on technology development and diffusion and innovation. In seeking to develop an understanding of innovation within a particular national context, the NSI and TS approaches have focussed on a range of institutions closely linked to the innovative process. For example, Carlsson and Stankiewicz (1995: 45) have referred to the institutions that constitute the technological system as the 'set of institutional arrangements (both regimes and organizations), which directly or indirectly, support, stimulate and regulate the process of innovation and diffusion of technology'. Definitions of the NSI tend to emphasize not only the institutions themselves, but their interactions. As such, Niosi, Saviotti, Bellon and Crow have defined the national system of innovation as:

> ... the system of interacting private and public firms (either large or small), universities, and government agencies aiming at the production of science and technology within national borders. Interaction among these units may be technical, commercial, legal, social and financial, in as much as the goal of the interaction is the development, protection, financing or regulation of new science and technology.
>
> (Niosi, Saviotti, Bellon and Crow 1993: 212)

It should be noted, however, that the traditions of comparative political economy (Kurzer 1993; Lazonick 1991; Porter 1990; Thurow 1993; Wilks and Wright 1987; Soskice 1990, 1997; Zysman 1983) and economic sociology (Dobbin 1994; Granovetter 1985; Swedberg 1997) and more recent work on comparative business systems (Whitley 1992, 1994, 1996, 2000; Kristensen 1996) have also emphasized the importance of institutional arrangements in influencing technology development and innovation, often incorporating a wider set of institutions within the framework of analysis (Zysman 1994: 265).

This literature has shown that institutional arrangements which have an important impact on innovation include those associated with the state, the education system, research infrastructure, the industrial relations and training system, financial markets, the system of labour relations and the organization of business itself, both within firms (intra-organizational) and between firms (inter-organizational). The cultural context, including codes of behaviour and values such as trust, attitudes to authority, and conceptions of fairness, also impact on the innovative behaviour of economic actors because they impose constraints and provide opportunities for owners, managers, workers and regulators (Kristensen 1996: 24–30). A nation's values and norms, state institutions, industrial relations system, finance sector, industry associations, trade unions and business organizations constitute a *system* within which innovation takes place.

The NSI and TS approaches have therefore contributed to an understanding of how institutions constitute an overall system of innovation within nations. A key debate that has emerged from this contribution concerns the relevance of adopting the nation as the unit of analysis in the study of technology development and diffusion or innovation. Contention over the appropriateness of the nation as a unit of analysis has been concerned with whether regions or technology fields are more suitable for the study of innovation. Studies of national systems have sometimes been criticized because they are unable to account for differences between sectors, regions or technology fields which may be inconsistent with broad understandings of the role of institutions in coordinating innovation at the national level.

Nations have become a focus of systems approaches to understanding innovation (Nelson 1992) because many of the institutions that impact on innovation – such as education, training and research institutions – are national in character and are influenced by the policies of national governments. Further, it is relevant to study national patterns of industrial specialization because to some extent they map out future directions of technological development (Edquist and McKelvey 2000: xv; Niosi *et al.* 1993: 211). Institutions, modes of behaviour and patterns of technological and industrial specialization within a nation combine as a system within which innovation takes place, and which potentially inhibits or encourages certain types of innovative activities. This is sometimes referred to as the path dependency of national patterns of industrial specialization.

The focus on the national context has also been criticized because of the increasing globalization of economic activity, which may render national systems less distinctive. However, there is a dearth of evidence of convergence in technology and innovation processes across nations, with indications that there are tendencies towards greater diversity between nations in terms of technological specialization. Further, as the previous chapter highlighted, the processes of technology development and diffusion still have strong national connections, further emphasizing the need for an understanding of the characteristics of nations which impact on the development and application of technology, an increasing source of competitiveness. As such, there is justification for research on the national context within which innovation takes place, which may be complemented by supra-national, regional, sectoral or technological studies (Edquist 1997: 12).

Coordinated and competitive systems

In adopting the nation as the unit of analysis in the study of economic processes, recent literature has categorized varieties of capitalism in terms of two distinctive types, usually referred to as 'coordinated' or 'competitive' capitalist economies. These are 'ideal types' of business systems, and countries depart from the ideal types to varying degrees.

There are many characteristics that make up the model of coordinated capitalism. These include particular forms of corporate organization often involving specialization on core competencies, close linkages between industry and banks resulting from cross-ownership and control between enterprises, long-term stable relationships with customers and suppliers and particular forms of inter-firm cooperation in relation to information sharing and the pooling of resources for research and development, design and marketing. In addition, the industrial relations system in the coordinated model is characterized by collective bargaining and labour market programmes and institutions that emphasize skills development in the workforce and security of tenure. Business associations are encompassing and well integrated with state policy making institutions. Culture is oriented towards cooperation, trust and equality. The discussion below seeks to elaborate on the coordinated system and the way in which it can enhance the process of innovation, particularly incremental innovations in medium technology industry sectors (Hall and Soskice 2001).

The competitive model is instead characterized by weakly-organized business groups and unions, decentralized determination of wages (at the level of enterprises), a highly competitive labour market with high labour turnover, a financial system heavily dependent on capital markets providing ready access to high-risk capital, hierarchical M-form diversified firms not typically categorized by decentralized inter-organizational relationships or participation in clusters, a strong emphasis on competition and anti-trust, and an unwillingness of the state to interfere with the investment and production decisions of private firms (Hall and Soskice 2001; Whitley 2000). As will be explained below, the competitive model has a tendency to favour certain industries, particularly those associated with radical innovations, such as computer systems or management consultancy.

Each of these different types of capitalism are associated with different processes of learning, knowledge transfer and innovation. The following discussion highlights the different institutions which impact on innovation and, in so doing, draws a distinction between the coordinated and competitive models. The implications of each of the institutional elements of the coordinated and competitive models for knowledge transfer and innovation are also discussed.

The state

The system of economic governance within a nation associated with state apparatus or publicly funded institutional arrangements has an impact on technology development and innovative activity. The state is important because of its capacity to direct resources to particular purposes through public research institutions and funding of the science base. It can influence the degree of cooperation between individual producers, and has the capacity to consolidate disparate interests towards common goals associated with industrial transformation, technological development and innovation (Weiss 1998). The state impacts on the time horizon adopted in economic decision-making, for example through the provision of public goods such as research or training of sufficient quality to overcome market deficiencies arising from positive externalities and the risk and uncertainty of returns on investment (Traxler and Unger 1994: 7). The state is also an important user of technology and establishes the regulatory environment within which innovation occurs. As Lundvall has highlighted:

> The public sector plays an important role in the process of innovation ... it is involved in direct support of science and development, its regulations and standards influence the rate and direction of innovation, and it is the single most important user of innovations developed in the private sector.
>
> (Lundvall 1992: 14)

Studies of new technology industries indicate that scientific knowledge developed in public research institutions and universities is critical to the successful development of new industries (McMillan, Narin and Deeds 2000). Public research institutes have been recognized as important knowledge intermediaries in high technology networks across Europe and Japan (Carlsson 1993; Fransman and Tanaka 1995; Storey and Tether 1998). The competitiveness of high technology firms, including their profitability and export performance, has been shown to relate to government support of the science base (Grupp 1997). For example, new firm entry and development in the biotechnology industry appears to be influenced to a large extent by the presence of a strong scientific research base (Prevezer 1997; Senker 1996; Swan and Prevezer 1996). The importance of university–industry linkages is demonstrated by recent OECD data which show that over 70 percent of US patent citations (references to published articles) in biotechnology were to papers that originated in public science institutions, and in the United Kingdom, co-authorship between academic and industry scientists increased from 20 percent to 40 percent from 1981 to 1991 (OECD 2000: 9).

Weiss has argued that the state is playing a central role in coordinating technological development in Japan by funding up to two thirds of the cost of commercializing research developed by public research institutes or universities. The amount of funds directed to technological development has increased significantly in the last few years. It is an area in which the state is playing an increasingly important role in coordinating industrial change (Weiss 1998: 200–1). In the United States, the Defence Department has played a role in technology development through its support of defence technology and weapons manufacturing, with significant implications for industries such as aeronautics and microelectronics (Hooks 1990). Chomsky has traced the role of the state as a funder and user of critical technologies in the United States, including microelectronics and the Internet (Chomsky 1998). Research by Carlsson and Jacobsson (1997a: 278–9) has shown that in Sweden the state has encouraged clusters of competence in the electronics sector; including radio and telecommunications, military electronics and power generation and distribution. Carlsson and Jacobsson identify two roles for the public sector – as a competent user of products in defence, power, communications and health, and in the establishment of a regulatory framework, including the common standard for mobile telephony in the Nordic region (Edquist, Hommen and McKelvey 2001: 134).

The state therefore plays a critical role in all systems of innovation, but its role in the coordinated system is quite distinctive. In some countries which fit the coordinated model, the state is prepared to regulate private firms and markets in the pursuit of pre-determined objectives. This emerges from a belief that private investment and production decisions have a significant impact on the economy and society, and should therefore be open to public scrutiny. Within the group of nations that fall within a coordinated model, there are some statist types that engage in strategic intervention that targets favoured industries with the objective of satisfying long term structural economic goals. As Weiss outlines, the state serves as an 'encompassing organizational complex' which is able to coordinate the multifarious activities of private industry which are often interdependent, (Weiss 1998). This need not take the form of state direction of economic activity, but might involve dialogue, communication and negotiation between the state and industry, as it has in the Danish negotiated economy, which has recognized that firms must act as responsible agents in an environment within which the actions of the state and industry are interdependent and in which the government and industry bodies often have common objectives and fates. Thus in Denmark policies affecting business have been coordinated in local communities by a multitude of agents, including industrial firms, banks, and public institutions at various levels of government, throughout the 1990s (Andersen and Kjaer 1993). In such, societies it is possible to identify state-based institutional coordination of the economy, emphasis on training and skills enhancement, promotion of research and development, and strategic interventions targeted at particular industries which have broader economic or social significance. However, the state does not necessarily play this role in all coordinated economies, as in some cases a national business system is regarded as coordinated because of the role of labour or financial institutions rather than the state.

For countries that fall within the competitive system, in contrast, the state limits its involvement in economic activity, and emphasizes instead deregulated labour markets, price competition through anti-trust laws, privatization, tax incentives and a reduction of business costs as strategies for enhancing the competitiveness of the private sector. This model does not incorporate state coordination of industrial renewal through sectoral interventions. There is an emphasis on managerial prerogatives, firm autonomy and market-led adjustment (Coleman 1997). There is a lack of centralized coordination of industrial modernization or continuous industrial improvement, because of the unwillingness of the state to interfere with the investment and production decisions of private firms, and because of the belief that economic incentives provide the best motivation for business competitiveness.

Weiss has argued that state capacity, typical of the coordinated regimes of Japan and Taiwan, explains the ability to rapidly adapt to international economic change by conquering new export markets or upgrading technological capabilities. A key characteristic of state capacity is the existence of policy linkages between the bureaucracy and industry, which are able to coordinate the investment decisions of industry. The state provides an 'encompassing organizational complex' that is able to organize industry around long term objectives and socialize the high risk associated with the development and diffusion of new technologies and production processes (Weiss 1998: 6). The coordinating role for the state is thought to facilitate the transfer of knowledge and the socialization of risk and uncertainty, thereby contributing to an environment of innovation.

In contrast, Audretsch and Thurik have emphasized the advantages of a competitive system in describing a shift from a 'managed' to an 'entrepreneurial' economy in contemporary societies. In Audretsch and Thurik's conceptualization of the entrepreneurial economy, there is an emphasis on individual motivation, new ideas and risk taking. According to this view, in the entrepreneurial economy, flexibility and innovation are more important than stability and control. Innovation is linked to entrepreneurial activity which depends on incentives and rewards for risk taking. The flexible and cost-competitive economic environments of the competitive model are seen as facilitating entrepreneurial activities and risk taking behaviour which are viewed as necessary for innovation (Audretsch and Thurik 2001).

In summary, the competitive model is thought to promote innovation by encouraging competition and allowing for high market rewards for entrepreneurial activity, while the coordinated model is thought to contribute to innovation through cooperation and the sharing of resources and information.

Although it is possible to identify differences in state – economy relations in the coordinated and competitive types, there are some common trends in the role and structure of the state that can be identified in both coordinated and competitive types. Many of these earlier approaches have described the role of the state in industrial development and transformation in terms of national coordination, bureaucratic hierarchies and centralized authority structures. More recent analysis has suggested that the role of the state in knowledge-based activities is somewhat different from that associated with the building of competitiveness in medium-technology manufacturing industries, which involved the state targeting 'national champions' or key large corporations in important industry sectors (Parker 1999). With respect to knowledge activities, the state's role is seen more in terms of the management of networks and interactions between a variety of actors within localized spaces.

Using Ireland as a case, O'Riain (2000) builds the concept of the 'flexible developmental state' to explain relatively recent success in knowledge activities such as ICT. According to O'Riain, the flexible developmental state takes on the role of linking local and global technology networks by embedding global business in local and regional economies, and by facilitating the integration of local business with global technology networks. The flexible developmental state does not depend on a tight or centralized organizational structure. Instead it depends on a 'loosely coupled' (O'Riain 2000: 167) organizational model in which different state agencies are able to become embedded in a diversity of local networks with different actors in the pursuit of common objectives of local industry development and linkage with national and global knowledge networks.

The shift of state economic management to local spaces is related to what Harvey (1989) has identified as an increased focus on the entrepreneurial basis of competitiveness in urban governance, which previously emphasized administration, transportation and housing. Brenner (2004) has described the Glocalizing Competition State Regime (GCSR) to highlight the focus on competition between urban spaces to position themselves in global value chains through marketing, the acquisition of subsidies from national or global institutions and property and infrastructure investment (Brenner 2004: 473). The concept of meta-governance is helpful in conceptualizing the state as an overarching institution, which, through legal and political authority, sets the rules of the game. Jessop (2002: 242) emphasizes the meta-governance role of the state in organizing dialogue within policy communities, shaping cognitive perceptions, mediating disputes, compensating for power differentials between actors, maintaining system integrity and moderating strategies in the pursuit of collective objectives. The changed role of the state captured in the concepts of the 'flexible development state', 'the entre-preneurial state' and 'meta-governance' reflects broader debates regarding a shift from hierarchies to networks. As such, there is an evolution in the role of the state in industrial transformation, although the way in which these trends develop in particular institutional contexts will most likely continue to vary.

Industrial relations institutions and the education and training system

Systems of labour relations have been identified as impacting on innovation because they create incentives and constraints which affect the behaviour of man-agers and employees (Zysman 1994). The education and training systems are also relevant (Patel and Pavitt 1991) because of their affect on the supply of highly skilled and trained employees.

The coordinated industrial relations system is characterized by a relatively equal distribution of wages achieved through a system of collective bargaining by encompassing organizations of labour, as well as long-term security of employ-ment. Security of employment or average tenure of employees varies significantly between nations depending on institutional influences over labour turnover. In countries such as Japan, the practice of lifetime employment in large corporations has fostered a sense of loyalty between employers and employees and discour-aged downsizing and job losses in periods of temporary economic decline. The state has played a role in promoting the system of lifetime employment in Japanese companies through a series of regulations, and by subsidizing employ-ers to avoid layoffs during periods of restructuring (Iwaki 1996). Societies with highly regulated industrial relations systems, such as Sweden, Germany and more recently France, have sought to deliberately develop rigid employment relation-ships that discourage layoffs in times of economic downturn. In Sweden, there has been a requirement that planned redundancies and layoffs be notified to the labour exchange and, if new work cannot be located, workers have been placed in training programmes oriented to 'future industries' (Delsen and van Veen 1992: 89; Kjellberg 1998: 93). These institutional rigidities have constrained the capacity of firms to adopt short term strategies for cost reduction that depend on large scale layoffs or downward wage pressures (Streeck 1996). In the coordi-nated model, processes and institutions of wage determination have played a major role in the realization of social aspirations such as fairness, justice and community cohesion, through either or both security of employment and the equi-table distribution of wages.

The coordinated model is also typically associated with an education and train-ing system that is funded and regulated through central public institutions and is broad-based and egalitarian (Lam 2002). This is a characteristic of the German system, which has provided for occupational qualifications that are portable across the workforce, because they are standardized and certified and therefore universally accepted. The national government has recognized around 400 apprenticed occupations, specifying the standard of knowledge and skill required for certification. Apprenticeship training has been widespread in Germany, covering about two thirds of young adults who spend between three and three and a half years in their training (Vitols 1997).

In contrast, in the competitive model, industrial relations is more decentralized and conflictual, with wages and conditions being determined through negotiations in individual workplaces, rather than being coordinated across the economy as a whole. As a result, wage differentials are higher than in coordinated systems (Traxler 1998). Firms retain less long term commitment to workers and labour turnover is also higher, reducing the incentive to invest in skills, the benefits of which might be easily and quickly procured by a competitor (Dahl 2002).

Reflecting the characteristics of the industrial relations system, the education and training system in the competitive model is less oriented towards equality. For example, in the United States, it has been suggested that education is divided between mass institutions and elite institutions (Lam 2002: 9–10). The former are oriented towards the promotion of behaviours, such as 'punctuality, obedience, regular and orderly work habits' (Hollingsworth 1997: 270), which are suitable for low and semi-skilled work at the bottom of an organizational hierarchy. There is little emphasis on cognitive or technical skills, which are instead promoted in elite institutions with wealthier students, whose employment paths are directed towards higher positions in organizational hierarchies and professional careers. As Hollingsworth explains, this model of education is highly supportive of mass production systems which rely on semi-skilled labour carrying out routine tasks and subject to control through organizational hierarchies (1997: 270–1).

The coordinated model of industrial relations and education and training has important implications for innovation. By reducing labour turnover, the system encourages investment in training, as workers are less likely to transfer skills to other companies (Lam 2002: 18). The benefits of investment in training are less likely to be reaped by competitors. At the same time, by discouraging cost reduction strategies including low wage employment, the system creates an incentive for investment in technology and new capital equipment, and the pursuit of quality-based competitiveness focussing on high technology, high skills, and productivity improvements. High wages can encourage firms to invest in new capital stock and to seek productivity enhancement through the adoption of new process technology, because they are precluded from competing on the basis of low wage costs (Streeck 1996).

Low wage differentials in the coordinated model can also encourage innovation. High wage differentials can be harmful to innovative firms, because they can be associated with high (excessive) wage claims in sectors of the economy that are highly innovative and highly profitable, reducing the rewards for risk taking entrepreneurs. At the same time, low profit non-entrepreneurial firms are advantaged by lower wage claims (Soskice 1990; Kleinknecht 1998). It follows that barriers to wage inequality can encourage innovative behaviour and discourage low productivity strategies. The broad based vocational training system and coordinated industrial relations system in Germany is thought to have resulted in low wage differentials and broad collective bargaining coverage, forcing German employers to adopt quality enhancing strategies rather than cost minimization strategies for competitive success. This is thought to be an important basis for innovation in medium technology industries such as automobiles (Streeck 1996: 145–6).

However, it is important to note that the highly flexible labour market and differentiated education institutions associated with the competitive model, and typical of the United States economy, are thought to contribute to learning and innovation in a different way. The flexible labour market facilitates inter-firm mobility of highly professional workers pursuing inter-firm career paths. This is thought to encourage innovation by transferring technological expertise across firms and encouraging entrepreneurial behaviour as professionals establish new firms (Saxenian 1996). The success of Silicon Valley is linked to this inter-firm mobility of professionals, but also depends on other institutions, including the presence of world-class universities which attract high quality students and act as a supplier of elite professionals to local networks of high technology firms (Lam 2002: 21). Thus, although the flexible labour market is thought to encourage transfer of knowledge and entrepreneurial activity, it is clear that it also depends on a supply of highly trained and skilled workers from educational institutions.

It should be noted that the coordinated model of industrial relations, based heavily on national collective bargaining systems, is experiencing some change, although the role of collective bargaining remains central. There are several trends which might result in longer term variation in the coordinated system of labour relations; these include 'opening' clauses in collective agreements which allow firms to depart from standards that have been established in collective agreements in particular situations, including economic crisis, in which a firm is unable to meet the standards, or in the case of small companies, which may not be able to afford the same conditions as larger firms. Further, as a result of the influence of the European Union, there has been a greater emphasis on the protection of labour rights through juridification rather than collective agreement (Visser 2005: 296–303). While these changes may result in variation in the coordinated systems of industrial relations in the longer term, the coordinated model remains distinctive from the competitive regime in its continued emphasis on collective agreements.

The finance sector

The importance of the finance sector to innovation has been explained in comparative studies of finance–industry relations (Christensen 1992). In coordinated systems, institutional arrangements have existed which have encouraged banks to support innovative activities through the provision of long term funds based on close and reciprocal long term relationships with firms. This has been characteristic of bank-based financial systems such as in Germany (Deeg 1997). These arrangements have enabled banks to have access to information that allows them to closely monitor industry. The rewards of learning associated with investment in training and technology are long term (Patel and Pavitt 1991). Bank-based financial systems have been regarded as more accepting of a long term outlook, because banks monitor firm strategies more closely and are therefore able to evaluate investments in intangibles such as training and research, both of which are important for innovation. In more recent times, these systems have been referred to as 'stakeholder' or 'control-oriented' systems because of their high concentration of debt and equity, and high level of investor control (Tylecote and Conesa 1999: 26–7).

This model also has direct benefits for innovation. As Soskice (1999: 109) explains, banks gather information from a variety of sources, including research institutions, customers and suppliers and business associations, ensuring the banks have access to information about industry-specific technologies and are able to evaluate projects with longer term potential. This results in a form of lending that can be described as 'relational', in which lending is part of a long-term relationship between the bank and the firm. This model is highly supportive of medium technology industries, such as mechanical engineering, in which innovation is decentralized. In these industries, innovation may occur at the point of production or in the nature of work organization, and is therefore difficult for outsiders to evaluate without the assistance of longer-term and well developed relationships (Visintin, Ozgen, Tylecote and Handscombe 2005: 622).

In contrast, the competitive system has a well developed capital market, traditionally referred to as a stock market based on arm's length financial system, in which industry has depended heavily on share holdings for investment support (Tylecote and Conesa 1999: 30–2). In this model, there has been a strong emphasis on short-term financial considerations, because of the dominance of portfolio holders who have no particular allegiance to any company or industry and demand short-term returns on investment. In this model, bank lending has been transactional, involving one-off relationships that tie lending to security. This has sometimes been associated with behaviour that is speculative in orientation and therefore discouraging of investment in technology and new capital equipment, which require large immediate outlays with returns in the long term. Further, the advantages of investments in intangibles such as research and training may not be easily visible to outsiders, and are therefore unlikely to be supported in this model (Zysman 1983; Tylecote 1994: 260–1).

However, the competitive system is usually also associated with well developed venture capital markets, which are important for new start-up firms. In this situation, the bank-based model may be of little help, as there is no pre-existing relationship between the firm and the bank. This would indicate that the stock market model, with its speculative orientation, might be more supportive of investment in new firm start-ups in high technology sectors, where the risks and potential rewards are both high. Further, the stock market model may be suitable in firms where research activity is centralized within the organization (such as with pharmaceuticals) and therefore more visible to outsiders with little relationship to the firm (Christensen 1992: 162; Tylecote 1994: 263–5; Visintin *et al.* 2005: 622).

The structure of firms

A further influence on innovation is the structure of firms (Nooteboom 2000). According to Whitley (1996: 43–5), firms in different societies can be categorized according to whether they demonstrate high levels of diversification (being engaged in a range of product lines or relying on a variety of resources, skills and technologies), or whether they specialize in activities that are closely-related and dependent on the same organizational capabilities. The former are the typical M-form (diversified and vertically integrated) firms, whereas the latter are more typical of holding companies (with loose relationships between specialized organizational units) or small specialized firms (Kristensen 1996).

In the competitive model, the M-form organization is thought to dominate. Williamson (1975), explained the emergence of the multi-divisional diversified (M-form) organization in capitalist economies as an attempt to reduce the costs of market transactions. Rather than transacting all business as isolated individuals in the market place, some transactions could be internalized within an organizational structure, reducing costs and the possibility for opportunistic behaviour (Granovetter 1985). Williamson's explanation of the emergence of firms remains true to the assumptions of neo-classical thought that considers the utility-maximizing behaviour of rational actors concerned with efficiency gains who formed organizations to reduce the costs of market transactions. This has been particularly important in mass production organizations, regarded as typical of the competitive system. These organizations have sought to reduce transaction costs through vertical integration, eliminating relations with customers and suppliers, which were highly transactional and focussed on price, by subsuming diverse functions within the firm (Hollingsworth 1997: 270).

In contrast, firms engaged in more specialized activities associated with core competencies or organizational capabilities are often embedded in supportive inter-organizational relationships with other firms, and are typical of the coordinated system. These relationships have been described as networks, and represent an alternative to pure market relationships and vertically integrated hierarchical organizational structures typical of the M-form firms. Inter-organizational relationships between firms can involve networks based on joint ventures or strategic alliances, or less formal relationships within geographical clusters of firms. These inter-organizational relationships coordinate economic behaviour through a diversity of decision-making processes and social relationships (Hage and Alter 1997). Networks might coordinate behaviour for the purposes of research, product development, setting of industry standards, financing, marketing or distribution. Clusters, which are typically informal geographically-based inter-organizational relationships, involve a range of relatively stable linkages between customers and suppliers, trade associations, universities, public research institutions and vocational training bodies (Porter 1998). These relationships allow for information sharing, more certain access to suppliers and trained employees, greater certainty in economic behaviour and shared risk.

Industry associations are also important institutions in the coordinated model, because they provide the possibility for mutual consultation and information-sharing, and for members to influence each others' decisions and therefore contribute to coordination in the innovation system. These associations facilitate cooperation between economic actors and encourage the identification of common goals. They provide an organizational complex within which economic decisions can be negotiated and future economic directions determined. Industry associations also provide an information gathering function, and constitute an institutional infrastructure for inter-organizational research and training (Coleman 1997). In coordinated economies, the role of centralized industrial associations is well developed, facilitating both cooperation between firms and cooperation with labour in the negotiation of wages and conditions across industries or the economy as a whole. In contrast, in the competitive system, the role of industrial associations is weak, both in coordinating the activities of firms and in cooperative relations with labour movements (Soskice 1999).

Differences in firm structures and the character of industry associations have implications for firm behaviour and innovation. Diversified firms that are vertically integrated, such as those typical of the competitive system, are more likely to dramatically alter current organizational capabilities through the radical adoption of new product lines, technologies or skills. This is because management remains autonomous both within the organization, in terms of its control over hiring, firing and work organization, and outside of the organization, in terms of its relative isolation and independence from relationships with other institutions or organizations. As such, organizations in the competitive model are thought to have a greater capacity for radical innovation than organizations in the coordinated model. The more specialized production units associated with the coordinated model are likely to adopt incremental approaches to change that are closely tied to current capabilities. This is because these firms are strongly embedded in relationships with other economic actors, including unions, banks, business associations or other firms in which mutual dependency constrains firms to specialized activities and renders radical new trajectories difficult to pursue (Whitley 1994: 56). In this model, organizations have a greater capacity for incremental innovation, which depends on the accumulated knowledge of loyal employees and long term relations with customers, suppliers and other institutions in the firm's business environment.

Values

Although the above discussion has highlighted institutional differences between the coordinated and competitive systems and explained the implications of those differences for the process and nature of innovation, it is important to note that prevailing values – norms, beliefs and codes of behaviour – also differ between the two types of capitalism and tend to reinforce cross-national institutional differences. Cultural factors may explain, among other things, socially-specific attitudes to science, industrialization, cooperation, and change.

In the coordinated system there is an emphasis on trust and cohesion (increasingly referred to as social capital) which impacts on organizational structures and inter-organizational relationships. Coordinated societies that are suspicious of authority are resistant to hierarchical organizational structures and favour the small specialized units of production typical of coordinated capitalism. The values of trust, cooperation, collectivism and uncertainty-avoidance usually associated with the coordinated model are compatible with inter-organizational relationships such as networks which depend on cooperation and are also typical of coordinated types of capitalism (Steensma, Marino, Weaver and Dickson 2000). These values therefore reinforce the institutional characteristics of the coordinated model.

In contrast, in the competitive model, greater importance is attributed to competition, profit and individualism, which are often associated with entrepreneurialism and therefore regarded as supportive of new and high risk activities characterized by a high level of uncertainty (Herbig, Golden and Dunphy 1994; Shane 1995). When alliances do occur, they are usually contractual in nature, because of a desire to retain arm's length association (Tiessen 1997). Further, these societies are more accepting of inequality, and therefore hierarchical business organizations typical of standardized production organizations and M-form organizations are compatible with prevailing social values. As with the coordinated model, values tend to reinforce key institutional arrangements which comprise the competitive system.

The performance of innovation systems

The above discussion has highlighted the various institutions that constitute the national system of innovation, and distinguished between the institutional characteristics of two types of capitalism – coordinated and competitive. The Northern European countries including Germany and Scandinavia are usually regarded as coordinated systems, and Japan is often regarded as a variation of the coordinated model. The United States and other English speaking countries more closely fit a competitive model. As these models are theoretical types, no country fits the coordinated or competitive system in its entirety, and regional and sectoral variations within countries are typical.

In seeking to understand the relationship between institutional contexts and the performance of national systems of innovation, it is useful to search for differences that might exist between the coordinated and competitive models. The following discussion highlights the different types of industries that are favoured by the institutional contexts of coordinated and competitive models of capitalism.

The literature on competitive and coordinated economies gives rise to a number of findings on the empirical relationship between systems of industrial coordination and economic performance. Vivien Schmidt's review of four studies of state–industry relations suggests that coordinated economies potentially produce positive outcomes for industry and the economy:

> … companies in cultures that emphasize community and cooperation benefit from more productive interfirm relations than companies in individualistic cultures … a history of government controlled or managed competition is more beneficial to long-term firm success than a laissez-faire approach that

increases adjustment difficulties during economic downturns ... centralized, statist policymaking processes of interventionist governments can under certain circumstances prove more successful than less interventionist governments ... governance systems with cooperative labor relations, quality worker training programs, large powerful unions, and close assembly–supplier relations tend to benefit firms competitiveness more than systems with weak unions, conflictual labor relations, poor training programs, and distant or unequal assembly–supplier relations.

(Schmidt 1996: 238–9)

However, much of the literature does not seek to develop an argument about the superiority of one system over the other. The suggestion is simply that particular systems give rise to competitiveness in different types of industries. In respect of innovation, coordinated and competitive models are thought to give rise to quite different innovative capacities.

As explained above, the coordinated model, typical of Germany and Sweden, is regarded as being oriented towards incremental innovations, particularly in medium technology industries. The high business costs in Germany and Sweden have been regarded as driving firms to adopt a strategy of diversified quality production that has involved the mass production of high quality products (Matraves 1997; Streeck 1997). This was seen as the basis of Germany and Sweden's industrial success, and was associated with good performance in a range of medium technology industries such as engineering and chemicals. The German and Swedish models are now viewed as highly conducive to the rapid diffusion of incremental innovations within existing industrial enterprises, rather than radical innovations in new industries (Carlsson 1996). The focus of innovation is on the development and application of new technologies to existing production activities, as opposed to the development of new products and processes.

In contrast, the competitive model, typical of the United States, is regarded as conducive to the rapid development of new technologies. In the United States, large venture capital markets, an entrepreneurial business culture, close linkages between universities and industry, and a highly mobile labour force have been regarded as critical elements of the business system which have encouraged the development of new technology firms in new industries (Walsh, Niosi and Mustar 1995). As Mowery and Rosenberg explain:

The successive waves of new product technologies that have swept through the postwar U.S. economy, including semiconductors, computers, and biotechnology, have been commercialized in large part through the efforts of new firms. The role of small firms in commercializing new technologies in the United States during this period appears to contrast with the pattern in both Japan and Western Europe, where established firms in electronics, pharmaceuticals, and other industries have played a more significant role in technology development.

(Mowery and Rosenberg 1992: 48)

The highly flexible external labour market in the United States may have constrained investment in training within firms, but it is thought to have facilitated the success of regional clusters of high technology firms, such as in Silicon Valley, by enabling technology diffusion between firms by highly skilled employees, and also by providing the possibility for researchers in public industrial laboratories and universities to move into industry and commercialize their innovations (Hollingsworth 1997: 292–4; Mowery and Rosenberg 1992: 49; Saxenian 1996). In addition, the well developed venture capital market in the United States, which has been willing to support risky new ventures, is regarded as having contributed to the development of new small firms in new industries, such as biotechnology (Casper 2000; Hollingsworth 1997: 293).

The above discussion has highlighted the general competitive orientation of the coordinated and competitive systems. Some recent work has questioned the findings of the varieties of capitalism literature regarding the association between the institutional environment and performance in different types of industries. The simple dichotomy sometimes drawn between competitive or liberal market economies and coordinated market economies, which suggests that the former have a comparative institutional advantage in high technology industries, is not reflected in the aggregate data. Recent longitudinal cross-national analysis of the innovation patterns of coordinated and competitive economies suggests that, if the United States is excluded from the group of liberal market economies, patterns of innovation do not conform to predictions of the Hall and Soskice (2001) varieties of capitalism model (Taylor 2004), suggesting that theoretical accounts of the strengths of liberal market economies are inadequate. Recently, Casper and Kettler (2001) have provided insights into the way in which public policies designed to compensate for deficiencies in the national institutional framework, such as insufficient sources of high risk capital, can interact with stable and core elements of the national institutional framework to result in a hybridization of business models. As such, public policy intervention may be able to compensate for deficiencies in the national institutional framework, which would otherwise impede the development of particular industries. Further, recent work indicates that the institutional variables incorporated within the varieties of capitalism approach need to be broadened to take into account regional-level institutions and policies as well as dimensions of the systems of innovation, as discussed in the previous chapter, in order to provide a fuller account of comparative performance in knowledge activities (Parker and Tamaschke 2005; Parker 2006).

It is possible to supplement this broad analysis of the competitive strengths of different varieties of capitalism with more specific quantitative measures of innovation performance. There are various quantitative measures that can be used to analyse national systems of innovation. These include inputs into the innovation system, such as expenditure on research and development by government and business. An alternative mechanism for measuring the performance of innovation systems is to examine the structure of the economic activity and the extent to which nations engage in knowledge intensive activities.

Expenditure on research and development (R&D) is used as a measure of input into the innovation system. Although new knowledge is often derived from less formal processes than those associated with public research institutions and research and development units within companies (Smith 2000), R&D measures are still of some importance because they indicate the extent to which public institutions and business corporations devote resources to the development of new knowledge. This is critical in industry sectors that are formally defined as high-technology sectors, such as pharmaceuticals, aircraft, computing, telecommunications equipment and medical instruments.

Figure 8.1 reports gross domestic expenditure on R&D (GERD) as a percentage of GDP. Sweden has high levels of expenditure on research and development at almost 4 percent of GDP. Sweden, Japan, the United States and Germany are the top performers in terms of expenditure on R&D. Italy and Australia fall well below the OECD average. In Figure 8.2, research and development expenditure is broken down by source of funds, indicating the balance between public and private funding of R&D. In Germany, Japan, Sweden and the United States, business enterprise contribution to R&D expenditure is at or above the average for the OECD area. In Australia and Italy, business contributes less than the OECD average; the data indicate that it is the business sector which is contributing to the poor overall R&D performance in these countries. The data on input into the innovation system do not reveal any clear differences between coordinated and competitive countries. The United States is regarded as the typical competitive economy and Sweden is a coordinated economy, but both have relatively high levels of R&D spending and similar levels of business contribution to total R&D.

R&D is a measure of inputs into the innovation system; the overall accumulated performance of the innovation system can be analysed with reference to a number of measures. One is the presence of knowledge-based industries, which produce technology, and knowledge-based services, which are critical users of technology (OECD 1999c: 18). Figure 8.3 shows that France, the United Kingdom, the United States and Germany perform above the OECD average in terms of value added in knowledge-based industries and services. The total contribution of knowledge-based industries and services to value added varies from around 24 percent in Canada to around 32 percent in Germany.

This measure can be broken down into two sectors – manufacturing sector producers of knowledge intensive goods, and service sector users of high technology products. An interesting picture emerges of the relative strengths and weaknesses of different countries when knowledge-based activities are broken down into the producer and user components. Figure 8.4 shows the contribution of major producers of knowledge products – high and medium-high technology manufacturing industries. These are industries which are regarded as contributing to rising profits and wages and are of increasing importance in international markets; as such, their contribution within the innovation system can be regarded as critical. The importance of these industries varies from around 9 to 12 percent of value added in Germany, Japan and Sweden to around 3 percent in Australia. It is

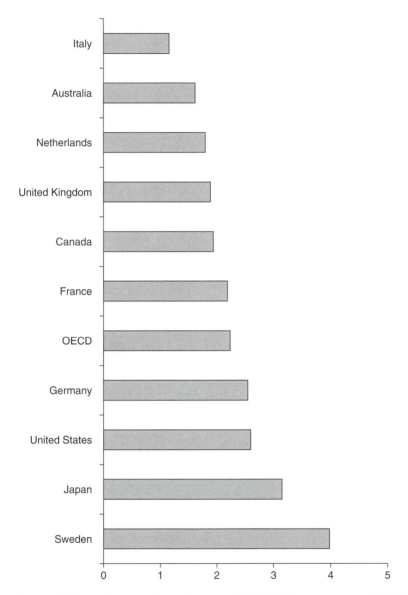

Figure 8.1 Gross Domestic Expenditure on R&D (GERD) as percentage GDP, 2003 or
nearest year.

Source: OECD (2005a), Table A.2.1, page 190.

important to note that the three best performers – Germany, Japan and Sweden –
are all coordinated economies as explained above. This perhaps indicates a
strength amongst coordinated economies in the production of knowledge intensive goods.

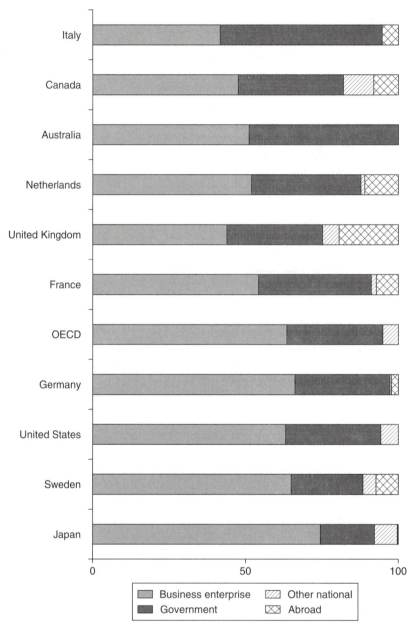

Figure 8.2 R&D expenditure by source of funds, percentages, 2003 or nearest year.
Source: Adapted from OECD (2005a), Table A.3.1, page 192.

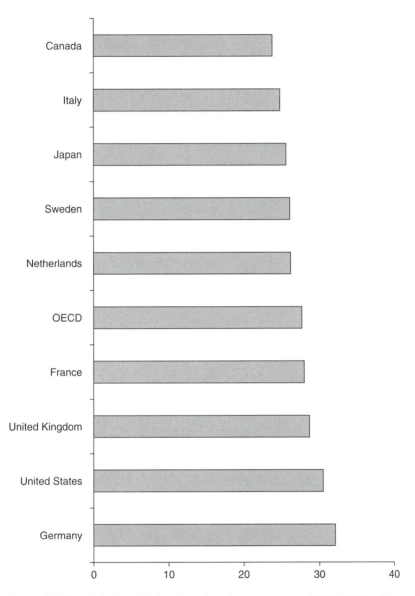

Figure 8.3 Knowledge based industries and services, percentage of GDP, 2002 or latest year.
Source: OECD (2005a), Table F.5, page 204.

Figure 8.5 reports the breakdown of services industries which the OECD has defined as critical users of technology. In the services area, the United States and the United Kingdom are the strongest performers. These are both competitive market economies, perhaps indicating a strength amongst competitive market

Figure 8.4 High and medium-high technology industries, share in business value added, percentages, 2002 or nearest year.

Source: Adapted from OECD (2005a), Table F.5, page 204.

economies in knowledge intensive services. While Sweden and Japan performed at a high level in relation to the production of knowledge intensive products, they perform below the OECD average in relation to knowledge intensive

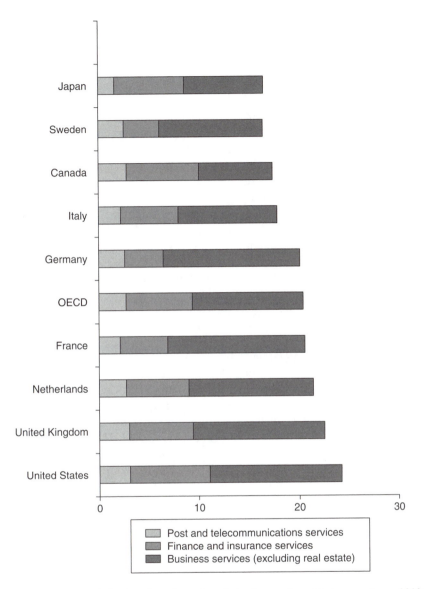

Figure 8.5 Knowledge based services, share in business value added, percentages, 2002 or
nearest year.

Source: Adapted from OECD (2005a), Table F.5, page 204.

services. Sweden performs particularly poorly in relation to finance and insurance
services – perhaps indicating a weakness in this coordinated economy. However,
it should be noted that both France and Germany perform at the OECD level in

terms of their orientation towards knowledge intensive services, and these countries do not fit the competitive model. An important distinction between the United States on the one hand and France and Germany on the other is that, in the United States the strength is in finance and insurance services, whereas in France and Germany the strength is in business services. This may reflect the more liberal financial structures of the United States and its central place in international financial markets.

While these data do not present a consistent picture of the comparative performance of coordinated and competitive economies, there is some indication that coordinated economies have a relative strength in the production of knowledge intensive goods, whereas competitive market economies such as the US have a strength in finance and insurance services – a sector that is regarded as a critical user of knowledge intensive products.

A final measure of the innovative environment might include the level of social cohesion, which provides an indirect measure of the breadth of participation in the knowledge economy and the extent of (what is increasingly referred to as) the 'digital divide', or gap between those with knowledge resources and those without. In societies with high social cohesion, it might be argued that there is broad participation in knowledge activities, and the benefits of the knowledge economy are broadly spread throughout the society. In contrast, in societies with low levels of cohesion, it might be argued that participation in the knowledge economy is restricted, and the benefits are reaped by a narrow segment of the population.

Figure 8.6 shows that, in the United States, wage inequality is higher than in coordinated economies such as Sweden and Germany. The level of inequality in the United States has increased dramatically over the last three decades. The ratio of CEO pay to that of the average production worker in the United States has risen from 42 to 1 in 1980 to 419 to 1 in 1998 (Evans 2000). This would suggest that certain groups, often high skilled knowledge workers and senior managers of major corporations, benefit from the growth of the new economy, while other less skilled groups are excluded from the rewards of knowledge activities.

It would seem that the level of inequality is related to the level of trust (Figure 8.7). The percentage of the population that believes that most people can be trusted is higher in Sweden and the Netherlands (with low levels of income inequality) than in the United States and the United Kingdom (competitive economies with high levels of income inequality).

The relationships discussed above are not perfect, and some countries depart from the general pattern. However, it seems that alongside success in medium-high and high technology production, coordinated economies have achieved social equality and cohesion. In contrast, while countries such as the United States have also achieved success in knowledge intensive activities, particularly in the finance and insurance sector, success has not always been linked to social cohesion and income equality. It might be argued that the benefits of the new economy have been more widely felt in the coordinated than the competitive economies.

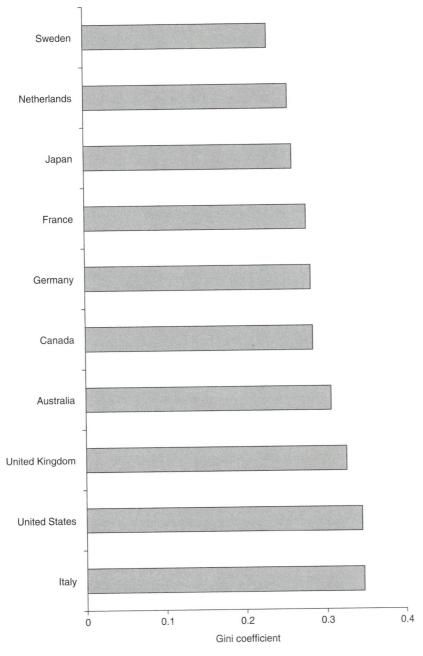

Figure 8.6 Income inequality for entire population, based on disposable income, mid-1990s.
Source: OECD (2001c), page 81.

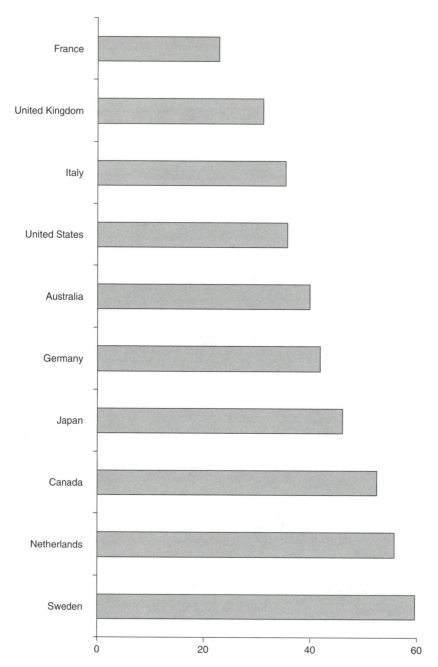

Figure 8.7 Trust – percentage of people saying that most people can be trusted, 1995–1996.
Source: World Values Survey reported in OECD (2001c), page 44.

Conclusion

This chapter has highlighted the continuing differences in advanced economies in key national institutions such as the state, the industrial relations system, the system of education and training, the structure of business organizations and the role of intermediary organization such as the finance sector and industry associations. These differences have been shown to be important in explaining the competitive orientation of different countries towards particular types of industries. National institutions have been shown to be important in terms of the way in which they affect innovation and ultimately influence the uptake of particular kinds of knowledge intensive activities. This chapter has therefore shown that, despite the global economic changes depicted in Chapter 7, the institutional configuration of society is still important to industry performance and social outcomes.

The chapter has drawn a conceptual distinction between competitive and coordinated market economies. The former have an emphasis on market relations and autonomous business units. In the latter, relations within corporations (between management and employees) and with external organizations and institutions (including other firms, suppliers, customers, research institutions and educational institutions) are more developed. Some of the coordinated economies have been shown to have an orientation towards success in the production of knowledge intensive goods, particularly in medium technology sectors. In contrast, some competitive economies have been shown to favour knowledge intensive service activities, particularly in the finance and insurance sector. However, not all competitive and coordinated economies fit that pattern. Further, it is difficult to draw any general conclusion about the relative innovative performance of competitive or coordinated economies. It would seem that some coordinated economies, such as Sweden, have been successful in new economy or knowledge intensive activities, particularly in medium and high technology manufacturing industries. However, it is also the case that the competitive economy of the United States has been successful in knowledge intensive activities, particularly in the finance and insurance service sector.

The chapter has shown that it is possible to capture knowledge intensive activities with either a competitive or coordinated institutional environment. However, the chapter has also shown that in coordinated economies, success in knowledge industries is more broadly felt throughout society through a high level of income equality and social cohesion. So, while the competitive and coordinated models might both have the capacity for engaging in knowledge intensive activities, it is only in the coordinated model that the rewards of the new economy translate into broader social benefits. It should also be noted that not all knowledge intensive activities are alike, and while participation in the knowledge economy has the potential to contribute to rising wages and profits, it does not necessarily result in widespread improvement in work and employment arrangements, as taken up in the next chapter.

9 New technology and the future of work

Employment restructuring, organizational change and the quality of jobs

Concerns about unemployment and technological change have a long history dating from the industrial revolution (see Ricardo 1821). However, the focus of attention has sharpened over the past three decades as the rapid introduction of new technologies, the ascendancy of neo-liberal economic policies and broader processes of globalization have been held responsible for perceived social changes in production and consumption and the relations and organization of work.

The aim of this chapter is to draw together many of the themes developed in previous chapters about one of these factors – the use of new technology in the workplace and the implications for the organization of contemporary work. The linking thread in this chapter is the manner in which both the quantity and the quality of jobs have changed as new technologies have been utilized to manage production. One of the key tasks of the chapter is to review, if not to reconcile, alternative accounts of technological change and employment that have developed almost independently in economics on the one hand and political economy and sociology on the other. Both approaches will be explored to develop an analytical framework to review the empirical evidence for long term structural changes in employment in industry sectors, and the dynamic changes in knowledge and skills that characterize the contemporary economy.

Long term structural changes in technology and employment in modern economies

The notion that technological innovation was embedded in the structural dynamics of the capitalist economy was introduced by Kondratieff (1935). His analysis of the historical patterns of capitalist investment concluded that it was possible to model long waves of economic development during which there is an increase in output and productivity associated with the take-up of technological innovation. In this model, productivity reaches a plateau after some decades, followed by a downturn in activity as the previous generation of technology and innovation loses its impact. The next upturn of the cycle is then driven by further technological discovery and implementation. While identification of these long waves has been subject to much conjecture, the model does draw attention to the discontinuous or cyclical nature of technological development and the social tensions and crises that it superintends, especially in its impact on jobs.

Kondratieff's analysis was taken up by Schumpeter (1939) who, more than any other economist, placed the dynamics of technological innovation at the centre of economic growth and employment. Schumpeter stressed that the characteristics of technological innovation and their diffusion throughout industry had the potential to bring about major disturbances in the economy centred on cyclical, technological unemployment. Schumpeter viewed the process of technological innovation as a major source of disequilibrium. He argued that innovation tended to be concentrated in key sectors or industries, giving rise to problems of structural adjustment between sectors as one grew and another declined. The process of diffusion of innovation was also shown to be an inherently uneven process with cyclical characteristics. A significant aspect of the patterns of innovation was the tendency for the mass take-up of new technologies to erode the profitability and opportunities for further investment by innovating firms.

Much of the contemporary economic debate has elaborated the Schumpeterian insights into the process of innovation and diffusion, and endeavoured to relate features of the process of technological change to long term changes in employment and unemployment (see Petit 1995). Contemporary analyses concentrate on the way in which technological change can affect the demand for labour in particular sectors or industries. The mechanism generally involves technological changes that increase the productivity of labour, and therefore reduce the amount of labour required per unit of output.

Soete (2001) summarizes the discussion, stating that the deployment of new technologies may have two effects: it may lead to more efficient production processes that reduce the costs of labour, capital or materials, or it may lead to the development of new products that generate new demand. The job losses that often follow the introduction of labour saving processes may be compensated by job creation associated with output growth, if organizations reduce prices as a result of productivity gains or increased investment in new products. Employment generation may also be created in other industries that are able to develop and supply these new technology-driven production processes as commodities, such as off-the-shelf software and hardware products. In this analysis, a great deal depends on the increase in demand following the reduction in prices. The linkages become more complex when temporal and spatial processes are considered. That is, a range of macro and micro-economic adjustment mechanisms impact on the time it takes for labour displaced from one industry to be re-employed in another. Moreover, the economy is not a closed system and the surplus value created by technological advancement in one society may well be mobilized in another society (Baldry 1988: 19). In a globalized framework, there is some likelihood that new employment may be generated in countries different to that in which the original organizational changes led to a decline in employment.

Modelling these outcomes needs to take into account demand elasticities in the industries affected, rates of factor substitution and augmentation with respect to the new technology, and labour and skill flexibilities. This includes the extent to which displaced employees are sufficiently mobile to be able to move from declining sectors to those in which employment opportunities are expanding (see Cyert and Mowery 1987: 51). All of these factors need to be set against possibly multiple trajectories and directions of technological change (Soete 1987: 34–5). Many contributors to the literature have begun to focus on the internal dynamics of organizational change; specifically the adjustments to industrial relations and work organization to make the most efficient use of new technologies at the local level have been considered (Petit 1995: 398). For Petit and Soete, these processes involve 'various coordination problems: how to bring about changes on the shop floor, at the organization level of production and distribution [and] at the institutional level' (2001: 3). However, these seemingly innocuous observations highlight some of the difficulties associated with assuming that technological change is an independent, external factor impacting on employment. This is an oversimplified theory of technological change that views new technologies as inexorable processes requiring consequential changes in particular patterns of social organization and social relations.

New technologies typically emerge not from instances of inspiration or discovery but from existing technology by a process of gradual change. They do not independently impose changes at the organizational level of production but may certainly be applied with that intent. It is less the invention of new products and processes and their initial commercial exploitation that generate changes in the process of production than their diffusion and application across industry. For most firms in manufacturing and services, buying and assimilating new technologies embodied in hardware and software is the main avenue of its diffusion. As MacKenzie and Wajcman correctly note 'technologies can be designed, consciously or unconsciously to open certain social options and to close others' (1999: 4). An important related aspect of the use of technologies is that technologies currently applied to the way work is organized have a significant influence on those new technologies that are adopted. Thus technologies that replace labour or reduce the cost of labour will be likely to prevail in those sectors or societies where there is an established, social and political pattern of acceptance of such changes. On the other hand, technologies that facilitate the interests of employees in protecting pay, job security, skill development and participation in decisions about work will be likely to prevail in sectors or societies in which labour interests have tended to be prominent.

The point is that these are political questions about which social groups have the power to influence decisions to develop and implement new technologies. Political power as it pertains to the organization of work will, in turn, be determined by: levels of unionization; the strength of institutions that represent employer or employee interests in industrial relations or broader policy arenas; dominant policy agendas; and the ideological predispositions of political parties in power.

There are two important questions that arise out of the previous discussion. The first concerns the *quality* of jobs and levels of skill and participation in workplace decision-making that have developed out of technological changes. The second question, to which we now turn, focusses on the impact of new technology on structural change and the *quantity* of jobs that are destroyed or generated in the process.

Table 9.1 Sectoral contributions to gross value added, percentages

	Industry		Manufacturing		Services	
	1991	2001	1991	2001	1991	2001
Australia	28.3	25.6	13.5	11.7	68.2	70.6
France	29.5	25.5	20.5	18.4	67.1	71.7
Germany	37.9	30.1	28.5	23.0	60.7	68.6
Italy	32.9	29.0	23.7	21.0	63.4	68.2
Japan	38.9	31.0	26.5	20.8	58.8	67.7
Netherlands	30.2	27.0	18.7	16.2	65.4	70.3
United Kingdom	33.1	27.6	21.6	17.4	65.1	71.6
United States	26.8	22.8	19.0	15.0	71.3	75.6

Source: OECD (2003).

Employment restructuring

Large historical shifts in the way in which production processes are organized and the technological changes that have facilitated them have promoted continuous structural changes in the economies of the major developed countries. Across the OECD countries there has been a general and significant decline in the contribution of industry to GDP which now accounts for approximately 27 percent across the top 20 OECD countries. This has been paralleled by an increase in the contribution of services which now account for approximately 70 percent across the same countries. Table 9.1 portrays the decline in industry (and manufacturing in particular) in eight large OECD economies over the decade from 1991 to 2001.

The table shows that manufacturing's contribution to gross value added fell by four to five percentage points in a relatively short time in Germany, Japan, the United Kingdom and the United States. The manufacturing sector has traditionally been the main driver of productivity growth in the OECD countries, and its decline in recent years has altered the quality and characteristics of aggregate employment, particularly in areas associated with skilled and semi-skilled work in manufacturing. In summary, the dynamism of the manufacturing sector can no longer be considered the pre-eminent factor in employment generation that it was in the first half of the twentieth century.

The reallocation of employment from industry to services is documented in Table 9.2. The table shows that in Australia, the Netherlands, Sweden, the United Kingdom and the United States the service sector now accounts for three quarters of all employment. Service sector employment as a percentage of civilian employment has also increased significantly by as much as 25 to 30 percentage points in countries such as Australia, France, Germany, Italy, Japan, and Sweden.

However, this structural transformation is clouded by a number of important factors. First, many activities such as human resources management, marketing, and financial accounting traditionally undertaken by integrated manufacturing firms have now been outsourced to firms located in the service sector. Decline in

Table 9.2 Civilian employment in industry and services

Industry as a percentage of civilian employment

	1965	1970	1975	1980	1985	1990	1995	2000	2005
Australia	40.2	36.4	33.5	30.9	27.3	24.9	22.8	21.7	21.0
France	39.1	39.2	38.6	35.7	32.0	29.7	26.3	24.1	22.6
Germany	49.3	49.3	45.4	43.7	41.0	38.6	36.3	33.7	30.0
Italy	37.0	39.5	39.2	37.9	33.6	32.3	34.1	32.4	31.1
Japan	32.4	35.7	35.9	35.3	34.9	34.1	33.6	31.2	27.9
Netherlands	–	–	34.9	31.4	28.1	26.3	22.6	21.2	20.3
Sweden	42.8	38.4	36.5	32.2	29.8	29.2	25.9	24.6	22.0
United Kingdom	33.2	30.7	40.4	37.6	34.8	32.3	27.3	25.2	22.1
United States	21.4	20.7	30.6	30.5	28.0	26.2	24.0	23.0	19.8

Services as a percentage of civilian employment

	1965	1970	1975	1980	1985	1990	1995	2000	2005
Australia	50.2	55.6	59.7	62.6	66.4	69.0	72.2	73.4	75.3
France	43.1	47.2	51.0	55.1	60.8	64.6	69.1	72.0	73.9
Germany	39.8	42.1	47.8	51.0	54.4	57.9	60.5	63.7	67.6
Italy	36.8	40.3	44.1	47.8	55.2	58.8	59.2	62.2	64.6
Japan	44.1	46.9	51.5	54.2	56.4	58.7	60.8	63.7	67.6
Netherlands	–	–	59.4	63.8	67.0	69.1	73.7	75.5	76.6
Sweden	45.9	53.5	57.1	62.2	65.3	67.4	71.0	73.0	76.0
United Kingdom	65.0	67.7	56.8	59.7	63.0	65.5	70.7	73.3	76.5
United States	75.3	77.2	65.3	65.9	68.8	70.9	73.1	74.4	78.6

Sources: OECD (1986); OECD (1999b: 32–4); OECD (2006: 32–5).

employment in one sector and growth in another may thus, in part, be a statistical artefact of the manner in which economic sectors are defined. Second, while manufacturing is declining both in terms of its share of GDP and of employment, the segment described as high technology manufacturing has expanded its share of GDP. In general, however, this expansion has not been accompanied by an increase in employment (OECD 1998: 37–8).

For the OECD area as a whole, service employment is rising rapidly in two contrasting areas: community, social and personal services; and finance, insurance and business services. Employment growth in services has involved some high skilled jobs and a preponderance of low skilled and low paid jobs – in such areas as shelf-filling, cleaning, domestic service, warehousing, security services, retailing, and hospitality services. In other words, manual labour has migrated to the service sector (Nolan and Wood 2003). In most of the advanced economies, we are witnessing the emergence of an hourglass economy characterized by highly-paid, two adult earner households in high skilled jobs, and a growing underclass of wage labourers in low skilled jobs (Nolan 2004). In manufacturing, the somewhat dramatic decline in employment (see Table 9.3) has been associated with a substantial decrease in blue-collar, routine jobs that are classified as low skilled. The once dominant manufacturing sectors of the OECD economies

Table 9.3 Civilian employment in manufacturing, percentages

	1965	1970	1975	1980	1985	1990	1995	2000	2005
Australia	30.5	26.4	23.4	19.7	16.4	15.1	13.5	12.5	10.7
Canada	33.2	22.3	20.2	19.7	–	15.6	14.3	15.2	13.6
Germany	38.3	39.4	35.6	34.3	–	–	25.2	23.8	22.1
Italy	37.0	39.5	39.2	26.8	–	–	24.7	23.5	21.6
Sweden	32.4	27.6	28.0	24.2	–	–	–	18.2	15.3
United Kingdom	31.4	28.8	23.7	20.5	–	–	19.0	17.0	13.3

Sources: OECD (1986); OECD (2006).

have been transformed over the past forty years into a much more diverse and complex service economy. These patterns of long term growth and decline in employment are broadly attributable to various kinds of structural changes (Petit 2001). These include: internationalization of production and distribution; the diffusion of new technologies; government regulatory policy; and institutions of labour management relations. The following material considers each of these factors in turn.

Changing patterns of *internationalization of production*, investment and research and development may act as an incentive for firms to adopt more efficient production processes. To the extent that such an outcome is achieved, there may be quite different implications for employment. In particular, if productivity gains are achieved by substituting capital for labour or by promoting low cost labour, there will be likely to be changes in the quality or quantity of jobs. The evidence for the employment effects of internationalization is mixed, but the available data suggests that productivity growth in medium to low technology firms in manufacturing can be mainly traced to labour shedding (OECD 1998: 46). Another matter at issue here is the fact that for most countries only a relatively small minority of the working population is involved in producing internationally traded goods and services, and the employment effects are therefore likely to be quite limited (Crouch 1997: 368).

The extent to which globalization has eclipsed the power of collective institutions to shape the character of labour is a question which remains unresolved. However, the emphasis in the contemporary literature concerning the role of footloose global corporations and the constraints of global market competition in limiting political regulation and public institutions is not supported by the available evidence (Boreham, Dow and Leet 1999). What can be stated with certainty is that, without a range of institutional and policy arrangements in place, there is little guarantee that free (international) markets will necessarily bring about a high skill, high productivity industry sector (Genoff and Green 1998: 5).

Most of the developed economies have been characterized by a changed *regulatory environment* which has involved increased liberalization of product, financial and labour markets. Since the 1980s, there has been a continuing emphasis on programmes to create a competitive environment along with an aspiration to moderate or phase-out industry-specific assistance packages. These policy settings have generally encompassed trade policy, industrial relations policy, labour market policy and the broader macroeconomic stance of government. The policy vocabulary is one of 'deregulated' labour market controls, thus increasing flexibility for management to redeploy labour outside of the constraints of custom or legal convention. Microeconomic reform also concentrates on intervening in the social and historical structures which have determined how work is done, and the social relations through which it is collectively organized. These *institutions of labour management relations* have played a key role in empowering labour, protecting labour rights and defending the pay and working conditions of employees. In general, the impact of 'reforms' to labour market and industrial relations institutions has been to greatly increase the capacity of managers to implement flexible work practices and flexible labour market arrangements with respect to hours of work and security of employment.

The impact of these changes has facilitated the diffusion of new technologies through removing customary, legal, regulatory and industrial relations impediments to their deployment. Common examples of these practices include: extended hours of work without overtime rates to enable continuous production processes; the replacement of face-to-face customer service with web-based or automated systems in banks and insurance companies; the creation of a range of positions including casual work, outsourcing, and subcontracting to provide management with the numerical flexibility to reduce or increase staff numbers at short notice to respond to volatile demand for new products; and performance management tools based on software built into new technological applications from check-outs, to call centres, to invoicing targets set as performance indicators for professional consultants in law and accounting.

The data that has been discussed above demonstrates that the use of new technologies has the potential to change the quantity of employment that is offered in particular industries and industry sectors. The dramatic changes in manufacturing and services employment and the associated decline in blue-collar jobs and growth in white-collar jobs attest to this. However, once these inter-industry flows are taken into account, the conditions under which the use of new technologies can be said to create employment or unemployment involve a complex set of interactions between the elasticity of demand for the industry's products or services, the process of innovation and diffusion, and the relative substitution and demand elasticities of capital and labour. All of this takes place in the dynamic context of national and international economic, social and political change that we have outlined above.

Information and communication technologies and employment in the services sector

Employment in the services sector now clearly predominates in most OECD countries. However, it is very important to make two observations about the implications for jobs that these changes have set in motion. First, while there is evidence of a long-term labour-displacing trajectory in the historical application of information processing technologies to routinized clerical work in service sector industries such as banking, insurance and travel, there has also been an increase in employment in ancillary white-collar occupations. The second observation is that, while many information processing systems now require labour-intensive support in specialist areas such as software maintenance and systems development, there is also an increased demand for low skilled repetitive clerical workers where human intervention is required in the cycle of information processing. Many of these operations, such as communications with customers, document handling, data entry and filing, are required to commence or complete the flow of work. It is not surprising, therefore, that claims clerks, insurance appraisers and call centre workers are among the fastest growing occupations in the financial services sector (Hecht 2001). In discussing the insurance industry, Hecht goes on to suggest that the trends in clerical/production employment broadly reflect 'both an intensification of the work process via increased supervisory monitoring and control' together with a 'drive to substitute semi-skilled clerks for *both* unskilled and higher paid claims personnel' (2001: 532). These changes lie behind the growth of such relatively new categories of employment as the 'customer service representative'.

These innovations in information and communications technologies (ICTs) are implicated in what has been termed the de-layering of organizations (see Purcell and Hutchinson 1996). ICTs have strongly influenced choices about the reorganization of work within contemporary firms. In particular, the strata of middle management formerly responsible for coordination and communication tasks has been diminished, as new computer-based information systems have enabled senior managers to directly access models of budgeting and financial performance data (Littler, Wiesner and Dunford 2003; Lapido and Wilkinson 2002: 9). It also needs to be emphasized that the proportion of managerial and supervisory jobs in each of the OECD economies varies from 7.6 percent (in France) to 16 percent (in Canada and the United States) (International Labour Office 2005). These data suggest that the size of the managerial workforce is much more likely to be tied to the historical evolution of human resource management practices associated with consultation and employee discretion, on the one hand, or control and surveillance, on the other. There is also evidence of the development of a new and growing category of ICT jobs that generally require more skills than unskilled office clerks, but less than middle level management and specialist positions.

Table 9.4 shows the percentage of ICT occupations in both 1995 and 2003 for major OECD countries. The term 'ICT employment' can be interpreted in two ways: first, employment in industries conventionally identified as belonging to the ICT sector including all occupations, even those with little use of ICTs, and, second, employment in occupations that use ICTs to various degrees across all industries. The latter approach emphasizes ICT specialists and advanced and basic ICT users. Those projects using the latter approach generally choose occupations on the basis of an assessment of the degree to which workers *are expected* to use ICTs (OECD 2004). The measure is entirely based on formal labour market characteristics rather than any detailed estimate of what the job actually involves. Using these definitions there is evidence of significant growth in occupations

Table 9.4 Employment in information and communication technology related occupations: ICT occupations as a percentage of total employment, 1995 and 2003

	ICT Specialists[a]		*ICT Users and Specialists*[a]	
	1995	*2003*	*1995*	*2003*
Australia[b]	3.38	3.75	20.98	21.08
Canada	3.03	4.03	20.72	19.91
France	2.90	2.92	18.63	19.74
Germany	2.22	3.04	20.38	21.63
Italy	2.44	2.84	20.91	25.74
Japan[c]	–	3.87	–	26.22
Netherlands[c]	3.28	2.13	23.04	25.26
Sweden[b]	2.87	4.68	20.38	23.92
United Kingdom	2.92	3.30	27.77	27.70
United States[d]	3.29	3.82	21.22	20.29

Source: OECD (2005a), Figures D2.1 and D2.2.

Notes
a   Narrow and broad definitions based on methodology described in Chapter 6 of OECD Information and Technology Outlook 2004. See also van Welsum, D., and G. Vickery (2005) 'New Perspectives on ICT skills and employment', Information Economy Working Paper DSTI/ICCP/IE (2004) 10/FINAL, OECD. Calculations based on EULFS, US Current Population Survey, Statistics Canada, Australia Bureau of Statistics, the Korean Work Information centre, Human Resource Development Service, Japanese Ministry of Public Management, Home Affairs, Post and Telecommunications, Statistics Bureau.
b   1997 instead of 1995.
c   2002 instead of 2003.
d   OECD estimates for 2003.

classified as 'computer workers' and 'high skilled ICT workers' in both the European Union and the United States (OECD 2002b).

As Table 9.4 shows, in 2003, ICT specialists together with ICT users represented 20–30 percent of total employment in most OECD countries. This is a very broad measure that includes as 'basic users' those who use basic word processing and other generic programs as a tool in the course of their employment. On the other hand, 'ICT specialists' who develop, operate and maintain ICT systems as the main part of their job constituted less than 5 percent of total employment in each of the OECD countries in 2003. Over the past decade, both categories have been a source of employment growth, and have grown faster than total employment in all but a few countries (OECD 2005a). There have been various assertions in the literature as to the status of these jobs and the rewards associated with them. Much of this analysis remains somewhat speculative, including the conclusions of those researchers who consistently estimate the wage differential associated with the use of computers at work at around 10–15 percent. However, as DiNardo and Pischke (1997) note, using a similar methodology, the wage differential associated with using a pencil is shown to be of similar magnitude (Brown and Campbell 2002). Nevertheless, ICTs are associated with the growth of the service sector, and there is prima facie evidence consistent with the view that, on balance, these new technologies are associated with a net gain in jobs (Campbell 2001). But what is the nature of these jobs?

Empirical studies reviewed by Brown and Campbell indicate that it is the combination of ICTs and work organization that is the major predictor of employment growth or decline, rather than the use of ICTs alone (2002: 24). In other words, the employment impact of new technologies depends on the organizational framework through which they are implemented. These firms-specific work practices are more important to the quantity and quality of jobs and the wage premiums they attract than the use of higher-skilled, specialist labour in its own right. Studies by Bresnahan, Brynjolfsson and Hitt (2002) also document the complex relationship between new technology and human resources management practices centred on employee involvement in developing higher levels of productivity and enterprise performance. A key aspect of these developments is that the influence of ICTs on the reshaping of organizations is quite pervasive, involving a wide range of jobs, not simply those in ICT-based industries and occupations. In summary, new technologies can have a broad array of outcomes on employment and the quality of jobs. The key variables influencing these outcomes are the institutional environment of the enterprise (organizational practices and the labour process) and the macro-environment in which the enterprise is embedded (industrial legislation and employment relations processes). There is no evidence that there is anything inherent in new technologies that increase or decrease skill. This is the issue that we turn to in the following section.

Technological change, employment and work organization: skills development and the quality of jobs

We have argued throughout this book that the way new technology is developed, the manner in which it is used in the workplace and the applications that it is used for are the result of essentially social and political rather than technical practices and processes. Nowhere is this more evident than in the characteristics of jobs that are developed in association with the implementation of technological innovations in the process of production. Two interconnected themes emerge concerning the skill requirements of the new jobs that are created, and the growth of what has been widely described as the knowledge economy. As the OECD put it: 'through its effects on production methods ... and the structure of economies, the spread of information and communications technologies is playing a key role in the transformation of OECD economies from industrial to knowledge-based' (OECD 1998: 36). In evaluating the evidence for such changes in the nature of work, we need to address the divergence that has grown between the rhetoric of the future of work and the reality of the contemporary workplace. While we have shown that there have been broad structural changes in employment attributable to economic and technological change, we do not believe that the evidence can sustain the conclusion that we are witnessing the emergence of a great social transformation, heralding the jobless economy (Dunkerly 1996) and the death of the career (Bridges 1995; Handy 1995b) in the new knowledge-based workplace (Leadbeater 2000).

That is not to say that there have not been important consequences for the way work is currently organized. The research highlights a new emphasis on the use of new technologies in most jobs and on raising the skill levels of the workforce (Taylor 2002: 16–17). Structures of control of work performance are being modified, and some positions have achieved an increase in autonomy and discretion. However, it is critical not to portray changes in the quality of the great majority of jobs as an inevitable outcome of technological developments. The character of jobs is dependent on the interaction of new technologies and other forces shaping employment, especially institutional and policy arrangements and labour relations. Before turning to an examination of the types of jobs that are being created in the contemporary economy, we need to broadly define the dimensions of job quality that might set a benchmark for workplaces of the future.

The term 'job quality' has a variety of meanings in the literature that are dependent on the standpoint of the author. Generally, issues of job quality centre on the employment relationship, work intensity and skills (see Green 2006). The major dimensions involve: the degree of autonomy or discretion over work processes available to employees; the nature and intensity of management surveillance and control; the intensity of the work; opportunities for participating in and contributing to decisions about work; the development, enhancement and exercise of skills and knowledge; and job security. In what follows, we focus on the major aspects of job quality that are influenced by the design and deployment of new technologies.

The knowledge economy: technology, work organization and skill

One of the problems encountered in the enthusiastic promotion of the knowledge economy literature is the tendency to read off the characteristics of jobs from the levels of education or types of qualifications that characterize the labour market. Graduate jobs become a proxy for skilled jobs. In this view, as graduates increasingly numerically dominate the labour market, the concept of a knowledge economy becomes true by default. However, as Crouch points out, if education standards are generally rising, then the educational level of the persons engaged in any particular occupation will be seen to rise. This has no implications for the skill levels of the work that is performed in these occupations (Crouch 1997: 369). In summary, it is the labour process and the type of work undertaken that determines the skill and knowledge content of jobs, not the qualifications held by their incumbents (see Thompson 2005).

As the previous section demonstrated, many more employees now use computer skills in the course of their work. As a consequence, there has been a tendency for researchers to focus on jobs associated with the emerging 'new economy' characterized by the development, diffusion and application of ICTs. For some employees, work may indeed have become more creative, more skilled and more focussed on high levels of knowledge. Most of the jobs in which these employees are engaged do involve expert labour using high level diagnostic skills for technical problem solving. However, the broader changes that are taking place in the labour process are much less striking. The evidence strongly suggests that 'employment growth does not appear to be concentrated in areas of creativity involving high thinking or diagnostic skills, but rather in the low wage, routine and unglamorous occupations that structured working lives in the early part of the twentieth century (Nolan 2000; Greenbaum 1998).

The transformation of the manufacturing sector into a much more diverse and complex service economy, and the emergence of new forms of organization using technological innovations, has had a much less profound effect on the quality of jobs. The saliency of deep-seated occupational differences in the use of knowledge, skills and discretion between manual and non-manual workers has not been significantly modified (Taylor 2002). As Warhurst, Lockyer and Dutton (2006) have pointed out, many jobs using ICTs have been inexorably fragmented and routinized, driven by developments in the technology itself, market pressures and managerial control systems. Contemporary work organizations, especially in the service sector, are producing a large number of jobs that require little or no skill. Many of these jobs are highly routinized and often involve a series of simple tasks, and even interactions with customers that are required to be performed in a prescribed manner and in a highly specified time-frame (Ritzer 1998: 60; Thompson *et al.* 2001).

While the tendency for jobs to be fragmented and routinized in this way remains at the forefront of modern management practices, there is a counter-tendency to facilitate organizational change that provides a framework to use the initiative and innovation of employees. This involves the use of tacit knowledge in the 'high performance workplace', enabling workers to share knowledge and solve problems. This process requires a set of skills to come to the fore that Thompson (2005) characterizes as 'person to person social competencies'. The context in which such knowledge intensive work is best facilitated involves higher levels of autonomy and discretion. The task for management then becomes one of capturing and controlling such tacit knowledge. The process of knowledge management is currently the focus of a great deal of technological intervention, through the application of networked systems of filing and 'matter control' in professional firms, which tend to shift the ownership of intellectual property from employee to employer. The following section brings some of these tensions between individual discretion and managerial control into focus.

Employee discretion and management control

As we have argued, new technologies present employers with an increased opportunity to codify knowledge that was previously only available in a tacit form, residing in the knowledge and analytical capacities of workers (Rubery and Grimshaw 2001). The development and commodification of codified knowledge renders the reproduction and verification of work skills and work processes able to be assessed by technological means. This allows for supervisory practices to be modified and replaced with less expensive forms of electronic monitoring

(Lapido and Wilkinson 2002). As a consequence, some researchers have argued that traditional forms of hierarchical management control are being dismantled, as the cost of monitoring and surveillance of workplace activity is diminished by new technologies. Organizations that are reliant on the development of high trust relations to take advantage of the skills and motivation of 'empowered workers' may also reframe employment relations that involved strict performance measurement. However, as Gallie, White, Cheng and Tomlinson (1998: 316) put it 'control remains pervasive and possibly more intense in the pressures it brings to bear on work effort'. Data from the 'Working in Britain in 2000 Survey' pointed to the same conclusion, noting that: 'despite the advance of new forms of work organization ... the degree of control and surveillance by management has also increased' (Taylor 2002: 18).

A broad range of studies have argued that organizations will be likely to externalize activities that are not central to their core business through outsourcing, sub-contracting, networking and partnerships. Such tendencies encompassing both sharing and control of knowledge have significant consequences for the development of employment relationships within organizational forms that may be characterized as networked at one end of the continuum to fragmented at the other (Rubery, Earnshaw, Marchington, Cooke and Vincent 2000). The empirical evidence suggests that many employers using sub-contracted services in networked or fragmented organizations will be likely to specify employment contracts that are tightly specified and based on 'low trust' forms of control over performance. Research reported by Rubery and Grimshaw, (2001: 170) and Grimshaw, Cooke, Grugulis and Vincent (2002) concludes that a diversity of organizational forms have developed in tandem with the advancement of ICTs, and that trends in the employment relationship that result are not necessarily unidirectional and may involve either more employee discretion or more managerial monitoring and control of performance. While we agree with these authors in rejecting a deterministic approach to the outcomes of technological change as either upskilling or deskilling, the weight of the research evidence, especially that from the United Kingdom, supports the development of a low trust, low discretion outcome. As Nolan puts it: 'evidence of the demise of hierarchy as a consequence of the diffusion of high commitment human resource management practices is in short supply' (Nolan 2000). The probability remains that these findings reflect the interaction between a range of factors shaping the future of employment and the quality of jobs, including the institutional, cultural, legal and political environment and the force of collective regulation.

Organizational change and work intensity

Competitive pressures in the market induce organizations to employ more flexible workers, and consequently to provide more insecure jobs in order to keep costs down and retain or increase market share. As Green concluded: 'an obvious factor driving competitive pressure is technological and organizational change which enable a greater control of work flows' (2001: 76). Green describes this process as 'effort biased technological change'. During the 1990s, research concerning labour market flexibility was to see a wider application of management practices, facilitated by the development of information and communication technologies that supported new forms of performance monitoring and raised the capacity of managers to control and intensify the flow of work.

The development of new methods of work organization facilitated by a range of techniques complementary to the expansion of new ICTs has generated new processes of production. Methods of production such as 'total quality management' and 'just-in-time' methods premised on minimization of inventories, require the rigorous control of workflows. Tailored software and the enhanced analytical capacity of computers offer the technical means to provide such levels of control, and are an important adjunct to these changes in work organization (Green 2004: 715). They offer management a heightened capacity for the efficient allocation of work. The manifestation of these changes for most employees is increased effort and work intensification, usually accompanied by a decline in employment security.

A number of recent empirical studies have pointed to the outcomes of organizational change enabled by new technologies as involving heavier workloads and a 'speed up' of activity (Edwards, Collinson and Rees 1998; Gallie *et al.* 1998; Green 2001; Sennett 1998). The process has become sufficiently widespread to have been labelled 'management by stress'. In discussing the results of a major study of work intensification and job insecurity in Britain, Lapido and Wilkinson (2002) report that the organizational flexibility associated with the use of new information technologies has led to calls for a corresponding flexibility in the workforce. Employers in their study reported pressure to modify the task content of jobs and the intensity of work. Not surprisingly, over 60 percent of employees in the same study described the intensification of their work (Burchell 2002: 72). Many contractual arrangements responding to flexibility imperatives involve part-time and casual jobs that also tend to involve intensified forms of self-imposed time and effort pressure.

Organizational change fostered by the utilization of new technologies also needs to recognize the permeable nature of organizations and the development of complex multi-employer relationships (Rubery *et al.* 2000). External agencies and sub-contractors are likely to be faced with increased job insecurity, pressures for time commitment and work intensification. These outcomes are likely to be exacerbated by management practices impacting on the employment relationship that often involve more intense and direct contractual systems of control for workers employed under these circumstances, and the loss of previous, collectively enforced norms regulating work intensity.

Technological changes introduced over recent decades have become an integral component of organizational change. These transformations in production have been associated with enhanced managerial control over the labour process designed to achieve higher effort levels. New technologies have been utilized to complement management practices that also impact on the flexible employment of labour. In many instances the result is an insecurity of employment that provides an incentive for engendering greater effort and the acceptance of work intensification, given the high cost of job loss (see Green 2004: 719–20). As we have noted previously, flexible employment conditions (casual and contract work) have been supported by political changes to labour market regulation and declining union power.

Conclusion

The application of new technologies to the production and distribution of goods and services has the potential to fundamentally change the way work is organized and the quantity and quality of jobs that are likely to characterize workplaces of the future. Throughout this volume we have painted a picture of different, often competing, scenarios that have emerged within and between nations, as employers, employees and regulatory institutions have set in train the process of design and implementation of information and communication technologies. New technologies are only one ingredient in this recipe for the future (national and international legal frameworks, national regulatory regimes governing employment, institutions for the collective representation of the interests of capital, labour and the state, the development of a culture and practice of management, and the political choices that emerge from these circumstances are all critical elements). An important consideration that underlies the debate about new technology at work is that these elements of political decision making are not arranged serendipitously, but are part of an ongoing process of change which will be very likely to constrain future choices and to set a trajectory for the workplace of the future.

References

Abel, J. and Pries, L. (2007) 'Shifting Patterns of Labor Regulation: Highly Qualified Knowledge Workers in German New Media Companies', *Critical Sociology*, 33, 1/2: 101–25.

Ackroyd, S. (2002) *The Organization of Business: Applying Organizational Theory to Contemporary Change*, Oxford: Oxford University Press.

Ackroyd, S. and Lawrenson, D. (1996) 'Knowledge Work and Organisational Transformation: Analysing Contemporary Change in the Social Use of Expertise', in Fincham, R. (ed.) *New Relationships in the Organised Professions: Managers, Professionals and Knowledge Workers*, Aldershot: Avebury, 149–70.

Ackroyd, S. and Procter, S. (1998) 'British Manufacturing Organization and Workplace Industrial Relations: Some Attributes of the New Flexible Firm', *British Journal of Industrial Relations*, 36, 2: 163–83.

Ackroyd, S. and Thompson, P. (2005) 'Paradoxes of Governance under Disconnected Capitalism', paper presented at conference on Governance in South Wales, Cardiff Business School, May.

Adami, L. (1999) 'Autonomy, Control and the Virtual Worker', in Jackson, P. (ed.) *Virtual Teleworking: Social and Organizational Dynamics*, London: Routledge, 131–49.

Adler, P.S. (ed.) (1992) *Technology and the Future of Work*, Oxford: Oxford University Press.

Ahmed, N. and Maddox, H. (1995) 'Managing the CIM–TQM Partnership', *Advanced Management Journal*, 60, 3: 19–29.

Alferoff, C. and Knights, D. (2002) 'Quality Time and the "Beautiful Call"', in Holtgrewe, U., Kerst, C. and Shire, K. (eds) *Re-organising Service Work: Call Centres in Germany and Britain*, Aldershot: Ashgate.

Alvarez, M.R., Garrett, G. and Lange, P. (1991) 'Government Partisanship, Labor Organization and Macroeconomic Performance', *American Political Science Review*, 85, 2: 539–56.

Alvesson, M. and Thompson, P. (2005) 'Post-bureaucracy?', in Ackroyd, S., Batt, R., Thompson, P. and Tolbert, P. (eds) *A Handbook of Work and Organization*, Oxford: Oxford University Press.

Ambrosini, V. and Bowman, C. (2001) 'Tacit Knowledge: Some Suggestions for Operationalization', *Journal of Management Studies*, 38, 6: 811–29.

Andersen, N.Å. and Kjaer, P. (1993) 'Private Industrial Policy in the Danish Negotiated Economy', in Hausner, J., Jessop, B. and Nielsen, K. (eds) *Institutional Frameworks of Market Economies: Scandinavian and Eastern European Perspectives*, Aldershot: Ashgate Publishing.

Anderson, H. (1988) 'Technological Trajectories, Cultural Values and the Labour Process', *Social Studies of Science*, 3, 1: 465–82.

Archibugi, D. and Michie, J. (1995) 'The Globalisation of Technology: A New Taxonomy', *Cambridge Journal of Economics*, 19: 121–40.

Archibugi, D. and Michie, J. (1997a) 'Technological Globalisation or National Systems of Innovation?', *Futures*, 29, 2: 121–37.

Archibugi, D. and Michie, J. (1997b) *Technology, Globalisation and Economic Performance*, Cambridge: Cambridge University Press.

Archibugi, D. and Immarino, S. (2002) 'The Globalization of Technological Innovation: Definition and Evidence', *Review of International Political Economy*, 9, 1: 98–122.

Armstrong, N.J. (1999) 'Flexible Work in the Virtual Workplace: Discourses and Implications of Teleworking', in Felstead, A. and Jewson, N. (eds) *Global Trends in Flexible Labour*, London: Macmillan Business, 41–63.

Armstrong, P., Marginson, P., Edwards, P. and Purcell, J. (1998) 'Divisionalization in the UK: Diversity, Size and the Devolution of Bargaining', *Organization Studies*, 19: 1–22.

Attewell, P. (1992) 'Skill and Occupational Changes in US Manufacturing', in Adler, P. (ed.) *Technology and the Future of Work*, New York: Oxford University Press.

Audretsch, D. and Thurik, R. (2001) 'What is New about the New Economy: Sources of Growth in the Managed and Entrepreneurial Economies', *Industrial and Corporate Change*, 10, 1: 25–48.

Australian Bureau of Statistics (ABS) (2001) *Locations of Work*, Australia 6275.0, Canberra: ABS.

Autor, D.H., Levy, F. and Murnane, R. (2002) 'Upstairs, Downstairs: Computers and Skills on Two Floors of a Large Bank', *Industrial and Labor Relations Review*, 55, 3: 432–47.

Axtmann, R. (2004) 'The State of the State: The Model of the Modern State and Its Contemporary Transformation', *International Political Science Review*, 25, 3: 259–79.

Badham, R.J. (2005) 'Technology and the Transformation of Work', in Ackroyd, S., Batt, R., Thompson, P. and Tolbert, P.S. (eds) *A Handbook of Work and Organization*, Oxford: Oxford University Press.

Baffour, G.G. and Betsey, C.L. (2000) 'Human Resources Management and Development in the Telework Environment', in U.S. Department of Labor, *Telework and the New Workplace of the Twenty-first Century*, New Orleans: U.S. Department of Labor. Available online: http://www.dol.gov/dol/asp/public/telework (accessed 30 March 2006).

Baily, M. (2000) 'Innovation in the New Economy', *OECD Observer*, Summer, 221–2: 98–100.

Bain, P. and Taylor, P. (2000) 'Entrapped by the "electronic panopticon"? Worker Resistance in the Call Centre', *New Technology, Work and Employment*, 15, 1: 2–18.

Baldry, C. (1988) *Computers, Jobs, and Skills: The Industrial Relations of Technological Change*, New York: Plenum Press.

Baldry, C. and Connelly, A. (1986) 'Drawing the Line: Computer Aided Design and the Organisation of the Drawing Office', *New Technology, Work and Employment*, 1, 1: 59–66.

Baldry, C., Bain, P.B., Taylor, P., Hyman, J., Scholarios, D., Marks, A., Watson, A., Gilbert, K., Gall, G. and Bunzel, D. (2007) *The Meaning of Work in the New Economy*, London: Palgrave.

Ball, K. (2002) 'Categorizing the Workers: Electronic Surveillance and Social Ordering in Call Centres', in Lyon, D. (ed.) *Surveillance as Social Sorting*, London: Routledge.

Bank for International Settlements (2002) *Triennial Central Bank Survey, Foreign Exchange and Derivatives Market Activity in 2001*, Basel: Bank for International Settlements.

Baran, B. (1988) 'Office Automation and Women's Work: The Technological Transformation of the Insurance Industry', in Pahl, R.H. (ed.) *On Work*, Oxford: Basil Blackwell.

Barker, J.R. (1993) 'Tightening the Iron Cage: Concertive Control in Self-Managing Teams', *Administrative Science Quarterly*, 38: 408–37.

Barker, J. and Downing, H. (1980) 'Word Processing and the Transformation of the Patriarchal Relations of Control in the Office', *Capital and Class*, 10: 64–99.

Barley, S.R. (2005) 'What we know (and mostly don't know) about technical work', in Ackroyd, S., Batt, R., Thompson, P. and Tolbert, P. (eds) *A Handbook of Work and Organization*, Oxford: Oxford University Press.

Barnes, A. (2004) 'Diaries, Dunnies and Discipline: Resistance and Accommodation to Monitoring in Call Centres', *Labour and Industry* 14/3: 127–38.

Barrett, R. (2004) 'Working at Webboyz: An Analysis of Control over the Software Development Labour Process', *Work, Employment and Society*, 38, 4: 777–94.

Barrett, R. (ed.) (2005) *Management, Labour Process and Software Development: Reality Bytes*, Milton Park, Oxon: Routledge.

Barrow, C. (2005) 'The Return of the State: Globalization, State Theory and the New Imperialism', *New Political Science*, 27, 2: 123–46.

Batt, R. (1999) 'Work Organization, Technology and Performance in Customer Service and Sales', *Industrial and Labour Relations Review*, 52, 4: 539–64.

Batt, R. and Moynihan, L. (2002) 'The Viability of Alternative Call Centre Production Models', *Human Resource Management Journal*, 12, 4: 14–34.

Batt, R., Christopherson, S., Rughtor, N. and van Jaarveld, D. (2001) *Net Working*, Washington: Economic Policy Institute.

Beatty, J. (2001) 'Cannibalistic Capitalism'. Online version cited: http://www.theatlantic.com/unbound/polipro/pp2001-06-07.htm. (accessed 30 June 2006).

Becker, M.C. (2000) 'The Constitution of Competence in a Call Centre: An Empirical Contribution of a Theory of Competences', unpublished paper, Judge Institute of Management, Cambridge University.

Beirne, M., Ramsay, H. and Panteli, A. (1998) 'Developments in Computing Work: Control and Contradiction in the Software Labour Process', in Thompson, P. and Warhurst, C. (eds) *Workplaces of the Future*, Basingstoke: Macmillan.

Bell, D. (1973) *The Coming of Post-Industrial Society*, New York: Basic Books.

Belt, V. (2002a) 'A Female Ghetto? Women's Careers in Call Centres', *Human Resource Management Journal*, 12, 4: 51–66.

Belt, V. (2002b) 'Capitalising on Femininity: Gender and the Utilisation of Social Skills in Telephone Call Centres', in Holtgrewe, U., Kerst, C. and Shire, K. (eds) *Re-organising Service Work: Call Centres in Germany and Britain*, Aldershot: Ashgate.

Belt, V. (2003) 'Work, Employment and Skill in the New Economy: Training for Call Centre Work in North East England', paper presented at the 21st Annual International Labour Process Conference, Bristol Business School, April.

Berggren, C. (1992) *Alternatives to Lean Production: Work Organisation in the Swedish Auto Industry*, Ithaca, NY: ILR Press.

Bienefeld, M. (1994) 'Capitalism and the Nation State in the Dog Days of the Twentieth Century', in Miliband, R. and Panitch, L. (eds) *Between Globalism and Nationalism: Socialist Register 1994*, London: Merlin Press.

Bijker, W.E. (1993) 'Do not Despair: There is Life After Constructivism', *Science, Technology and Human Values*, 18, 4: 113–38.

Blackler, F. (1995) 'Knowledge, Knowledge Work and Organizations: An Overview and Interpretation', *Organization Studies*, 16, 6: 1021–46.

Blauner, R. (1964) *Alienation and Freedom: The Factory Worker and his Industry*, Chicago: University of Chicago Press.

Block, F. (1977) *The Origins of International Economic Disorder: A Study of United States International Monetary Policy from World War II to the Present*, Berkeley: University of California Press.

Bloomfield, B. and Coombs, R. (1992) 'Information Technology, Control and Power: The Centralization and Decentralization Debate Revisited', *Journal of Management Studies*, 29: 459–84.

Boddy, D. and Buchanan, D. (1986) *Managing New Technology*, Oxford: Blackwell.

Boddy, D. and Gunson, N. (1997) 'Organizations in the Network Age', *Organization Studies*, 18, 5: 880–1.

Bolton, S. (2005) *Emotion Management in the Workplace*, London: Palgrave.

Boreham, P. (2002) 'Governance of the Labour Market: The Declining Role of the State', in Bell, S. (ed.) *Economic Governance and Institutional Dynamics*, Melbourne: Oxford University Press.

Boreham, P. (2003) 'The Australian Labour Market: Social Consequences of Political Change', in Boreham, P., Stokes, G. and Hall, R. (eds) *The Politics of Australian Society: Political Issues for the New Century*, Sydney: Longman.

Boreham, P., Hall, R. and Harley, B. (1996) 'Two Paths to Prosperity: Work Organization and Industrial Relations Decentralization in Australia', *Work, Employment and Society*, 10, 3: 449–68.

Boreham, P., Dow, G. and Leet, M. (1999) *Room to Manoeuvre: Political Aspects of Full Employment*, Melbourne: Melbourne University Press.

Borland, V.S. (2003) 'Global Technology in the 21st Century', *Textileworld.com*, 153, 1: 52–7.

Boyer, R. (2005) 'How and Why Capitalisms Differ', *Economy and Society*, 34, 4: 509–57.

Boyer, R. and Drache, D. (1996) States Against Markets: *The Limits of Globalization*, London: Routledge.

Braham, P. (1985) 'The Effects of IT on Employment', in Open University course booklet *IT and Change in the Workplace*, Milton Keynes: Open University Press.

Braithwaite, J. and Drahos, P. (2000) *Global Business Regulation*, Cambridge: Cambridge University Press.

Braverman, H. (1974) *Labor and Monopoly Capital: The Degradation of Work in the Twentieth Century*, New York: Monthly Review Press.

Brenner, N. (2004) 'Urban Governance and the Production of New State Spaces in Western Europe, 1960–2000', *Review of International Political Economy*, 11, 3: 447–88.

Bresnahan, T., Brynjolfsson, E. and Hitt, L. (2002) 'Information Technology, Work Organization, and the Demand for Skilled Labor: Firm Level Evidence', *Quarterly Journal of Economics,* 117, 1: 339–76.

Bridges, W. (1995) *Jobshift: How to Prosper in a Workplace without Jobs*, London: Nicholas Brealey.

Brigham, M. and Corbett, M. (1996) 'Trust and the Virtual Organization: Handy Cyberias', in Jackson, P.J. and Van der Wielen, J. (eds) Proceedings of the workshop *New International Perspectives on Telework: From Telecommuting to the Virtual Organization*, London, July–August 1996, Tilburg, The Netherlands: Tilburg University Press.

Brigham, M.J. and Corbett, J.M. (1997) 'E-mail, Power and the Constitution of Organisational Reality', *New Technology, Work and Employment*, 12, 1: 25–35.

Brown, C. and Campbell, B. (2001) 'Technical Change, Wages, and Employment in Semiconductor Manufacturing', *Industrial and Labor Relations Review*, 54, 2A: 450–65.

Brown, C. and Campbell, B. (2002) 'The Impact of Technological Change on Work and Wages', *Industrial Relations,* 41, 1: 1–33.

Brown, J.S. and Duguid, P. (1991) 'Organisational Learning and Communities of Practice: Towards a Unified View of Working, Learning and Innovation', *Organization Science*, 2, 1: 40–51.

Brown, P. and Hesketh, A. (2004) *Playing to Win: Managing Employability in the Knowledge-Based Economy*, Oxford: Oxford University Press.

Bruun, H. and Hukkinen, J. (2003) 'Crossing Boundaries: An Integrative Framework for Studying Technological Change', *Social Studies of Science*, 33, 1: 95–116.

Bryan, D. (1992) 'International Accumulation and the Contradictions of National Monetary Policy', *Science and Society*, 56, 3: 324–52.

Bryan, D. and Rafferty, M. (1999) *The Global Economy in Australia: Global Integration and National Economic Policy*, Sydney: Allen and Unwin.

Buchanan, D. and Boddy, D. (1983) *Organisations in the Computer Age: Technological Imperatives and Strategic Choice*, Aldershot: Gower.

Buchanan, J. and Hall, R. (2003) *Beyond VET: The Changing Skill Needs of the Victorian Services Sector*, report for the Department of Education and Training, Government of Victoria, Melbourne: Department of Education and Training.

Burawoy, M. (1979) *Manufacturing Consent: Changes in the Labor Process under Monopoly Capitalism*, Chicago: University of Chicago Press.

Burchell, B. (2002) 'The Prevalence and Redistribution of Job Insecurity and Work Intensification', in Burchell, B., Lapido, D. and Wilkinson, F. (eds) *Job Insecurity and Work Intensification*, London: Routledge.

Burgess, J. and Campbell, I. (1998) 'The Nature and Dimensions of Precarious Employment in Australia', *Labour and Industry*, 8, 3: 5–21.

Burris, B. (1993) *Technocracy at Work*, Albany, NY: State of New York Press.

Butler, D. (1988) 'Secretarial Skills and Office Technology', in Willis, E. (ed.) *Technology and the Labour Process: Australasian Case Studies*, Sydney: Allen and Unwin.

Callaghan, G. (2002) 'Call Centres: The Latest Industrial Office?', paper presented at the 20th Annual International Labour Process Conference, University of Strathclyde, April.

Callaghan, G. and Thompson, P. (2001) 'Edwards Revisited: Technical Control and Call Centres', *Economic and Industrial Democracy*, 22: 13–37.

Callaghan, G. and Thompson, P. (2002) 'We Recruit Attitude: The Selection and Shaping of Call Centre Labour', *Journal of Management Studies*, 39, 2: 233–54.

Callon, M. (1986) 'The Sociology of an Actor Network', in Callon, M., Law, J. and Rip, A. (eds) *Mapping the Dynamics of Science and Technology*, London: Macmillan.

Campbell, D. (2001) 'Can the Digital Divide be Contained?', *International Labour Review*, 140 (2): 11–141.

Carlsson, B. (1993) 'Technological Systems and Industrial Development: Four Swedish Case Studies', *MTEU Studies in Development*, 20, 4: 475–502.

Carlsson, B. (1996) 'Innovation and Success in Sweden: Technological Systems', in de la Mothe, J. and Paquet, G. (eds) *Evolutionary Economics and the New International Political Economy*, New York: Pinter.

Carlsson, B. and Stankiewicz, R. (1991) 'On the Nature, Function and Composition of Technological Systems', *Journal of Evolutionary Economics*, 1, 2: 93–118.

Carlsson, B. and Stankiewicz, R. (1995) 'On the Nature, Function and Composition of Technological Systems', in Carlsson, B. (ed.) *Technological Systems and Economic Performance: The Case of Factory Automation*, Dordrecht: Kluwer.

Carlsson, B. and Jacobsson, S. (1997a) 'Diversity Creation and Technology Systems: A Technology Policy Perspective', in Edquist, C. (ed.) *Systems of Innovation: Technologies, Institutions and Organizations*, London: Pinter.

Carlsson, B. and Jacobsson, S. (1997b) 'The Technological System for Factory Automation', in Carlsson, B. (ed.) *Technological Systems and Industrial Dynamics*, London: Kluwer.

Casey, C. (1995) *Work, Self and Society after Industrialism*, London: Routledge.

Casper, S. (2000) 'Institutional Adapativeness, Technology Policy and the Diffusion of New Business Models: The Case of German Biotechnology', *Organization Studies*, 21, 5: 887–914.

Casper, S. and Kettler, H. (2001) 'National Institutional Frameworks and the Hybridization of Entrepreneurial Business Models: The German and UK Biotechnology Sectors', *Industry and Innovation*, 8, 1: 5–30.

Castells, M. (1996) 'The Rise of the Network Society', *The Information Age: Economy, Society and Culture*, Volume 1, Oxford: Blackwell.

Castells, M. (1997) 'The Power of Identity', *The Information Age: Economy, Society and Culture*, Volume 2, Oxford: Blackwell.

Castells, M. (1998) 'End of Millennium', *The Information Age: Economy, Society and Culture*, Volume 3, Oxford: Blackwell.

Castells, M. (2000) 'Information Technology and Global Capitalism', in Hutton, W. and Giddens, A. (eds) *On the Edge: Living with Global Capitalism*, London: Jonathan Cape.

Castells, M. (2001) *The Internet Galaxy: Reflections on the Internet, Business, and Society*, Oxford: Oxford University Press.

Caulkin, S. (2003) 'Time to Reroute Call Centres', *The Observer*, 2 March: 8.

Cerny, P.G. (1996) 'International Finance and the Erosion of State Capacity', in Cerny, P.G. (ed.) *Globalization and Public Policy*, Cheltenham: Edward Elgar.

Chandler, A. (1977) *The Visible Hand*, Cambridge, MA: Harvard University Press.

Child, J. (1973) *Man and Organization: The Search for Explanation and Social Revelance*, London: Allen and Unwin.

Child, J. (1984) 'Microelectronics and employment in the service sector', in Marstrand, P. (ed.) *New Technology and the Future of Work and Skills*, London: Pinter.

Child, J. (1985) 'Managerial Strategies, New Technology and the Labour Process', in Knights, D., Willmott, H. and Collinson, D. (eds) *Job Redesign: Critical Perspectives on the Labour Process*, Aldershot: Gower.

Chomsky, N. (1998) 'Power in the Global Era', *New Left Review*, 230: 3–27.

Christensen, J.L. (1992) 'The Role of Finance in National Systems of Innovation', in Lundvall, B. (ed.) *National Systems of Innovation: Towards a Theory of Innovation and Interactive Learning*, London: Pinter.

Ciscel, D. and Smith, B.E. (2005) 'The Impact of Supply Chain Management on Labor Standards: The Transition to Incessant Work', *Journal of Economic Issues*, 39 (2): 429–37.

Clark, J., McLoughlin, I., Rose, H. and King, R. (1988) *The Process of Technological Change: New Technology and Social Choice in the Workplace*, Cambridge: Cambridge University Press.

Clarke, T. and Rollo, C. (2001) 'Capitalizing Knowledge: Corporate Knowledge Management Investments', *Creativity and Innovation Management*, 10, 3: 177–88.

Clegg, S., Boreham, P. and Dow, G. (1986) *Class, Politics and the Economy*, London: Routledge and Kegan Paul.

Coleman, W.D. (1997) 'Associational Governance in a Globalizing Era: Weathering the Storm', in Hollingsworth, J.R. and Boyer, R. (eds) *Contemporary Capitalism: The Embeddedness of Institutions*, Cambridge: Cambridge University Press.

Coleman, W. and Porter, T. (1994) 'Regulating International Banking and Securities: Emerging Co-operation Among National Authorities', in Stubbs, R. and Underhill, G. (eds) *Political Economy and the Changing Global Order*, London: Macmillan.

Collin-Jacques, C. (2003) 'Professionals at Work: A Cross-National Study of Nurse Call Centres in England and Quebec', in Deery, S. and Kinnie, N. (eds) *Human Resource Management and Call Centre Work*, London: Palgrave.

Collinson, D. and Collinson, M. (1997) 'Delayering Managers: Time-Space Surveillance and its Gendered Effects', *Organization*, 4, 3: 375–411.

Conti, R. and Warner, M. (1994) 'Taylorism, Teams and Technology in "Reengineering" Work-organization', *New Technology, Work and Employment*, 9, 2: 93–102.

Cooley, M. (1980) *Architect or Bee: The Human/Technology Relationship*, Boston, MA: South End Press.

Coombs, R., Knights, D. and Willmott, H.C. (1992) 'Culture, Control and Competition: Towards a Conceptual Framework for the Study of Information Technology in Organizations', *Organization Studies*, 13, 1: 51–72.

Cooper, C.L. and Rousseau, D.M. (eds) (1999) *The Virtual Organization*, London: Wiley.

Counter Information Services (CIS) (1980) *Report on New Technology*, London: Counter Information Services.

Cousins, C. (1999) 'Changing Regulatory Frameworks and Non-standard Employment: A Comparison of Germany, Spain, Sweden and the UK', in Felstead, A. and Jewson, N. (eds) *Global Trends in Flexible Labour*, London: Macmillan.

Cox, R.W. (1994) 'Global Restructuring: Making Sense of the Changing International Political Economy', in Stubbs, R. and Underhill, G. (eds) *Political Economy and the Changing Global Order*, London: Macmillan.

Cramton, C.D. (2002) 'Attribution in Distributed Work Groups', in Hinds, P.J. and Kiesler, S. (eds) *Distributed Work*, Cambridge, MA: MIT Press.

Crompton, R. and Jones, G. (1984) *White Collar Proletariat, Deskilling and Gender*, London: Macmillan.

Crouch, C. (1997) 'Skills-based Full Employment: the Latest Philosopher's Stone', *British Journal of Industrial Relations*, 35, 3: 367–91.

Cyert, R.M. and Mowery, D.C. (eds) (1987) *Technology and Employment: Innovation and Growth in the U.S. Economy*, Washington: National Academy Press.

Dahl, M. (2002) 'Embedded Knowledge Flows Through Labour Mobility in Regional Clusters in Denmark', paper presented at DRUID Summer Conference 'Industrial Dynamics of the New and Old Economy', Copenhagen, June.

Darrow, W. (1987) 'An International Comparison of Flexible Manufacturing Systems Technology', *Interaces*, 17, 6: 86–91.

Davenport, T. (2000) *Mission Critical: Realizing the Promise of Enterprise Systems*, Boston, MA: Harvard Business School Press.

Davidow, W.H. and Malone, M.S. (1992) *The Virtual Corporation, Structuring and Revitalizing the Corporation for the 21st Century*, New York: Harper Business.

Davies, M. (1979) 'A Women's Place is at the Typewriter', in Eisenstein, Z.R. (ed.) *Capitalist Patriarchy and the Case for Socialist Feminism*, London: Monthly Review Press.

Dawson, P., Drinkwater, R., Gunson, N. and Atkins, M. (2000) 'Computer-Mediated Communication and the Virtual Workplace: the Social and Political Processes of Change', *Labour and Industry*, 10, 3: 17–36.

Deeg, R. (1997) 'Banks and Industrial Finance in the 1990s', *Industry and Innovation*, 4, 2: 53–74.

Deery, S. and Kinnie, N. (2002) 'Call Centres and Beyond: A Thematic Evaluation', *Human Resource Management Journal*, 12, 4: 3–13.

Deery, S., Iverson, R. and Walsh, J. (2002) 'Work Relationships in Telephone Call Centres: Understanding Emotional Exhaustion and Employee Withdrawal', *Journal of Management Studies*, 39, 4: 471–96.

Delsen, L. and van Veen, T. (1992) 'The Swedish Model: Relevant for Other Countries?', *British Journal of Industrial Relations*, 30, 1: 85–105.

Dent, M. and Barry, J. (2004) 'New Public Management and the Professions in the UK: Reconfiguring Control?', in Dent, M., Chandler, J. and Barry, J. (eds) *Questioning the New Public Management*, London: Ashgate.

Dery, K., Hall, R. and Wailes, N. (2006) 'ERPs as "Technologies-in-Practice": Social Construction, Materiality and the Role of Organisational Factors', *New Technology, Work and Employment*, 21, 3: 229–41.

DeSanctis, G. and Poole, M.S. (1994) 'Capturing the Complexity in Advanced Technology Use: Adaptive Structuration Theory', *Organization Science*, 5, 2: 121–47.

Despres, C. and Hiltrop, J.M. (1995) 'Human Resource Management in the Knowledge Age: Current Practices and Perspectives on the Future', *Employee Relations*, 7: 9–23.

Dicken, P. (1992) *Global Shift: The Internationalization of Economic Activity*, London: Paul Chapman.

DiNardo, J.E. and Pischke, J.S. (1997) 'The Returns to Computer Use Revisited: Have Pencils Changed the Wage Structure too?', *Quarterly Journal of Economics*, 112, 1: 291–304.

Dobbin, F. (1994) *Forging Industrial Policy: The United States, Britain and France in the Railway Age*, New York: Cambridge University Press.

Drucker, P. (1955) The Practice of Management, New York: Harper and Row.

Dunkerley, M. (1996) *The Jobless Economy? Computer Technology in the World of Work*, Cambridge: Polity Press.

Dvorak, P. (2000) 'Digital Factories Foster New Vision of Manufacturing', *American Machinist*, 144, 4: 16–20.

Eckstein, A.L.H. and Rohleder, T.R. (1998) 'Incorporating Human Resources in Group Technology/Cellular Manufacturing', *International Journal of Production Research*, 36, 5: 1199–222.

Edquist, C. (1997) 'Systems of Innovation Approaches – Their Emergence and Characteristics', in Edquist, C. (ed.) *Systems of Innovation: Technologies, Institutions and Organisations*, London: Pinter.

Edquist, C. and McKelvey, M. (2000) 'Introduction', in Edquist, C. and McKelvey, M. (eds) *Systems of Innovation: Growth, Competitiveness and Employment*, volume 1, Cheltenham: Edward Elgar.

Edquist, C., Hommen, L. and McKelvey, M. (1998) 'Product Versus Process Innovation: Implications for Employment', in Michie, J. and Reati, A. (eds) *Employment, Technology and Economic Needs: Theory, Evidence and Public Policy*, Cheltenham: Edward Elgar.

Edquist, C., Hommen, L. and McKelvey, M. (2001) *Innovation and Employment: Process versus Product Innovation*, Cheltenhan: Edward Elgar.

Edwards, L.N. and Field-Hendrey, E. (1996) 'Home-based Workers: Data from the 1990 Census of Population', *Monthly Labor Review*, 119, 11: 26–34.

Edwards, P.K., Collinson, M. and Rees, C. (1998) 'The Determinants of Employee Responses to Total Quality Management: Six Case Studies', *Organization Studies*, 19: 449–75.

Edwards, R. (1979) *Contested Terrain: The Transformation of the Workplace in the Twentieth Century*, New York: Basic Books.

Ellis, V. and Taylor, P. (2006) 'You Don't Know What You've Got Till it's Gone: Re-contextualising the Origins, Development and Impact of the Call Centre', *New Technology, Work and Employment*, 212: 107–22.

European Electronic Commerce and Telework Trends (ECaTT) (2000a) *Telework Data Report (Population Survey): Ten Countries in Comparison*, Bonn: ECaTT. Available online: http://www.ecatt.com (accessed 1 March 2006).

European Electronic Commerce and Telework Trends (ECaTT) (2000b) *Telework Data Report (Establishment Survey): Ten Countries in Comparison*, Bonn: ECaTT. Available online: http://www.ecatt.com (accessed 12 March 2006).

Evans, J. (2000) 'Workers in the New Economy', *OECD Observer*, December 1999: 219.

Felstead, A., Gallie, D. and Green, F. (2004) 'Job Complexity and Task Discretion: Tracking the Direction of Skills at Work in Britain', in Warhurst, C., Grugulis, I. and Keep, E. (eds) *The Skills That Matter*, London: Palgrave.

Fernie, S. and Metcalf, D. (1998) '(Not) Hanging on the Telephone: Payment Systems in the New Sweatshops', Discussion Paper 390, Centre for Economic Performance, London School of Economics.

Filby, M. (1992) 'The Figures, The Personality and The Bums: Service Work and Sexuality', *Work Employment and Society*, 6, 1: 23–42.

Fincham, R. (2000) 'Knowledge Work as Occupational Strategy: The Cases of IT and Management Consultancy', paper presented at European Institute for Advanced Studies in Management (EIASM) workshop on Management Consultancy, Brussels, 17–18 November.

Findlay, P., McKinlay, A., Marks, A. and Thompson, P. (2000) 'In Search of Perfect People: Teamwork and Team Players in the Scottish Spirits Industry', *Human Relations*, 53, 12: 1549–74.

Fine, L. (1990) *The Souls of the Skyscraper: Female Clerical Workers in Chicago, 1970–1930*, Philadelphia: Temple University Press.

Fleck, J. (1994) 'Learning by Trying: The Implementation of Configurational Technology', *Research Policy* 23, 6: 637–52.

Florida, R. (2002) *The Rise of the Creative Class*, New York: Basic Books.

Foucault, M. (1977) *Discipline and Punish: The Birth of the Prison*, Harmondsworth: Penguin.

Fox, A. (1974) *Beyond Contract: Work, Power and Trust Relations*, London: Faber and Faber.

Fransman, M. and Tanaka, S. (1995) 'Government, Globalization and Universities in Japanese Biotechnology', *Research Policy*, 24, 1: 13–50.

Fraser, J.A. (2001) *White Collar Sweatshop: The Deterioration of Work and its rewards in Corporate America*, New York: W.W. Norton & Co.

Freeman, C. (1995) 'The "National System of Innovation" in Historical Perspective', *Cambridge Journal of Economics*, 19: 5–24.

Frenkel, S.J., Tan, M., Korcyznski, M. and Shire, K. (1998) 'Beyond Bureaucracy? Work Organization in Call Centres', *International Journal of Human Resource Management*, 9, 6: 957–79.

Frenkel, S.J., Korczynski, M., Shire, K.A. and Tan, M. (1999) *On the Front Line: Organization of Work in the Information Economy*, Ithaca, NY: Cornell University Press.

Frieden, J.A. (1991) 'Invested Interests: the Politics of National Economic Policies in a World of Global Finance', *International Organization*, 45, 4: 425–51.

Friedman, A. (1977) 'Responsible Autonomy versus Direct Control over the Labour Process', *Capital and Class*, 1, Spring: 43–58.

Friedman, A. and Cornford, D. (1989) *Computer Systems Development: History, Organisation and Implementation*, Chichester: John Wiley and Sons.

Friedman, T. (1999) *The Lexus and the Olive Tree: Understanding Globalization*, New York: Farrar, Straus, Giroux.

Fröbel, F., Heinrichs, J. and Kreye, O. (1980) *The New International Divison of Labour*, Cambridge: Cambridge University Press.

Gale, H.F., Wojan, T.R. and Olmsted, J.C. (2002) 'Skills, Flexible Manufacturing Technology, and Work Organization', *Industrial Relations*, 41, 1: 48–79.

Gallie, D., White, M., Cheng, Y. and Tomlinson, M. (1998) *Restructuring the Employment Relationship*, Oxford: Clarendon Press.

Gareis, K. (2002) 'The Intensity of Telework in 2002 in the EU, Switzerland and the USA', Paper presented at the Annual International Telework Forum Congress, Badajoz, Spain, 3–5 September. Available online: http://www.sibis-eu.org/publications/articles. htm (accessed: 2 February 2007).

Gareis, K. and Kordey, N. (2000) 'The Spread of Telework in 2005', Bonn: European Electronic Commerce and Telework Trends (ECaTT). Available online: http://www. ecatt.com (accessed 27 April 2006).

Garrett, G. (1998) 'Global Markets and National Politics: Collision Course or Virtuous Circle', *International Organization*, 52, 4: 787–812.

Garrett, G. and Lange, P. (1991) 'Political Responses to Interdependence: What's "Left" for the Left?', *International Organisation*, 45, 4: 539–64.

Garson, B. (1988) *The Electronic Sweatshop: How Computers are Transforming the Office of the Future into the Factory of the Past*, New York: Simon and Schuster.

Genoff, R. and Green, R. (eds) (1998) *Manufacturing Prosperity: Ideas for Industry, Technology and Employment*, Sydney: Federation Press.

Giddens, A. (1984) *The Constitution of Society*, Los Angeles: University of California Press.

Giddens, A. (1998) *The Third Way: The Renewal of Social Democracy*, Cambridge: Polity Press.

Gill, C. (1985) *Work, Unemployment and the New Technology*, Oxford: Polity Press.

Gittleman, M., Horrigan, M. and Joyce, M. (1998) ' "Flexible" Workplace Practices: Evidence from a Nationally Representative Survey', *Industrial and Labor Relations Review*, 52, 1: 99–115.

Glenn, E.K. and Feldberg, R.L. (1979) 'Proletarianising Office Work', in Zimbalist, A. (ed.) *Case Studies on the Labor Process*, New York: Monthly Review Press.

Godard, J. and Delaney, J.T. (2000) 'Reflections on the "High Performance" Paradigm's Implications for Industrial Relations as a Field', *Industrial and Labor Relations Review*, 52: 99–113.

Golding, P. (1996) 'World Wide Wedge: Division and Contradiction in the Global Information Infrastructure', *Monthly Review*, July–August, 48, 3: 70–85.

Goodman, J.B. and Pauly, L.W. (1993) 'The Obsolescence of Capital Controls? Economic Management in the Age of Global Markets', *World Politics*, 46: 50–82.

Gordon, D.M. (1996) *Fat and Mean: The Corporate Squeeze of Working Americans and the Myth of Managerial 'Downsizing'*, New York: Free Press.

Granovetter, M. (1985) 'Economic Action and Social Structure, the Problem of Embeddedness', *American Journal of Sociology*, 91, 3: 481–510.

Granstrand, O., Patel, P. and Pavitt, K. (1999) 'Multi-technology Corporations: Why they have "Distributed" rather than "Distinctive Core" Competencies', in Pavitt, K. (ed.) *Technology, Management and Systems Innovation*, London: Edward Elgar, 87–103.

Grassman, S. (1980) 'Long-term trends in openness of national economies', *Oxford Economic Paper*, 32, 1: 123–33.

Green, F. (2001). 'It's Been a Hard Day's Night: The Concentration and Intensification of Work in Late Twentieth Century Britain', *British Journal of Industrial Relations*, 39: 53–80.

Green, F. (2004) 'Why Has Work Effort Become More Intense?', *Industrial Relations*, 43, 4: 709–41.

Green, F. (2006) *Demanding Work: The Paradox of Job Quality in the Affluent Economy*, Princeton: Princeton University Press.

Greenbaum, J. (1995) *Windows on the Workplace – Computers, Jobs and the Organization of Office Work in the Late Twentieth Century*, New York: Monthly Review Press.

Greenbaum, J. (1998) 'The Times they are A'Changin: Dividing and Recombining Labour through Computer Systems', in Thompson, P. and Warhurst, C. (eds) *Workplaces of the Future*, Basingstoke: Macmillan.

Grimshaw, D., Cooke, F.L., Grugulis, I. and Vincent, S. (2002) 'New Technology and Changing Organisational Forms: Implications for Managerial Control and Skills', *New Technology, Work and Employment*, 17 (3): 186–203.

Grint, K. (1995) *Management: A Sociological Introduction*, Cambridge: Polity Press.

Grint, K. and Woolgar, S. (1997) *The Machine at Work: Technology, Work and Organization*, London: Polity Press.

Grupp, H. (1997) 'The Links between Competitiveness, Firms' Innovative Activities and Public R&D Support in Germany: An Empirical Analysis', *Technology Analysis and Strategic Management*, 9, 1: 19–33.

Giuliano, V.E. (1982) 'The Mechanization of Office Work', *Scientific American*, 66–75.

Gunasekaran, A. (1999) 'Agile Manufacturing: A Framework for Research and Development', *International Journal of Production Economics*, 62: 87–105.

Hage, J. and Alter, C. (1997) 'A Typology of Interorganizational Relationships and Networks', in Hollingsorth, J.R. and Boyer, R. (eds) *Contemporary Capitalism: The Embeddedness of Institutions*, Cambridge: Cambridge University Press.

Hales, C. (2002) '"Bureaucracy-lite" and Continuities in Managerial Work', *British Journal of Management*, 13: 51–66.

Hales, C.P. (1999) 'Why Do Managers Do What They Do? Reconciling Evidence and Theory in Accounts of Managerial Work', *British Journal of Management*, 10: 335–50.

Hall, P. and Sockice, D. (2001) *Varieties of Capitalism: The Institutional Foundations of Comparative Advantage*, Oxford: Oxford University Press.

Hall, R. (2002) 'Enterprise Resource Planning Systems and Organisational Change: Transforming Work Organisation?', *Strategic Change*, 11, 5: 263–70.

Hall, R. (2005) 'The Integrating and Disciplining Tendencies of ERPs: Evidence from Australian Organisations', *Strategic Change*, 14, 5: 245–54.

Hallier, J. (2004) 'Embellishing the Past: Middle Manager Identity and Informality in the Implementation of New Technology', *New Technology, Work and Employment*, 19, 1: 43–62.

Hallman, A. (2003) 'Flexible Manufacturing for Auto Parts', *Tooling and Production*, 69, 1: 32–4.

Hamid, Z. (2005) *Knowledge Workers: Evaluating the Impact and Management of Knowledge Workers*, unpublished PhD thesis, Department of Human Resource Management, University of Strathclyde.

Hampson, I. (1999) 'Lean Production and the Toyota Production System – Or, the Case of the Forgotten Production Concepts', *Economic and Industrial Democracy*, 20, 3: 369–91.

Handy, C. (1995a) *The Future of Work*. WH Smith Contemporary Papers, 8.

Handy, C. (1995b) 'Trust and the Virtual Organization', *Harvard Business Review*, May–June: 40–50.

Harley, B., Wright, C., Hall, R. and Dery, K. (2006) 'Management Reactions to Technological Change: the Example of Enterprise Resource Planning', *Journal of Applied Behavioral Science*, 42, 3: 58–75.

Harris, M. (1998) 'Rethinking the Virtual Organization', in Jackson, P.J. and Van der Wielen, J.M. (eds) *Teleworking: International Perspectives: From Teleworking to the Virtual Organization*, London: Routledge.

Harrison, B. (1994) *Lean and Mean: The Changing Landscape of Corporate Power in the Age of Flexibility*, New York: Basic Books.

Harvey, D. (1989) *The Urban Experience*, Oxford: Basil Blackwell.

Hay, C. (2004) 'Common Trajectories, Variable Paces, Divergent Outcomes? Models of European Capitalism Under Conditions of Complex Economic Interdependence', *Review of International Political Economy*, 11, 2: 231–62.

Hecht, J. (2001) 'Classical Labour-Displacing Technological Change: The Case of the U.S. Insurance Industry', *Cambridge Journal of Economics,* 25: 517–37.

Heckscher, C. and Donnellon, A. (eds) (1994) *The Post-Bureaucratic Organisation: New Perspectives on Organisational Change*, London: Sage.

Hedley, R. (2002) *Running Out of Control* – Dilemmas of Globalisation, Bloomfield: Kumarian Press.

Heery, E. and Salmon, J. (eds) (2000) *The Insecure Workforce*, London: Routledge.

Helleiner, E. (1995) 'Explaining the Globalisation of Financial Markets: Bringing the States Back In', *Review of International Political Economy*, 2, 2: 315–41.

Helling, A. (2000) 'A Framework for Understanding Telework', in U.S. Department of Labor, *Telework and the New Workplace of the Twenty-first Century*, New Orleans: U.S. Department of Labor. Available online: http://www.dol.gov/dol/asp/public/telework (accessed 5 June 2006).

Henwood, D. (1997) *Wall Street: How It Works and For Whom*, London: Verso.

Herbig, P., Golden, J. and Dunphy, S. (1994) 'The Relationship of Structure to Entrepreneurial and Innovative Success', *Marketing Intelligence and Planning*, 12, 9: 37–48.

Higa, K. and Wijayanayake, J. (1998) 'Telework in Japan: Perceptions and Implementations', paper presented at the Thirty-first Annual Hawaii International Conference on System Sciences'. Available online: http://ieeexplore.ieee.org/iel4/5217/14270/00655272.pdf?arnumber=655272 (accessed 17 March 2007).

Hinds, P.J. and Kiesler, S. (eds) (2002) *Distributed Work*, Cambridge, MA: MIT Press.

Hirschhorn, L. and Mokray, J. (1992) 'Automation and Competency Requirements in Manufacturing: A Case Study', in Adler, P. (ed.) *Technology and the Future of Work*, New York: Oxford University Press.

Hirst, P. and Thompson, G. (1992) 'The Problem of "Globalization": International Economic Relations, National Economic Management and the Formation of Trading Blocs', *Economy and Society*, 21, 4: 357–96.

Hirst, P. and Thompson, G. (1999) *Globalisation in Question: the International Economy and the Possibilities of Governance*, Cambridge: Polity Press.

Hochschild, A.R. (1983) *The Managed Heart: The Commercialisation of Human Feeling*, Berkeley: University of California Press.

Hochschild, A.R. (1997) *The Time Bind: When Work Becomes Home and Home Becomes Work*, New York: Metropolitan Books.

Hodson, R. (1990) 'Symposium: Dispelling the Japanese Mystique? Quality Circles: Are They America's Future?', *Contemporary Sociology*, 19, 6: 792–5.

Hofstede, G.H. (1991) *Cultures and Organizations: Software of the Mind*, New York: McGraw-Hill.

Hollingsworth, J.R. (1997) 'Continuities and Changes in Social Systems of Production: The Cases of Japan, Germany and the United States', in Hollingsworth, J.R. and Boyer, R. (eds) *Contemporary Capitalism: The Embeddedness of Institutions*, Cambridge: Cambridge University Press.

Hollingsworth, J.R. and Boyer, R. (1997) 'Coordination of Economic Actors and Social Systems of Production', in Hollingsworth, J.R. and Boyer, R. (eds) *Contemporary Capitalism: The Embeddedness of Institutions*, Cambridge: Cambridge University Press.

Holloway, J. (1994) 'Global Capital and the Nation State', *Capital and Class*, 52: 23–50.

Holman, D., Batt, R. and Holtgrewe, U. (2007) *The Global Call Centre Report: International Perspectives on Management and Employment*, Sheffield: Global Call Centre Research Network.

Holton, R.J. (1998) *Globalization and the Nation-State*, London: Macmillan.

Hood, C. (1995), 'The "New Public Management" in the 1980s: Variations on a Theme', *Accounting, Organizations and Society*, 20, 2/3: 93–109.

Hooks, G. (1990) 'The Rise of the Pentagon and U.S. State Building: The Defense Program as Industrial Policy', *American Journal of Sociology*, 96, 2: 358–404.

Houlihan, M. (2000) 'Eyes Wide Shut? Querying the Depth of Call Centre Learning', *Journal of European Industrial Training*, 24, 2/4: 228–40.

Houlihan, M. (2001) 'Managing to Manage? Stories from the Call Centre Floor', *Journal of European Industrial Training*, 25, 2/3/4: 208–20.

Houlihan, M. (2002) 'Tensions and Variations in Call Centre Management Strategies', *Human Resource Management Journal*, 12, 4: 67–85.

Howell, C. (2003) 'Varieties of Capitalism: And then there was one?', *Comparative Politics*, 36: 103–24.

Howells, J. (1996) 'Tacit Knowledge, Innovation and Technology Transfer', *Technology Analysis and Strategic Management*, 8, 2: 91–106.

Howkins, J. (2001) *The Creative Economy*, London: Penguin.

Huber, G.P. (1990) 'A Theory of the Effects of Advanced Information Technologies on Organizational Design, Intelligence, and Decision Making', *Academy of Management Review*, 15 (1): 47–71.

Hughes, J.A., O'Brien, J., Randall, D., Rouncefield, M. and Tolmie, P. (2001) 'Some "Real" Problems of "Virtual" Organisation', *New Technology, Work and Employment*, 16, 1: 4–64.

Hughes, J.A., Rouncefield, M. and Tolmie, P. (2002) 'The Day-to-Day Work of Standardization: A Sceptical Note on the Reliance on IT in a Retail Bank', in Woolgar, S. (ed.) *Virtual Society: Technology, Cyberbole, Reality*, Oxford: Oxford University Press.

Hughes, T.P. (1979) 'The Electrification of America: The System-builders', *Technology and Culture*, 20: 125–39.

Hunt, V.D. (1987) *Dictionary of Advanced Manufacturing Technology*, New York: Elsevier.

Huq, F. (1992) 'Labor Issues in the Implementation of Group Technology Cellular Manufacturing', *Production and Inventory Management Journal*, 33, fourth quarter: 15.

Hutton, W. (1995) 'Reviving Bretton Woods: Social Democracy Needs a New International Exchange Rate Regime', *New Economy*, 1, 4: 207–12.

Huws, U. (2003) *The Making of a Cybertariat: Virtual Work in a Real World*, New York: Monthly Review Press.

Igbaria, M. and Tan, M. (1998) *The Virtual Workplace*, Hershey, PA: Idea Group.

Immarino, S. and Michie, J. (1998) 'The Scope of Technological Globalisation', *International Journal of Economics and Business*, 5, 3: 335–53.

International Labour Office (2005) *Yearbook of Labour Statistics*, Geneva: International Labour Office.

International Monetary Fund (2002) *World Economic Outlook*, New York: International Monetary Fund.

Iwaki, H. (1996) 'Labour Market Mechanisms in Japan', in Michie, J. and Grieve Smith, J. (eds) *Creating Industrial Capacity: Towards Full Employment*, Oxford: Oxford University Press.

Jackson, P. (ed.) (1999) *Virtual Working: Social and Organizational Dynamics*, London: Routledge.

Jackson, P.J. and van der Wielen, J.M. (1998a) 'Actors, Approaches and Agendas from Telecommuting to the Virtual Organization', in Jackson, P.J. and van der Wielen, J.M. (eds) *Teleworking: International Perspectives: From Telecommuting to the Virtual Organization*, London: Routledge, 1–18.

Jackson, P.J. and van der Wielen, J.M. (eds) (1998b) *Teleworking: International Perspectives: From Teleworking to the Virtual Organization*, London: Routledge.

Jaikumar, R. (1986) 'Postindustrial Manufacturing', *Harvard Business Review*, November–December: 69–76.

James, N. (1989) 'Emotional Labour', *Sociological Review*, 37: 15–42.

Jenkins, C. and Sherman, B. (1979) *The Collapse of Work*, London: Eyre Methuen.

Jessop, B. (2002) *The Future of the Capitalist State*, Cambridge: Polity Press.

Jessop, B. (2003) 'Informational Capitalism and Empire: The Post-Marxist Celebration of US Hegemony in a New World Order', *Studies in Language and Capitalism*. Available online: http://www.languageandcapitalism.info/Inc/papers/ (accessed 03 May 2006).

Jones, M. (1999) 'Structuration Theory', in Currie, W. and Galliers, B. (eds) *Rethinking Management Information Systems*, Oxford: Oxford University Press, 103–35.

Jones, M., Orlikowski, W. and Munir, K.A. (2004) 'Structuration Theory and Information Systems: A Critical Reappraisal', in Willcocks, L. and Mingers, J. (eds) *Social Theory and Philosophy for Information Systems*, Chichester: Wiley, 297–328.

Jones, O. (1997) 'Changing the Balance? Taylorism, TQM and Work Organization', *New Technology, Work and Employment*, 12, 1: 13–24.

Jordan, M. (2003) 'Pulling Widgets into Lean Success', *Industrial Engineer*, 35, 3: 34–9.

Jürgens, U. (1993) *Breaking from Taylorism: Changing Forms of Work in the Automobile Industry*, Cambridge: Cambridge University Press.

Jürgens, U., Naumann, K. and Rupp, J. (2000) 'Shareholder Value in an Adverse Environment: The German Case', *Economy and Society*, 29, 1: 54–79.

Kalleberg, A.L. (2001) 'Organizing Flexibility: The Flexible Firm in a New Century', *British Journal of Industrial Relations*, 39, 4: 479–504.

Katzenstein, P.J. (1985) *Small States in World Markets: Industrial Policy in Europe*, Ithaca, NY: Cornell University Press.

Keating, M. (2000) 'The Pressures for Change', in Davis, G. and Keating, M. (eds) *The Future of Governance: Policy Choices*, Sydney: Allen and Unwin.

Keefe, J.H. (1991a) 'Do Unions Influence the Diffusion of Technology?', *Industrial and Labor Relations Review*, 44, 2: 261–74.

Keefe, J.H. (1991b) 'Numerically Controlled Machine Tools and Worker Skills', *Industrial and Labor Relations Review*, 44, 3: 503–19.

Kern, H. and Schumann, M. (1992) 'New Concepts of Production and the Emergence of the Systems Controller', in Adler, P. (ed.) *Technology and the Future of Work*, New York: Oxford University Press.

Kitay, J. (1999) 'Change in Tandem: Employment Relations in Australian Retail Banks', in Regini, M., Kitay, J. and Baethge, M. (eds) *From Tellers to Sellers*, Cambridge, MA: MIT Press.

Kjellberg, A. (1998) 'Sweden: Restoring the Model?', in Ferner, A. and Hyman, R. (eds) *Changing Industrial Relations in Europe*, Oxford: Blackwell.

Klein, H. and Kleinman, D. (2002) 'The Social Construction of Technology: Structural Considerations', *Science, Technology and Human Values*, 27 (1): 28–52.

Kleinknecht, A. (1998) 'Is Labour Market Flexibility Harmful to Innovation?', *Cambridge Journal of Economics*, 22: 387–96.

Kling, R. (1996) *Computerization and Controversy: Value Conflicts and Social Choices*, 2nd edition, San Diego: Academic Press.

Knights, D. and Murray, F. (1994) *Managers Divided: Organisation Politics and Information Technology Management*, Chichester: John Wiley & Sons.

Knights, D., Noble, F., Willmott, H. and Vurdubakis, T. (1999) 'Constituting the CSR: Consumption, Production and the Labour Process in Call Centres', paper presented at the 17th International Labour Process Conference, Royal Holloway College, March.

Kochan, T. and Osterman, P. (1994) *The Mutual Gains Enterprise: Forging a Winning Partnership Among Labor, Management and Government*, Boston, MA: Harvard Business School Press.

Kominski, R. (2000) 'The Rise of Computing Technology and Working at Home: Data from Current Population Survey Supplements', in U.S. Department of Labor, *Telework and the New Workplace of the Twenty-first Century*, New Orleans: U.S. Department of Labor. Available online: http://www.dol.gov/dol/asp/public/telework (accessed: 15 August 2006).

Kondratieff, N.D. (1935) 'The Long Waves in Economic Life', *Review of Economic Statistics*, 17 (6).

Korczynski, M. (2002) *Human Resource Management and Service Work: The Fragile Social Order*, London: Palgrave.

Kotha, S. and Swamidass, P.M. (1998) 'Advanced Manufacturing Technology Use: Exploring the Effect of the Nationality Variable', *International Journal of Production Research*, 36, 11: 3135–46.

Kotter, J.P. (1982) *The General Managers*, New York: Free Press; London: Collier MacMillan.

Kraft, P. (1977) *Programmers and Managers: The Routinisation of Computer Programming in the United States*, New York: Springer Verlag.

Kraft, P. (1979) 'The Industrialization of Computer Programming: From Programming to Software Production', in Zimbalist, A. (ed.) *Case Studies in the Labor Process*, New York: Monthly Review Press.

Krippner, G.R. (2005) 'The Financialisation of the American Economy', *Socio-Economic Review*, 3: 173–208.

Kristensen, P.H. (1996) 'Variations in the Nature of the Firm in Europe', in Whitley, R. and Kristensen, P.H. (eds) *The Changing European Firm: Limits to Convergence*, London: Routledge.

Kumar, K. (1978) *Prophecy and Progress: The Sociology of Industrial and Post-Industrial Society*, Harmondsworth: Penguin Books.

Kurzer, P. (1993) *Business and Banking: Political Change and Economic Integration in Western Europe*, Ithaca, NY: Cornell University Press.

Lam, A. (1997) 'Embedded Firms, Embedded Knowledge: Problems of Collaboration and Knowledge Transfer in Global Cooperative Ventures', *Organization Studies*, 18, 6: 973–96.

Lam, A. (2000) 'Tacit Knowledge, Organizational Learning and Societal Institutions: An Integrated Framework', *Organization Studies*, 21, 3: 487–514.

Lam, A. (2002) 'Alternative Societal Models of Learning and Innovation in the Knowledge Economy', paper presented at DRUID Summer Conference 'Industrial Dynamics of the New and Old Economy', Copenhagen, June.

Lapido, D. and Wilkinson, F. (2002) 'More Pressure, Less Protection', in Burchell, B., Lapido, D. and Wilkinson, F. (eds) *Job Insecurity and Work Intensification*, London: Routledge.

Lash, S. and Wittell, A. (2002) 'Shifting New Media: From Content to Consultancy, from Heterarchy to Hierarchy', *Environment and Planning A*, 34, 11: 1985–2001.

Latour, B. (1996) *Aramis*, Cambridge, MA: Harvard University Press.

Latour, B. (2004) 'Using ANT for Studying Information Systems: A (Somewhat) Socratic Dialogue', in Avgerou, C., Ciborra, C. and Land, F. (eds) *The Social Study of Information and Communications Technology*, Oxford: Oxford University Press.

Law, J. and Callon, M. (1992) 'The Life and Death of an Aircraft: A Network Analysis of Technological Change', in Bijker, W. and Law, J. (eds) *Shaping Technology/Building Society: Studies in Socio-technical Change*, Cambridge MA: MIT Press.

Lazonick, W. (1991) *Business Organisation and the Myth of the Market Economy*, Cambridge: Cambridge University Press.

Lazonick, W. and O'Sullivan, M. (2000) 'Maximising Shareholder Value: A New Ideology for Corporate Governance', *Economy and Society*, 29, 1: 13–35.

Leadbeater, C. (2000) *Living on Thin Air: The New Economy*, London: Viking.

Leidner, R. (1993) *Fast Food, Fast Talk: Service Work and Routinization of Everyday Life*, Berkeley: University of California Press.

Lessard, B. and Baldwin, S. (*c.* 2000) *Net Slaves: True Tales of Working the Web*, New York: McGraw-Hill.

Liker, J.K., Haddad, C.L. and Karlin, J. (1999) 'Perspectives on Technology and Work Organization', *Annual Review of Sociology*, 25: 575–96.

Lindblom, C.E. (1959) 'The Science of Muddling Through', *Public Administration Review*, 19: 79–88.

Lingle, J.H. and Schiemann, W.A. (1996) 'From Balanced Scorecard to Strategic Gauges: Is Measurement Worth It?', *Management Review*, 85: 56–61.

Littler, C., Wiesner, R. and Dunford, R. (2003) 'The Dynamics of Delayering: Changing Management Structures in Three Countries', *Journal of Management Studies*, 40 (2): 225–56.

Lockwood, D. (1958) *The Blackcoated Worker: A Study in Class Consciousness*, London: Allen and Unwin.

Lowi, T. (2001) 'Our Millennium: Political Science Confronts the Global Corporate Economy', *International Political Science Review*, 22, 2: 131–50.

Lund, J. and Wright, C. (2003) 'Integrating the Supply Chain: Industrial Relations Implications in US Grocery Distribution', *New Technology, Work and Employment*, 18 (2): 101–14.

Lundvall, B. (1992) 'Introduction', in B. Lundvall (ed.) *National Systems of Innovation: Towards and Theory of Interactive Learning*, London: Pinter.

Lyon, D. (1988) *The Information Society: Issues and Illusions*, Cambridge: Polity Press.

Lyytinen, K.J. and Ngwenyama, O.K. (1992) 'What Does Computer Support for Co-operative Work Mean? A Structurational Analysis of Computer Supported Co-operative Work', *Accounting, Management and Information Technologies*, 2, 2: 19–37.

MacDonald, C.L. and Sirriani, C. (1996) *Working in the Service Society*, Philadelphia: Temple University Press.

MacKenzie, D. and Wajcman, J. (eds) (1985) *The Social Shaping of Technology*, London: Open University Press.

MacKenzie, D. and Wajcman, J. (eds) (1999) *The Social Shaping of Technology*, 2nd edition, London: Open University Press.

MacKenzie, R. (2002) 'The Migration of Bureaucracy: Contracting and the Regulation of Labour in the Telecommunications Industry', *Work, Employment and Society*, 16, 4: 599–616.

McKinlay, A. (2002) 'The Limits of Knowledge Management', *New Technology, Work and Employment*, 17, 2: 76–88.

McKinlay, A. (2004) 'Knowledge Management', in Ackroyd, S., Batt, R., Thompson, P. and Tolbert, P. (eds) *A Handbook of Work and Organization*, Oxford: Oxford University Press.

Mackintosh, J. (2003) 'Ford Learns to Bend with the Wind', *Financial Times*, 14 February: 9.

McLaughlin, J., Rosen, P., Skinner, D. and Webster, A. (1999) *Valuing Technology: Organisations, Culture and Change*, London: Routledge.

McLoughlin, I. (1989) 'CAD and the Taylorisation of Drawing Office Work', *New Technology, Work and Employment*, 4, 1: 29–39.

McLoughlin, I. (1990) 'Management, Work Organisation and CAD: Towards Flexible Automation?', *Work, Employment and Society*, 4, 2: 217–37.

McLoughlin, I. (1999) *Creative Technological Change: The Shaping of Technologies and Organisations*, London: Routledge.

McLoughlin, I. and Clark, J. (1994) *Technological Change at Work*, 2nd edition, Buckingham: Oxford University Press.

McMahon, P. (2001) 'Technology and Globalisation: An Overview', *Prometheus*, 19, 3: 211–22.

McMillan, G., Narin, F. and Deeds, D. (2000) 'An Analysis of the Critical Role of Public Science in Innovation: The Case of Biotechnology', *Research Policy*, 29: 1–8.

McSweeny, B. (2005) 'Are We Living in a Post-Bureaucratic Epoch?', *Journal of Organizational Change Management*, 19/1: 22–37.

Maglen, L. and Shah, C. (1999) 'Emerging Occupational Patterns in Australia in the Era of Globalization and Rapid Technological Change: Implications for Education and Training', Working Paper No. 21, Melbourne: Centre for the Economics of Education and Training, Monash University.

Malone, T.W. and Rockart, J.F. (1993) 'How Will Information Technology Reshape Organizations? Computers as Coordination Technology?', in Bradley, S.P., Hausman, J.A. and Nolan, R.L. (eds) *Globalization, Technology, and Competition*, Boston, MA: Harvard Business School Press, 37–56.

Mandla, E. (2006) 'Life's a Beach and So is Work', *Sydney Morning Herald*, 6–19 March: 3.

Marceau, J. and Manley, K. (2001) 'Australia's System of Innovation', in Dow, G. and Parker, R. (eds) *Business Work and Community into the New Millennium*, Melbourne: Oxford University Press.

Marshall, J. and Richardson, R. (1996) 'The Impact of "Telemediated" Services on Corporate Structures: The Example of "Branchless" Retail Banking in Britain', *Environment and Planning*, 28: 1843–58.

Mason, D., Button, G., Lankshear, G. and Coates, S. (2002) 'Getting Real About Surveillance and Privacy at Work', in Woolgar, S. (ed.) *Virtual Society: Technology, Cyberbole, Reality*, Oxford: Oxford University Press.

Mathews, J. (1989) *Tools of Change: New Technology and the Democracy of Work*, Sydney: Pluto Press.

Matraves, C. (1997) 'German Industrial Structure in Comparative Perspective', *Industry and Innovation*, 4, 2: 37–52.

May, C. (2002) *The Information Society: A Sceptical View*, Cambridge: Polity Press.

Mayer-Ahuja, N. and Wolf, H. (2007) 'Beyond the Hype: Working in the German Internet Industry', *Critical Sociology*, 33, 1: 73–99.

Mazmanian, M., Yates, J. and Orlikowski, W. (2006) 'Ubiquitous Email: Individual Experiences and Organizational Consequences of Blackberry Use', in *Proceedings of the 65th Annual Meeting of the Academy of Management*, Atlanta, GA, August, St Louis, MO: The Academy of Management.

Meder, D. (2004) 'Automated Credit Systems Take the Heavy Lifting Out of Business-to-Business Credit Decisions', *Credit and Financial Management Review* 10, 1.

Michie, J. and Reati, A. (eds) (1998) *Employment, Technology and Economic Needs: Theory, Evidence and Public Policy*, Cheltenham: Edward Elgar.

Milkman, R. (1997) *Farewell to the Factory: Auto Workers in the Late Twentieth Century*, Berkeley: University of California Press.

Milkman, R. (1998) 'The New American Workplace: High Road or Low Road', in Thompson, P. and Warhurst, C. (eds) *Workplaces of the Future*, Basingstoke: Macmillan.

Milkman, R. and Pullman, C. (1991) 'Technological Change in an Auto Assembly Plant: The Impact on Workers' Tasks and Skills', *Work and Occupations*, 18, May: 123.

Mills, C.W. (1951) *White Collar*, New York: Oxford University Press.

Milner, H.V. and Keohane, R.O. (1996) 'Internationalization and Domestic Politics: An Introduction', in Keohane, R.O. and Milner, H.V. (eds) *Internationalization and Domestic Politics*, Cambridge: Cambridge University Press.

Mintzberg, H. (1973) *The Nature of Managerial Work*, New York: Harper and Row.

Mitchell, H. (2000) 'How Many Teleworkers?', European Telework Development Initiative. Available online: http://www.eto.org.uk/faq/faq-numb (accessed 19 January 2006).

Monk, E. and Wagner, B. (2006) *Concepts in Enterprise Resource Planning*, 2nd edition, Boston, MA: Thomson Course Technology.

Morrin, F. (2000) 'A Transformation in the French Model of Shareholding and Management', *Economy and Society*, 29, 1: 36–54.

Moses, J.W. (1994) 'Abdication from National Policy Autonomy: What's Left to Leave?', *Politics and Society*, 22, 2: 125–48.

Moss, P., Salzman, H. and Tilly, C. (2003) *Under Construction: the Continuing Evolution of Job Structures in Call Centers*, Lowell, MA: Center for Industrial Competitiveness, Boston, MA: University of Massachusetts.

Mowery, D.C. and Rosenberg, N. (1992) 'The U.S. National Innovation System', in Nelson, R. (ed.) *National Innovation Systems: A Comparative Analysis*, New York: Oxford University Press.

Mutch, A. (2000) 'Managers and Information: Agency and Structure', *Information Systems Review*, 1: 169–80.

Mutch, A. (2002) 'Actors and Networks or Agents and Structures: Towards a Realist View of Information Systems', *Organization*, 9, 3: 477–96.

Nelson, R. (1992) 'National Innovation Systems: A Retrospective on a Study', *Industrial and Corporate Change*, 1, 2: 347–74.

Nelson, R. and Rosenberg, N. (1992) 'Technical Innovation and National Systems', in Nelson, R. (ed.) *National Innovation Systems: A Comparative Analysis*, New York: Oxford University Press.

Newman, R. and Newman, J. (1985) 'Information Work: The New Divorce?', *British Journal of Sociology*, 36, 4: 497–515.

Nilles, J.M. (1998) *Managing Telework: Strategies for Managing the Virtual Workforce*, New York: Wiley.

Niosi, J., Saviotti, P., Bellon, B. and Crow, M. (1993) 'National Systems of Innovation: In Search of a Workable Concept', *Technology in Society*, 15, 2: 207–27.

Noble, D. (1979) 'Social Choice in Machine Design: The Case of Automatically Controlled Machine Tools', in Zimbalist, A. (ed.) *Case Studies in the Labour Process*, New York: Monthly Review Press.

Nolan, J. (2002) 'The Intensification of Everyday Life', in Burchell, B., Lapido, D. and Wilkinson, F. (eds) *Job Security and Work Intensification*, London: Routledge.

Nolan, P. (2000) 'Back to the Future of Work', plenary paper, 50th Anniversary Conference of the British Universities Industrial Relations Association, University of Warwick.

Nolan, P. (2004) 'Editorial, Shaping the Future: The Political Economy of Work and Employment', *Industrial Relations Journal,* 35, 5: 378–87.

Nolan, P. and Wood, S. (2003) 'Mapping the Future of Work', *British Journal of Industrial Relations,* 41, 2: 165–74.

Nonaka I. (1991) 'The Knowledge Creating Company', *Harvard Business Review*, November–December: 96–104.

Nooteboom, B. (2000) 'Institutions and Forms of Co-ordination in Innovation Systems', *Organization Studies*, 21, 5: 915–39.

OECD (1986) *Labour Force Statistics 1964–1984*, Paris: OECD.

OECD (1998) *Technology, Productivity and Job Creation: Best Policy Practices*. Paris: OECD.

OECD (1999a) *The Knowledge Based Economy: A Set of Facts and Figures*, Paris: OECD.

OECD (1999b) *Labour Force Statistics 1979–1998*, Paris: OECD, 32–4.

OECD (1999c) *Science, Technology and Industry Scoreboard: Benchmarking Knowledge Based Economies*, Paris: OECD.

OECD (2000) *A New Economy: The Changing Role of Innovation and Information Technology in Growth*, Paris: OECD.

OECD (2001a) *OECD Science, Technology and Industry Scoreboard: Towards a Knowledge Based Economy*, Paris: OECD.

OECD (2001b) *Measuring Globalisation: The Role of Multinationals in OECD Countries, Volume I: Manufacturing Sector, Volume II: Service Sector*, Paris: OECD.

OECD (2001c) *The Well-Being of Nations: The Role of Human and Social Capital*, Paris: OECD.

OECD (2002a) *Economic Outlook No. 72*, Paris: OECD.

OECD (2002b) 'The ICT Sector', in *Measuring the Information Economy*, OECD: Paris.

OECD (2003) *National Accounts of OECD Countries*, OECD: Paris.

OECD (2004) 'ICT Skills and Employment', in *OECD Information Technology Outlook 2004,* Paris: OECD.

OECD (2005a) *OECD Science, Technology and Industry Scoreboard*, Paris: OECD.

OECD (2005b) *Main Science and Technology Indicators*, Paris: OECD.

OECD (2006) *Labour Force Statistics 1985–2005*, Paris: OECD, 32–5.

Ogbonna, E. and Wilkinson, B. (1990) 'Corporate Strategy and Corporate Structure: the View from the Checkout', *Personnel Review*, 19, 4: 9–15.

Ohmae, K. (1990) *The Borderless World*, London: Collins.

OMIS Research (2006) 'Contact Centres and Offshoring', Research Newsletter Number 10, March.

O'Riain, S. (2000) 'The Flexible Developmental State: Globalization, Information Technology, and the "Celtic Tiger"', *Politics and Society*, 28, 2: 157–93.

Orr, J.E. (1997) *Talking about Machines: An Ethnography of a Modern Job*, Ithaca, NY: ILR Press.

Orlikowski, W.J. (1988) 'The Data Processing Occupation: Professionalization or Proletarianization?', *Research in the Sociology of Work*, 4: 95–124.

Orlikowski, W.J. (1991) 'Integrated Information Environment or Matrix of Control? The Contradictory Implications of Information Technology', *Accounting, Management and Information Technologies*, 1, 1: 9–42.

Orlikowski, W.J. (1992) 'The Duality of Technology: Rethinking the Concept of Technology in Organizations', *Organization Science*, 3, 3: 398–427.

Orlikowski, W.J. (2000) 'Using Technology and Constituting Structures: A Practice Lens for Studying Technology in Organizations', *Organization Science*, 11, 4: 404–28.

Orlikowski, W. and Iacono, S. (2001) 'Research Commentary: Desperately Seeking the "IT" in IT Research – A Call to Theorizing the IT Artefact', *Information Systems Research*, 12, 2: 121–34.

Osterman, P. (1994) 'How Common Is Workplace Transformation and Who Adopts It?', *Industrial and Labor Relations Review*, 47, 2: 173–88.

Parker, R. (1999) 'From National Champions to Small and Medium Sized Enterprises: The Changing Focus of Industry Policy in France, Germany and Sweden', *Journal of Public Policy*, 19, 1: 63–89.

Parker, R. (2006) 'Small Business and Entrepreneurship in the Knowledge Economy: A Comparison of Australia and Sweden', *New Political Economy* 11, 2: 201–26.

Parker, R. and Tamaschke, L. (2005) 'Explaining Regional Departures from National Patterns of Industrial Specialisation: Bringing the State Back in to Innovation Systems and Comparative Capitalism', *Organization Studies*, 26, 12.

Patel, P. and Pavitt, K. (1991) 'Large Firms in the Production of the World's Technology: An Important Case of Non-globalisation', *Journal of International Business Studies*, 22, 1: 91–102.

Patel, P. and Vega, M. (1999) 'Patterns of Internationalisation of Corporate Technology: Location vs. Home Country Advantages', *Research Policy*, 28: 145–55.

Pauly, L.W. and Reich, S. (1997) 'National Structures and Multinational Behaviour: Enduring Differences in the Age of Globalization', *International Organization* 51, 1: 1–30.

Pavitt, K. (ed.) (1999) *Technology, Management and Systems Innovation*, London: Edward Elgar.

Petit, P. (1995) 'Employment and Technological Change', in Stoneman, P. (ed.) *Handbook of the Economics of Innovation and Technological Change*, Oxford: Blackwell, 366–404.

Petit, P. (2001) 'Europe in the Triad: Growth Pattern and Structural Changes', in Petit, P. and Soete, L. (eds) *Technology and the Future of European Employment*, Cheltenham: Edward Elgar.

Petit, P. and Soete, L. (eds) (2001) *Technology and the Future of European Employment*, Cheltenham: Edward Elgar

Pinch, T.J. and Bijker, W.E. (1984) 'The Social Construction of Facts and Artefacts – Or How the Sociology of Science and the Sociology of Technology Might Benefit Each Other', *Social Studies of Science*, 14, 3: 399–441.

Pink, D. (2001) *Free Agent Nation*, New York: Warner Business.

Piore, M. and Sabel, C. (1984) *The Second Industrial Divide: Possibilities for Prosperity*, New York: Basic Books.

Pocock, B. (2003) *The Work/Life Collision: What Work Is Doing To Australians and What To Do About It*, Annandale: Federation Press.

Polanyi, K. (1944) *The Great Transformation: The Political and Economic Origins of Our Time*, Boston, MA: Beacon Press.

Porter, M. (1990) *The Competitive Advantage of Nations*, London: Macmillan.

Porter, M. (1998) 'Clusters and the New Economics of Competition', *Harvard Business Review*, November–December: 77–90.

Powell, W.W. and Snellman, K. (2004) 'The Knowledge Economy', *Annual Review of Sociology*, 30: 199–230.

Poynter, G. (2000) 'Thank You for Calling: The Ideology of Work in the Service Economy', *Soundings*, 14, Spring: 151–160.

Pratt, A. (2002) 'New Economy: a Cool Look and the Hot Economy', unpublished mimeo, London School of Economics.

Pratt, A. (2003) 'A "Third Way" for the Creative Industries?', unpublished mimeo, London School of Economics.

Pratt, J. (1999) 'Cost Benefits of Teleworking to Manage Work/Life Responsibilities', Telework America National Telework Survey for the International Telework Association and Council. Available online: http://web.archive.org/web/20060509170052/ www. workingfromanywhere.org/telework/twa1999.htm (accessed 6 July 2006).

Pratt, J. (2000) 'Telework and Society Implications for Corporate and Societal Cultures', U.S. Department of Labor, *Telework and the New Workplace of the Twenty-first Century*, New Orleans: U.S. Department of Labor. Available online: http://www.dol. gov/dol/asp/public/telework (accessed 11 April 2006).

Preece, D. (1995) *Organisations and Technical Change: Strategy, Objectives and Involvement*, London: Routledge.

Prevezer, M. (1997) 'The Dynamics of Industrial Clustering in Biotechnology', *Small Business Economics*, 9, 3: 255–71.

Purcell, J. and Hutchinson, S. (1996) 'Lean and Mean', *People Management*, 2, 20: 27–33.

Purcell, J., Hutchinson, S. and Kinnie, N. (2000) 'Fun and Surveillance: The Paradox of High Commitment Management in Call Centres', *International Journal of Human Resource Management*, 11/2: 967–85.

Putzell, J. (2005) 'Globalization, Liberalization and Prospects for the State', *International Political Science Review*, 26, 1: 5–16.

Radice, H. (ed.) (1984) *International Firms and Modern Imperialism*, Harmondsworth: Penguin.

Radice, H. (1998) ' "Globalisation" and National Differences', *Competition and Change*, 3, 4: 263–91.

Radice, H. (2000) 'Globalisation and National Capitalisms: Theorizing Convergence and Differentiation', *Review of International Political Economy*, 7, 4, 719–42.

Randle, K. (1996) 'The Whitecoated Worker: Professional Autonomy in a Period of Change', *Work, Employment and Society*, 10, 4: 737–53.

Randle, K. (1998) 'Managing Intellect: The Dysfunctions of Post-bureaucracy', paper presented at the Work, Employment and Society Conference, Cambridge, September.

Reed, M.I. (2001) 'Organization, Trust and Control: A Realist Analysis', *Organization Studies*, 22, 2: 201–28.

Regini, M., Kitay, J. and Baethge, M. (eds) (1999) *From Tellers to Sellers*, Cambridge, MA: MIT Press.

Reich, R. (1991) *The Work of Nations*, London: Simon and Schuster.

Reid, S. (1978) 'Computers and De-skilling: Some Preliminary Observations from a Case-Study in Local Government', Oxford: Nuffield Research Paper.

Ricardo, D. (1821) *On the Principles of Political Economy and Taxation*, 3rd edition, London: John Murray.

Rifkin, J. (1995) *The End of Work: The Decline of the Global Work Force and the Dawn of the Post-Market Era*, London: Penguin.

Rifkin, J. (2000) *The Age of Access: How the Shift from Ownership to Access is Transforming Capitalism*, Harmondsworth: Penguin.

Riley, P., Mandavilli, A. and Heino, R. (2000) 'Observing the Impact of Communication and Information Technology on "Net-Work"', U.S. Department of Labor, *Telework and the New Workplace of the Twenty-first Century*, New Orleans: U.S. Department of Labor. Available online: http://www.dol.gov/dol/asp/public/telework (accessed 07 May 2006).

Ritzer, G. (1998) *The McDonaldization Thesis: Explorations and Extensions*, London: Sage Publications.

Robey, D. and Azevedo, A. (1994) 'Cultural Analysis of the Organizational Consequences of Information Technology', *Accounting, Management and Information Technologies*, 4: 23–37.

Roberts, K.H. and Grabowski, M. (1995) 'Organizations, Technology, and Structuring', in Clegg, S.R., Hardy, C. and Nord, W.R. (eds) *Handbook of Organization Studies*, Thousand Oaks, CA: Sage Publications.

Rothschild, J. and Ollilainen, M. (1999) 'Obscuring but Not Reducing Managerial Control: Does TQM Measure Up to Democracy Standards?', *Economic and Industrial Democracy*, 20, 4: 583–623.

Rowe, C. (1986) *People and Chips: The Human Implications of Information Technology*, London: Paradigm Press.

Rubery, J. and Grimshaw, D. (2001) 'ICTs and Employment: The Problem of Job Quality', *International Labour Review*, 140 (2): 165–92.

Rubery, J., Earnshaw, J., Marchington, M., Cooke, F.L. and Vincent, S. (2000) 'Changing Organizational Forms and the Employment Relationship', Working Paper 14, ESRC Future of Work Programme.

Sackmann, S. (1992) 'Culture and Subcultures: an Analysis of Organizational Knowledge', *Administrative Science Quarterly*, 37: 140–61.

Sandberg, Å. and Augustsson, F. (2002) *In-house Production, Ordering and Subcontracting of Interactive Media Among Swedish Firms and Government Agencies*, Stockholm: Arbetslivsinstitutet.

Sandel, M.J. (1996) *Democracy's Discontent: America in Search of a Public Philosophy*, Cambridge, MA: Harvard University Press.

Saxenian, A. (1996) 'Beyond Boundaries: Open Labour Markets and Learning in Silicon Valley', in Arthur, M.B. and Rousseau, D.M. (eds) *The Boundaryless Career: A New Employment Principle for a New Organisational Era*, New York: New York University Press.

Scarborough, H. and Burrell, G. (1996) 'The Axeman Cometh: the Changing Roles and Knowledges of Middle Management', in Clegg, S. and Palmer, G. (eds) *The Politics of Management Knowledge*, London: Sage, 113–89.

Scarbrough, H. and Swan, J. (2001) 'Explaining the Diffusion of Knowledge Management: The Role of Fashion', *British Journal of Management*, 12: 3–12.

Scase, R. and Goffee, R. (1989) *Reluctant Managers*, London: Unwin Hyman.

Scase, R. and Davis, H. (2001) *Managing Creativity*, Milton Keynes: Open University Press.

Schiller, D. (1999) *Digital Capitalism: Networking the Global Market System*, Cambridge, MA: MIT Press.

Schmidt, V. (1996) 'Industrial Policy and Policies of Industry in Advanced Industrialized Nations', *Comparative Politics*, 28, 2: 225–48.

Schneider, B. and Bowen, D.E. (1999) 'Understanding customer delight and outrage', *Sloan Management Review*, 41: 35–46.

Schoenberger, E. (1988a) 'Multinational Corporations and the New International Division of Labour: A Critical Appraisal', *International Regional Science Review*, 11: 105–19.

Schoenberger, E. (1988b) 'The Ambiguous Future of Professional and Technical Workers in Manufacturing: Some Hypotheses', *Acta Sociologica*, 31, 3: 241–47.

Schumpeter, L. (1939) *Business Cycles: A Theoretical, Historical and Statistical Analysis of the Capitalist Process*, New York: McGraw-Hill.

Senker, P.J. (1992) 'Automation and Work in Britain', in Adler, P. (ed.) *Technology and the Future of Work*, New York: Oxford University Press.

Senker, P.J. (1996) 'National Systems of Innovation, Organizational Learning and Industrial Biotechnology', *Technovation*, 16, 5: 219–30.

Sennett, R. (1998) *The Corrosion of Character: The Personal Consequences of Work in the New Capitalism*, New York: W.W. Norton & Co.

Sewell, G. (1998) 'The Discipline of Teams: The Control of Team-Based Industrial Work Through Electronic and Peer Surveillance', *Administrative Science Quarterly*, 43, 406–69.

Sewell, G. and Wilkinson, B. (1992) 'Someone to Watch over Me: Surveillance, Discipline and the Just-in-Time Labour Process', *Sociology*, 26, 2: 271–89.

Shadbolt, N. and Milton, N. (1999) 'From Knowledge Engineering to Knowledge Management', *British Journal of Management*, 10: 309–22.

Shane, S. (1995) 'Uncertainty Avoidances and the Preference for Innovation Championing Roles', *Journal of International Business Studies*, 26: 47–68.

Shipman, A. (2002) *The Globalisation Myth*, Cambridge: Cambridge University Press.

Shire, K., Holtgrewe, U. and Kerst, C. (2002) 'Re-Organising Customer Service Work: An Introduction', in Holtgrewe, U., Kerst, C. and Shire, K. (eds) *Re-organising Service Work: Call Centres in Germany and Britain*, Aldershot: Ashgate.

Sindell, M.T. (2001) 'KM Conversations', *Training*, 55, 11: 20–2.

Sinden, A. (1996) 'The Decline, Flexibility and Geographical Restructuring of Employment in British Retail Banks', *The Geographical Journal*, 162, 1: 25–40.

Smith, K. (2000) 'What is the "Knowledge Economy"? Knowledge-intensive Industries and Distributed Knowledge Bases', paper presented at DRUID Summer Conference 'Learning Economy', Rebild, Denmark, June.

Smith, S. and Wield, D. (1987) 'New Technology and Bank Work: Banking on IT as an "Organizational Technology"', in Finnegan, R., Salaman, G. and Thompson, K. (eds) *Information Technology: Social Issues, A Reader*, Sevenoaks: Hodder and Stoughton.

Soete, L. (1987) 'Employment, Unemployment and Technical Change: A Review of the Economic Debate', in Freeman, C. and Soete, L. (eds) *Technical Change and Full Employment*, Oxford: Basil Blackwell.

Soete, L. (2001) 'ICTs, Knowledge Work and Employment: The Challenges to Europe', *International Labour Review*, 140 (2): 143–92.

Solvell, O. and Zander, I. (1995) 'Organization of the Dynamic Multinational Enterprise: The Home-based and the Heterarchical MNE', *International Studies of Management and Organization*, 25, 1–2: 17–38.

Songini, M. (2000) 'Just-In-Time-Manufacturing', *Computerworld*, 34, 47: 50.

Soskice, D. (1990) 'Reinterpreting Corporatism and Explaining Unemployment: Co-ordinated and Non-co-ordinated Market Economies', in Brunetta, R. and Dell, C.A. (eds) *Labour Relations and Economic Performance*, London: Macmillan.

Soskice, D. (1997) 'German Technology Policy, Innovation and National Institutional Frameworks', *Industry and Innovation*, 4, 2: 75–96.

Soskice, D. (1999) 'Divergent Production Regimes: Coordinated and Uncoordinated Market Economies in the 1980s and 1990s', in Kitschelt, H., Lange, P., Marks, G. and Stephens, J. (eds) *Continuity and Change in Contemporary Capitalism*, London: Cambridge University Press.

Sowinski, L. (2001) 'Move Over, JIT', *World Trade*, 14, 4: 54–5.

Sparrow, P.R. and Daniels, K. (1999) 'Human Resource Management and the Virtual Organization: Mapping the Future Research Issues', in Cooper, C.L. and Rousseau, D.M. (eds) *The Virtual Organization*, London: Wiley.

Stanworth, C. (1998) 'Telework and the Information Age', *New Technology, Work and Employment*, 13, 1: 51–62.

Statistical Indicators Benchmarking the Information Society (SIBIS) (2003) 'Benchmarking Work, Employment and Skills in the Information Society in Europe and the US', prepared by Empirica, Bonn: SIBIS.

Steensma, H., Marino, L., Weaver, K. and Dickson, P. (2000) 'The Influence of National Culture on the Formation of Technology Alliances by Entrepreneurial Firms', *Academy of Management Journal*, 43, 5: 951–73.

Stewart, R. (1967) *The Reality of Management*, London: Pan.

Storey, D. and Tether, B. (1998) 'Public Policy Measures to Support New Technology-based Firms in the European Union', *Research Policy*, 26: 1037–57.

Storey, J., Mabey, C. and Thomson, A. (1997) 'What a Difference a Decade Makes', *People Management*, 12, June: 28–30.

Strange, S. (1997) 'The Future of Global Capitalism – Or Will Divergence Persist Forever?', in Crouch, C. and Streeck, W. (eds) *Political Economy of Modern Capitalism: Mapping Convergence and Divergence*, London: Sage, 182–91.

Strange, S. (1998) *Made Money: When Markets Outgrow Governments*, Ann Arbor, MI: University of Michigan Press.

Streeck, W. (1996) 'Lean Production and the German Automobile Industry: A Test Case for Convergence Theory', in Berger, S. and Dore, R. (eds) *National Diversity and Global Capitalism*, Ithaca, NY: Cornell University Press.

Streeck, W. (1997) 'German Capitalism: Does it Exist? Can it Survive?', *New Political Economy*, 2, 2: 237–56.

Streeten, P. (1996) 'Free and Managed trade', in Berger, S. and Dore, R. (eds.) *National Diversity and Global Capitalism*, Ithaca, NY: Cornell University Press.

Sturdy, A. (2001) 'Servicing Societies? – Colonisation, Control, Contradiction and Contestation', in Study, A., Gregulis, I. and Willmott, H. (eds) *Customer Service: Empowerment and Entrapment*, Houndmills, Basingstoke: Palgrave.

Swan, P. and Prevezer, M. (1996) 'A Comparison of the Dynamics of Industrial Clustering in Computing and Biotechnology', *Research Policy*, 25, 7: 1139–57.

Swedberg, R. (1997) 'New Economic Sociology: What has been Accomplished, What is Ahead', *Act Sociologica*, 40, 2: 161–82.

Taplin, I.M. (1995) 'Flexible Production, Rigid Jobs: Lessons from the Clothing Industry', *Work and Occupations*, 22, 4: 412–38.

Tapscott, D. (1998) *Growing up Digital: The Rise of the Net Generation*, New York: McGraw-Hill.

Taylor, M.Z. (2004) 'Empirical Evidence Against Varieties of Capitalism: Theory of Technological Innovation', *International Organization*, 58: 601–31.

Taylor, P. and Bain, P. (1999) 'An Assembly Line in the Head: Work and Employee Relations in the Call Centre', *Industrial Relations Journal*, 30, 2: 101–17.

Taylor, P. and Bain, P. (2003) *Call Centres in Scotland and Outsourced Competition from India*, Glasgow: Scottish Enterprise.

Taylor, P. and Bain, P. (2005) 'India Calling to the Far Away Towns: the Call Centre Labour Process and Globalisation', *Work, Employment and Society*, 19, 2: 261–82.

Taylor, R. (2002) 'Britain's World of Work – Myths and Realities', ESRC Future of Work Seminar Series, London: ESRC. Available online: http://www.esrc.ac.uk/ESRCInfoCentre (accessed 21 November 06).

Taylor, S. (1998) 'Emotional Labour and the New Workplace', in Thompson, P. and Warhurst, C. (eds) *Workplaces of the Future*, Basingstoke: Macmillan, 84–103.

Teresko, J. (2002) 'Robots Revolution', *Industry Week*, 251, 8: 24–8.

Terranova, T. (2000) 'Free Labor: Producing Culture for the Digital Economy', *Social Text*, 63, 18, 2: 33–58.

Tether, B.S. (1997) 'Growth Diversity Amongst Innovative and Technology-based New and Small Firms: An Interpretation', *New Technology, Work and Employment*, 12, 2: 91–107.

Thilmany, J. (2003) 'Shaking Hands Again', *Mechanical Engineering*, 125, 4: 34–7.

Thompson, G. (2003) *Between Hierarchies and Markets: The Logic and Limits of Network Forms of Organization*, Oxford: Oxford University Press.

Thompson, P. (1989) *The Nature of Work: An Introduction to Debates on the Labour Process*, 2nd edition, London: Macmillan.

Thompson, P. (2005) *Skating on Thin Ice: The Knowledge Economy Myth*, Glasgow: University of Strathclyde.

Thompson, P. and Warhurst, C. (eds) (1998) *Workplaces of the Future*, Basingstoke: Macmillan.

Thompson, P. and McHugh, D. (2002) *Work Organisations*, 3rd edition, London: Palgrave.

Thompson, P. and Harley, B. (2007) 'HRM and the Worker: Labor Process Perspectives', in Boxall, P., Purcell, J. and Wright, P. (eds), *The Oxford Handbook of Human Resource Management*, Oxford: Oxford University Press, 147–65.

Thompson, P., Warhurst, C. and Callaghan, G. (2001) 'Ignorant Theory and Knowledgeable Workers: Interrogating the Connections Between Knowledge, Skills and Services', *Journal of Management Studies*, 38, 7: 923–42.

Thompson, P., Callaghan, G. and van den Broek, D. (2004) 'Keeping up Appearances: Recruitment, Skills and Normative Controls in Call Centres', in Deery, S. and Kinnie, N. (eds) *Call Centres and Human Resource Management: A Cross-National Perspective*, London: Palgrave.

Thompson, P., Jones, M. and Warhurst, C. (2007) 'From Conception to Consumption: Creativity and the Missing Managerial Link', *Journal of Organizational Behavior*, 28, 5: 625–40.

Thurow, L. (1993) *Head to Head: The Coming Economic Battle Among Japan, Europe and Germany*, Sydney: Allen and Unwin.

Thurow, L. (1999) *Building Wealth: The New Rules for Individuals, Companies and Nations in a Knowledge-Based Economy*, New York: HarperCollins.

Tiessen, J.H. (1997) 'Individualism, Collectivism, and Entrepreneurship: A Framework for International Comparative Research', *Journal of Business Venturing*, 12: 267–364.

Toffler, A. (1970) *Future Shock*, New York: Bantam Books.

Tomaney, J. (1990) 'The Reality of Workplace Flexibility', *Capital and Class*, 40: 29–60.

Tomaney, J. (1994) 'A New Paradigm of Work Organisation and Technology', in Amin, A. (ed.) *Post-Fordism: A Reader*, Oxford: Blackwell.

Tomaskovic-Devey, D. and Risman, B. (1993) 'Telecommuting Innovation and Organisation: A Contingency Theory of Labor Process Change', *Social Science Quarterly*, 74: 367–85.

Traxler, F. (1998) 'Collective Bargaining in the OECD: Developments, Preconditions and Effects', *British Journal of Industrial Relations*, 4, 2: 207–26.

Traxler, F. and Unger, B. (1994) 'Governance, Economic Restructuring and International Competitiveness', *Journal of Economic Issues*, 28, 1: 1–23.

Trinca, H. and Fox, C. (2004) *Better Than Sex: How a Whole Generation Got Hooked on Work*, Milons Point: Random House Australia.

Truett, R. (2002) 'Mechanical Muscle', *Automotive News*, 76.5996: 36.

Tsoukas, H. (1993) 'Analogical Reasoning and Knowledge Generation in Organization Theory', *Organization Studies*, 14 (3): 323–46.

Tylecote, A. (1994) 'Financial Systems and Innovation', in Dodgson, M. and Rothwell, R. (eds) *The Handbook of Industrial Innovation*, Cheltenham: Edward Elgar.

Tylecote, A. and Conesa, E. (1999) 'Corporate Governance, Innovation Systems and Industrial Performance', *Industry and Innovation*, 6, 1: 25–50.

United Nations Conference on Trade and Development (UNCTAD) (2002) *Handbook of Statistics*, Geneva: UNCTAD.

United Nations Economic Commission for Europe (UNECE) (2002) 'World Robotics Survey', press release, 3 October, Geneva: United Nations.

Vallas, S.P. (1998) 'Manufacturing Knowledge: Technology, Culture, and Social Inequality at Work', *Social Science Computer Review*, 16, 4: 353–69.

Vallas, S.P. and Beck, J.P. (1996) 'The Transformation of Work Revisited: The Limits of Flexibility in American Manufacturing', *Social Problems*, 43, 3: 339–61.

van den Broek, D. (2002) 'Monitoring and Surveillance in Call Centres: Some Responses from Australian Workers', *Labour and Industry*, 12, 3: 43–58.

van den Broek, D. (2004) 'Call to arms? Collective and individual responses to call centre labour management', in Deery, S. and Kinnie, N. (eds) *Call Centres and Human Resource Management: A Cross-National Perspective*, London: Palgrave, 267–84.

Van Horn, C.E. and Storen, D. (2000) 'Telework: Coming of Age? Evaluating the Potential Benefits of Telework', U.S. Department of Labor, *Telework and the New Workplace of the Twenty-first Century*, New Orleans: U.S. Department of Labor. Available online: http://www.dol.gov/dol/asp/public/telework (accessed 28 June 2006).

Visnic, B. (2002) 'Toyota Adopts New Flexible Assembly System', *Ward's Auto World*, 38, 11: 30–1.

Visintin, F., Ozgen, B., Tylecote, A. and Handscombe, R. (2005) 'Italian Success and British Survival: Case Studies of Corporate Governance and Innovation in a Mature Industry', *Technovation*, 25: 621–9.

Visser, J. (2005) 'Beneath the Surface of Stability: New and Old Modes of Governance in European Industrial Relations', *European Journal of Industrial Relations*, 11, 3: 287–306.

Vitols, S. (1997) 'German industrial policy: an overview', *Industry and Innovation*, 4, 1: 15–36.

Wachtel, H. (1995) 'Taming global money', *Challenge: The Magazine of Economic Affairs*, 38, 1: 36–40.

Wade, R. (1996) 'Globalization and its Limits: Reports of the Death of the National Economy are Greatly Exaggerated', in Berger, S. and Dore, R. (eds) *National Diversity and Global Capitalism*, Ithaca, NY: Cornell University Press.

Walker, C.R. and Guest, R.H. (1952) *Man on the Assembly Line*, Cambridge, MA: Harvard University Press.

Wallace, C.M., Eagelson, G. and Waldersee, R. (2000) 'The Sacrificial HR Strategy in Call Centres', *International Journal of Service Industry Management*, 11, 2: 174–84.

Walsh, V., Niosi, J. and Mustar, P. (1995) 'Small Firm Formation in Biotechnology: A Comparison of France, Britain and Canada', *Technovation*, 15, 5: 303–28.

Warhurst, C., Lockyer, C. and Dutton, E. (2006) 'IT Jobs for All?', *New Technology, Work and Employment,* 21, 1: 75–88.

Warhurst, C. and Thompson, P. (1998) 'Hands, Hearts and Minds: Changing Work and Workers at the End of the Century', in Thompson, P. and Warhurst, C. (eds) *Workplaces of the Future*, Basingstoke: Macmillan.

Watson, A., Bunzel, D., Lockyer, C.J. and Scholarios, D. (2000) 'Changing Constructions of Career, Commitment and Identity: The Call Centre Experience', paper presented at the 15th Annual Employment Research Unit Conference: 'Work Futures', Cardiff, September.

Watt, S.E., Lea, M. and Spears, R. (2002) 'How Social is Internet Communication? A Reappraisal of Bandwidth and Anonymity Effects', in Woolgar, S. (ed.) *Virtual Society: Technology, Cyberbole, Reality*, Oxford: Oxford University Press.

Webb, M.C. (1991) 'International Economic Structures, Government Interests and International Co-ordination of Macro-economic Adjustment Policies', *International Organization*, 45, 3: 309–42.

Webster, F. (2002) *Theories of the Information Society*, 2nd edition, London: Routledge.

Webster, J. (1990) *Office Automation: The Labour Process and Women's Work and in Britain*, Hemel Hempstead: Harvester Wheatsheaf.

Weick, K.E. (1990) 'Technology as Equivoque', in Goodman, P.S., Sproull, L.S. and Associates (eds) *Technology and Organisations*, San Francisco, CA: Jossey-Bass.

Weimer, G. (2000) 'Robots Storm Factory World: Is This the Age of Robots', *Material Handling Management*, 55, 5: 63–6.

Weiss, L. (1998) *The Myth of the Powerless State: Governing the Economy in a Global Era*, Cambridge: Polity Press.

Wenger, E., McDermott, R. and Synder, W. (2002) *Cultivating Communities of Practice*, Boston, MA: Harvard Business School Press.

Went, R. (2004) 'Economic Globalization Plus Cosmopolitanism', *Review of International Political Economy*, 11, 2: 337–55.

Whitfield, K. and Poole, M. (1997) 'Organizing Employment for High Performance', *Organization Studies*, 18, 5: 745–64.

Whitley, R. (1992) 'Societies, Firms and Markets: The Social Structuring of Business Systems', in Whitley, R. (ed.) *European Business Systems: Firms and Markets in their National Contexts*, London: Sage.

Whitley, R. (1994) 'Dominant Forms of Economic Organisation in Market Economies', *Organization Studies*, 15, 2: 153–82.

Whitley, R. (1996) 'The Social Construction of Economic Actors: Institutions and Types of Firm in Europe and Other Markets', in Whitley, R. and Kristensen, P. (eds) *The Changing European Firm: Limits to Convergence*, London: Routledge.

Whitley, R. (1998) 'Internationalization and Varieties of Capitalism: the Limited Effects of Cross-National Coordination of Economic Activities on the Nature of Business Systems', *Review of International Political Economy*, 5: 445–81.

Whitley, R. (2000) 'The Institutional Structuring of Innovation Strategies: Business Systems, Firm Types and Patterns of Technical Change in Different Market Economies', *Organization Studies*, 21, 5: 885–6.

Wilkinson, B. (1983) *The Shop Floor Politics of New Technology*, London: Heinemann Educational.

Wilks, S. (1996) 'Class Compromise and the International Economy: The Rise and Fall of Swedish Social Democracy', *Capital and Class*, 58: 89–111.

Wilks, S. and Wright, M. (eds) (1987) *Comparative Government-Industry Relations: States, Sectors and Networks*, Oxford: Oxford University Press.

Williams, K. (2000) 'From Shareholder Value to Present Day Capitalism', *Economy and Society*, 29, 1: 1–12.

Williams, R. and Edge, D. (1996) 'The Social Shaping of Technology', *Research Policy*, 25: 865–99.

Williamson, O. (1975) *Markets and Hierarchies, Analysis and Antitrust Implications: A Study in the Economics of Internal Organization*, New York: Free Press.

Winner, L. (1977) *Autonomous Technology*, Cambridge, MA: MIT Press.

Winner, L. (1980) 'Do Artefacts have Politics?', *Daedalus*, 109: 121–36.

Winner, L. (1993) 'Upon Opening the Black Box and Finding it Empty: Social Constructivism and the Philosophy of Technology', *Science, Technology, & Human Values*, 18, 3: 362–78.

Witz, A., Warhurst, C. and Nickson, D. (2003) 'The Labour of Aesthetics and the Aesthetics of Organization', *Organization*, 10, 1: 33–54.

Womack, J., Jones, D. and Roos, D. (1990) *The Machine that Changed the World*, New York: Rawson.

Wood, S. (1982) *The Degradation of Work? Skill, Deskilling and the Labour Process*, London: Hutchinson.

Wood, S. (1999a) 'Human Resources Management and Performance', *International Journal of Management Reviews*, 1: 367–413.

Wood, S. (1999b) 'Getting the Measure of the Transformed High-Performance Organization', *British Journal of Industrial Relations*, 37, 3: 391–417.

Woodward, J. (1958) *Management and Technology*, London: HMSO.

Woodward, J. (1965) *Industrial Organisation*, Oxford: Oxford University Press.

Woolgar, S. (ed.) (2002a) *Virtual Society: Technology, Cyberbole, Reality*, Oxford: Oxford University Press.

Woolgar, S. (2002b) 'Five Rules of Virtuality', in Woolgar, S. (ed.) *Virtual Society: Technology, Cyberbole, Reality*, Oxford: Oxford University Press.

Woolley, A. (2005) 'Evaluating Value: A Historical Case Study of the Capacity of Alternative Billing Methods to Reform Unethical Hourly Billing', *International Journal of the Legal Profession*, 12 (3): 339–66.

World Trade Organization (2000) *International Trade Statistics*, Geneva: World Trade Organisation.

WorldatWork (2006) 'WorldatWork Telework Trendlines for 2006', Scottsdale, Arizona: WorldatWork. Available online: http://www.workingfromanywhere.org/ (accessed 07 February 2007).

Wright, C. and Lund, J. (1996) 'Best-Practice Taylorism: "Yankee Speed-Up", in Australian Grocery Distribution', *Journal of Industrial Relations*, 38, 2: 196–212.

Wright, C. and Lund, J. (1997) 'Under the Clock: Trade Union Responses to Computerised Control in the US and Australian Grocery Warehousing', *New Technology Work and Employment*, 13, 1: 3–15.

Yarbrough, B.V. and Yarbrough, R.M. (1997) 'The "Globalization" of Trade: What's Changed and Why?', in Gupta, S.D. (ed.) *The Political Economy of Globalization*, Boston, MA: Kluwer Academic Publishers.

Youssef, M. and Al-Ahmady, B. (2002) 'Quality Management Practices in a Flexible Manufacturing Systems (FMS) Environment', *Total Quality Management*, 13, 6: 877–90.

Zuboff, S. (1988) *In the Age of the Smart Machine: the Future of Work and Power*, New York: Basic Books.

Zysman, J. (1983) *Government, Markets and Growth: Financial Systems and the Politics of Industrial Change*, Oxford: Martin Robertson.

Zysman, J. (1994) 'How Institutions Create Historically Rooted Trajectories of Growth', *Industrial and Corporate Change*, 3, 1: 243–83.

Zysman, J. (1996) 'The Myth of a Global Economy: Enduring National Foundations and Emerging Regional Realities', *New Political Economy*, 1, 2: 157–84.

Index